W9-BSV-971

TABÉ
2016

McGraw-Hill Education
TABE*

Test of Adult Basic Education

Level A

Second Edition

Phyllis Dutwin, MA

Richard Ku, MA

Carol G. Altreuter, MEd

Kathleen A. Peno, PhD

3 2298 00181 3502

New York Chicago San Francisco Athens London Madrid
Mexico City Milan New Delhi Singapore Sydney Toronto

1 2 3 4 5 6 7 8 9   RHR   21 20 19 18 17 16

ISBN   978-1-259-58779-5
MHID   1-259-58779-7

e-ISBN   978-1-259-58780-1
e-MHID   1-259-58780-0

The TABE is administered by Data Recognition Corporation/CTB, which was not involved in the
production of, and does not endorse, this product.

McGraw-Hill Education products are available at special quantity discounts to use as premiums
and sales promotions or for use in corporate training programs. To contact a representative,
please visit the Contact Us pages at www.mhprofessional.com.

CONTENTS

TO THE READER

The Test of Adult Basic Education is an academic test that measures a person's ability and skill in mathematics, reading, and language. This book has been designed to help you succeed on the TABE by acquiring more than just test-taking skills. When you finish the book, you will have identified some of your goals. You will also know more about your learning preferences and the strategies that make learning and test taking easier for you. In other words, the book will help you succeed in the challenges of work and study that follow.

HOW TO USE THIS BOOK

The TABE tests cover basic skills that you use in your everyday life. You may be surprised to find that you know more than you think you do. You may also be surprised to discover skill gaps you do not know about.

This book is all about helping you target and master the skills you need to succeed

- On the TABE
- In future situations as a lifelong learner

Before You Begin

Before you begin to use this book, take some time to explore it. The book offers much more than question and answer material. Read the table of contents. As you browse through the book, notice the following:

- Skills Assessments beginning each section
- Scenarios recalling students the authors have known
- Skill building in every subject
- Word study
- Study Tips, Test Tips, and FYI's

All of these elements give you a process, or way of learning. In fact, because each section builds skills, you should read and do all the exercises in the order given in the book.

What if you think you have great strength in one of the subjects? Take the Skills Assessment for that subject anyway. If your results are 90 to 95 percent correct, you probably don't have to study that section. However, be sure to take all the posttests when you have finished all the sections.

One section, "Spelling," needs a special comment. *You should not study this section straight through* from first page to last. Correct spelling is best learned slowly and through repetition. Take the pretest. If you find that spelling is not your strong subject, start the "Spelling" section. No matter what else you are working on, study a *small* part of the spelling section at the same time. If you use the tips provided and study consistently, you can improve your spelling.

 FYI

Learning how to succeed in test-taking situations makes good career sense.

You will be expected to take tests throughout your adult life, both on and off the job. Standardized tests are everywhere you look: drivers' licenses, technical certification, educational placement tests, financial aid qualifying tests, job placement, and advancement exams.

Use This Book as Your Personal Trainer

You should approach this book as you would any fitness regimen you start.

Step 1: Develop a fitness plan.
Complete Section 1: "Work Smarter, Not Harder."

Step 2: Warm up:
Take each of the subject area Skills Assessments.
Target skills you need to strengthen.

Step 3: Work out:
Pace yourself through the exercises.
Achieve optimum results.

 TEST TIP

Do not study for the Skills Assessments that begin each subject section. The results of each assessment will help you

- Compare what you already know with what you need to know
- Make a learning plan for choosing and using the lessons that follow.

Look for these tips throughout this book:

 **STUDY TIP**   **TEST TIP**   **FYI**

Succeed at Learning

Before reading about what *other* people have to say about learning, how would you complete this sentence?

"The best learning experience I ever had was _____."

You do not have to write it—just think what you would say if someone asked

> "I *see* and I forget, I *hear* and I remember, I *do* and I understand."
> *An Old Chinese proverb*

Research about how people learn and remember has proven the truth of this ancient proverb. When we learn something new, and do something with that knowledge, understanding comes more quickly.

After two weeks, we tend to remember:

- 10% of what we read
- 20% of what we hear
- 30% of what we see

- 50% of what we hear *and* see
- 70% of what we say
- 90% of what we say and do
- 95% of what we help someone else learn and understand

The higher our level of involvement, the more likely we will remember.

Increase Your Percentage of Success

- **Put it to work.** *Doing* something with new knowledge means *putting it to work* and getting results.
- **Results are valuable feedback.** You may be unhappy with your first results, but making mistakes is part of the learning process.
- **Mistakes** are *learning opportunities*. Welcome mistakes as a chance to figure out "what is not working and why." Then make it your business to try again.
- **Just do it, step by step.** The path to acquiring new knowledge or skills is a series of steps. Sometimes these steps are baby steps, especially if you have had no previous experience in this area. Other times these steps may be giant steps, as when a new bit of information connects with knowledge you already possess.
- **Use it to make it yours.** The understanding of how to do something new is first stored, *temporarily,* in your short-term memory. Perhaps it will stay there for a minute, an hour or a day. If you do not take it out of temporary storage, and *use it within that time period*, it will not be there when you need to use it again. You will have to start the process over again.
- **3 may be the magic number.** Each time you put a new bit of knowledge to work, you help guarantee that it will move from *temporary* storage to *permanent* storage in your memory. *Rule of thumb:* Use your new skill successfully 3 times, on 3 different occasions, and you'll probably find yourself saying, "I've got it."
- **Use it again, or risk losing it.** A stored skill, like a stored metal tool, may rust or become stiff with time. Then, when you need to use it, you'll find it doesn't do the job easily or well. Then again, you may forget where you left the key! Plan to open that storage door regularly, and put your skill to work.

How do you prefer to learn something new?

- See it; read about it; write it down?   (See TIPS A)
- Hear it; talk about it?   (See TIPS B)
- Watch it done, then do it yourself?   (See TIPS C)

Lead with your strength. If you have a strong preference for a certain style of learning, it makes sense to connect with new information in that way *first*.

TIPS A

1 Think in pictures, colors, and shapes. Make movies in your mind about new ideas.
2 Think on paper. Organize your thoughts by making diagrams, charts, and flash cards.
3 Watch videos, TV, or films about subjects you are learning. Search for study books that have lots of graphics and photographs.
4 Ask yourself questions in writing; reply to yourself in writing. Doodle your ideas.
5 Work in a quiet place, with a clear study space that is pleasing to your eyes.

TIPS B

1 Think out loud. Explain things out loud to yourself as you study.
2 Read out loud. Read *under your breath*—as you move your lips, you will *hear* the sound of the words in your head.
3 Make your own tapes of information you want to remember. Get the *sound* of standard English *in your ear* by taping your voice reading from a textbook or novel.
4 Study with other people. Talk things over. Hold question-and-answer sessions.
5 Listen to information about a topic on video, TV, film, or recorded books.

TIPS C

1 Connect to things you are studying with *movement* and *touch*. Act out ideas. "Talk" with your hands.
2 Watch someone *do* what you need to learn. Then, *do* it yourself.
3 Use the computer as a learning tool. Go for programs that are multimedia and interactive. Create your own study notes on your computer or tablet.
4 Write about, draw, or build models of what you are learning.
5 Exercise before you sit down to study. Take 5-minute *movement breaks* between 30-minute study sessions. Play background music as you study.

Don't Limit Your Options

Learning different subjects may mean using different approaches. Consider all the tips above. Ask others about their tips for learning. Watch for study and learning tips in the subject lessons that follow.

On Your Own, or with Others?

If you work together with a partner, or with a small study group, you can benefit in these ways. You have the opportunity to

- Pool your experience and knowledge
- Exchange strategies and study tips

- Ask and answer questions of each other without fear of embarrassment
- Give and get suggestions when the going gets tough

Ask

Questions are like fishhooks.

Information you hook with your own questions tends to "stick around" in your memory better than information you have received without fishing for it.

Learn how to ask good questions. Keep your hook baited and in the water long enough to catch some information.

Take time to do some fishing. Chances are, you will be hooked on learning for a lifetime.

One Final Observation

The more you understand about the way you learn best, the more you will be able to get what you need to succeed.

Good luck at discovering how to unlock your potential!

Work Smarter, Not Harder

LESSON 1 Identify Your Target

Where Are You Headed?

My Goals

I am studying to score well on the Test of Adult Basic Education, Level A, and upgrade my basic academic skills to (*check all that apply*):

☐ Enroll in an associate degree program
☐ Enter a vocational certificate program
☐ Obtain admission to a job training program
☐ Obtain admission to a career advancement program
☐ Qualify for a promotion at my workplace
☐ Be eligible for federal financial aid under Ability to Benefit guidelines
☐ Qualify for certification in _____
☐ Complete graduation requirements for _____
☐ Successfully exit the Welfare to Work Program _____
☐ Become more independent in handling my affairs
☐ Attain personal satisfaction
☐ Help family members with their schooling
☐ _____
☐ _____
☐ _____

After I upgrade my skills and/or score well on the TABE, I plan to _____
_____
_____.

A vision I have for my future is _____
_____
_____.

When Do You Want to Get There?

My Timeline

Today's date: _____

I want to upgrade my skills by (this date) _____ because that is when _____.

That date is _____ (months, weeks, days) from today.

If I do not improve my skills as much as I want to by that date, my options will be to _____.

Do You Need to Achieve a Certain Score?

Programs vary in their TABE score requirements.

Are you already in a program with TABE score requirements? _____

Do you want to enroll in, or qualify for, a program that has TABE score requirements? _____

Do you need to take the TABE test to qualify for scholarship aid? _____

If you answer yes to any of these questions, make sure you know what those specific requirements are. Take the time to find out this information right now. It will help you focus on your goals for studying the subjects in this book. The information will help you be realistic as you plan your timeline.

Turn to Appendix A (p. 323) for specific information on TABE scoring.

Do Your Research

Complete the statement that fits your situation.

1. The program *I am already working in* requires me to_____
   _____.

2. The program *I want to get into* requires me to_____
   _____.

For my own satisfaction, I would like to _____.

What Do You Already Know About Your Skills?

Take a moment to think in general about the academic subject areas covered in this book and tested on the TABE: Reading, Math, and Language.

Would you say your level of skill is about the same in each area or quite different? _____

How about your level of comfort using and learning about these subjects? Are you just as comfortable learning in one subject area as another, or is there a significant difference in the way you feel about them? _____

Rank Your Levels of Skill and Comfort

Skill Level:
Strongest subject area first

1. _____

2. _____

3. _____

Comfort Level:
Most comfortable subject area first

1. _____

2. _____

3. _____

Why do you think your skills are stronger in some of these areas than others?

_____

_____

_____

Why do you think you are more comfortable with some subjects than others?

_____

_____

_____

What Do You Need to Succeed as a Test-Taker?

Reflection: Past Experiences with Tests

The last time I took a standardized test was _____.

My results were ____OK ____Good ____Excellent ____A disaster.

I think my performance on that test was due to _____.

In general, I consider myself a ____Good ____Fair ____Poor test-taker.

My biggest problem with taking tests is _____.

To improve my performance I think I need to _____.

Test-Taking Strategies
I am familiar with, and am able to put into practice, the following test-taking strategies. I know how to

Visualize success for self-confidence ____Yes ____No ____Need Practice and best results.

Prepare physically for the test day. ____Yes ____No ____Need Practice

Identify key words in questions and directions.	____Yes	____No	____Need Practice
Recognize pitfalls of multiple-choice tests.	____Yes	____No	____Need Practice
Use process of elimination to check multiple-choice questions.	____Yes	____No	____Need Practice
Relax by using breathing techniques.	____Yes	____No	____Need Practice
Take 1-minute vacations to relieve stress during the test.	____Yes	____No	____Need Practice
Pace myself during the test to finish within the time limit.	____Yes	____No	____Need Practice
Know when to leave a question that is giving me trouble.	____Yes	____No	____Need Practice
Use time that is left at the end to check my work.	____Yes	____No	____Need Practice

 FYI

Don't worry yet about getting ready for any of the assessments or tests in this book or the TABE. There are test-taking tips throughout the lessons. See Appendix A for an explanation of each of the strategies mentioned in the preceding list.

Take time to complete the next unit: Analyze yourself as a learner. You will meet another student in the next few pages. Learn how she uses this analysis to help herself prepare for studying to be test-ready.

LESSON 2 Analyze Yourself as a Learner

Self-Assessment and Planning

In this section you will take steps to better understand yourself as a learner. You also need to examine and manage the time you have to prepare for the TABE. In addition, you will be able to identify, understand, and develop strategies to overcome the barriers that many adults face as learners. The result will be a plan of action that will help you target success.

To help you through this process, read Alice's story, and then walk through the worksheets with her. Once you see how the process is done, complete your own.

Alice

Alice has been employed for the past 18 years in a small safety products manufacturing plant as an assembler. She recently saw a supervisor's position opening in her department posted in the lunchroom. Alice thought about applying for the job. The poster said to see the Human Resources Department Manager for job specifications. She went to the department and picked up the qualifications statement.

Assembly Supervisor

Qualifications:

The qualified applicant will possess

- Excellent communication skills (oral and written)
- Leadership abilities (able to manage the different personalities in the department)
- Ability to schedule workers, understand department budgets, and operate within them
- Ability to assist with new product setup
- Ability to read, analyze, and report on computer printout data regarding scrap rates
- Ability to implement the quality control process on a daily basis
- Ability to make adjustments to work processes

The successful candidate will

- Assist department employees with information regarding the performance of their jobs
- Provide employees in his or her charge with an annual review of their performance, including goals and professional development activities
- Possess specific skills to be used in the quality control and process improvement including ability to
    - Understand algebraic equations used in the quality control process
    - Compute fractions (used in measurement of product outcomes)
    - Understand the geometry (area, perimeter, volume) needed to set up new products
    - Understand the basic statistics used in this process

Alice had been working in the assembly department for many years; however, she lacked many of the skills the supervisor's job required. She was especially worried about her lack of math skills and wasn't sure that she could do that job.

What Kind of a Learner Are You?

Because people learn in different ways, it is important for you to understand how *you* learn best. This information will help you develop a learning plan that targets success on the TABE and helps you achieve your other learning goals. Alice reflected on her learning experiences. The last math class she took was a disaster. She remembered having trouble, being confused, and feeling alone. The way the teacher expected her to learn did not work for her.

The following is an example of how Alice might complete this worksheet.

Learner Preference Worksheet

1. *What time(s) of day or night do you feel better able to study/work/read/write?*
   Early morning _✓_ Afternoon ___ Early evening ___ Late night

2. *Do you prefer to study or learn by yourself or with others? (Check one)*
   I like learning about new things with a study group. ___
   I like learning about new things by myself. ___
   I like learning something new with one other person to help me. ___
   It depends on the subject matter. _✓_ (I need help with Math.)

3. *Do you learn best by (Check all that apply)*
   Reading about something? _✓_
   Seeing a picture or graph? _✓_
   Hearing someone explain something? ___
   Doing what I'm learning about? ___
   Writing it down? ___
   Talking about it with or without someone else? _✓_

4. *What length of time do you prefer to spend studying?*
   I prefer to work for periods of 2 hours or more. _✓_
   I prefer to work for shorter periods of time (less than an hour). ___
   I can work whenever time permits. ___

5. *How's your concentration?*
   I need complete quiet when I study or read. _✓_
   I can study or read with some background noise. ___
   I can study or read in any environment, quiet or noisy. ___

Examine the items you have checked to get a picture of how you best learn. Use the information to fill in the blanks in the Learner Preference Statement that follows.

Learner Preference Statement

I prefer to study in the _early morning_ with _the help of others (when I'm doing math)_. I learn best when I _see something in a picture or graph_ and by _talking about it with other people_. I prefer to spend _at least 2 hours_ studying, and I prefer to study _in complete silence_.

Now that you have seen an example of a completed worksheet, complete this one on your own to get an idea how *you* prefer to learn.

Learner Preference Worksheet

1. *What time(s) of day or night do you feel better able to study/work/read/write?*
    Early morning _____ Afternoon _____ Early evening _____ Late night _____

2. *Do you prefer to study or learn by yourself or with others? (Check one)*
    I like learning about new things with a study group. _____
    I like learning about new things by myself. _____
    I like learning something new with one other person to help me. _____
    It depends on the subject matter. _____

3. *Do you learn best by (Check all that apply)*
    Reading about something? _____
    Seeing a picture or graph? _____
    Hearing someone explain something? _____
    Doing what I'm learning about? _____
    Writing it down? _____
    Talking about it with or without someone else? _____

4. *What length of time do you prefer to spend studying?*
    I prefer to work for periods of 2 hours or more. _____
    I prefer to work for shorter periods of time (less than an hour). _____
    I can work whenever time permits. _____

5. *How's your concentration?*
    I need complete quiet when I study or read. _____
    I can study or read with some background noise. _____
    I can study or read in any environment, quiet or noisy. _____

Review the items you have checked above to get a picture of how you learn best. Use this information to fill in your Learner Preference Statement.

Learner Preference Statement

I prefer to study in the (1) _____ with (2) _____.
I learn best by (3) _____.
I prefer to spend (4) _____ studying.
I study best with (5) _____.

We will use this information to develop your Personal Learning Plan later in this chapter.

You have thought about how you learn and study best. Now you should be aware of, and plan for, obstacles that might get in the way of your success.

As adults, we are all faced with a variety of life issues and challenges that can, if we let them, sabotage the accomplishment of our goals. We can overcome these barriers if we are aware of the supports that we can draw upon to help us deal with them.

You can categorize barriers in three ways: institutional, circumstantial, and individual. Read the discussion of barriers that follows. An exercise follows the discussion to help you plan for and overcome some of these barriers to your success.

Barriers

Institutional barriers are those over which we have no control. They are put in place by a school, a program, or a class. Institutional barriers may include inconvenient class times, detailed registration procedures, financial aid deadlines, and other things that prevent us from taking a class or continuing with one. In some cases we can overcome these barriers.

Circumstantial barriers may be difficult but are more often within our control to overcome. These barriers may include lack of time, money, child-care, or transportation. They may make it difficult for us to achieve our learning goals.

Personal barriers are often within our control to overcome, yet they are typically the most difficult for us to overcome. They include our own long-held beliefs about our abilities as a learner or student.

Examples of personal barriers include the following:

- Feelings of being too old to take classes or to learn
- Feelings that we are not smart enough to do well in class or even in one particular subject (many people have a fear of math and feel they cannot do well in that subject)
- Negative feelings about school or learning because of bad experiences with school earlier in life

These barriers may prevent some people from even attempting to return to school or take a course. They might also be why someone drops out of a class or program. The good news is that there are ways to deal with, and overcome, many of these barriers.

Supports

You have many sources of support. Identify these within your own family, your circle of friends, and your neighborhood and community.

Family
Identify people within your close or extended family you can ask for help. Ask yourself these questions:

1. Do I have a parent, sibling, aunt, uncle, or other relative who can provide child-care, even on a short-term basis, so I can study, go to the library, or attend a class?
   I can ask _____. Telephone: _____.
   I can ask _____. Telephone: _____.
2. Is there any family member I can call on short notice to help me if I need a ride, last-minute child-care, or financial assistance?
   I can call _____. Telephone: _____.
   I can call _____. Telephone: _____.

Friends

Identify those people closest to you who may be able to help you with child-care, studying, or a ride if you need one. What can you offer these people in exchange? Can you offer them child-care or other support in exchange when they need it? Sometimes friends set up an informal child-care exchange program and develop a schedule of support for one another.

I will ask my friend _____ for help with _____.

In exchange, I can offer _____. Telephone: _____.

I will ask my friend _____ for help with _____.

In exchange, I can offer _____. Telephone: _____.

Neighbors

Do you have neighbors who might be willing to help you on short notice if you need it?

A neighbor I might call on for help is _____. Telephone: _____.
A neighbor I might call on for help is _____. Telephone: _____.

Community

Many social services are available in the community to assist you. These services include child-care, transportation, clothing, food, shelter, financial aid, and counseling. Check the community service telephone numbers listed in the front of your telephone directory or search online for services. Many communities offer:

- Heath center services
- Family services
- Educational financial aid services

I will check out the following community services:

_____

_____

_____

_____

_____

Before you identify your own barriers, read what Alice has identified as her barriers. See how she plans to overcome some of these barriers by tapping into her support system.

Balancing Barriers and Supports Worksheet

Barriers	Supports
Institutional	**Family, Friends, Neighbors, Community**
Some of my classes will be at work, but I've never taken classes anywhere else before. So I'm not sure where I go to register.	I will ask the Human Resources director at work how to register for classes outside the office.
Circumstantial	
I'm not sure I can afford these classes. I'll need help with my kids while I'm in class.	I will try to get financial aid from the school or try to find out if I qualify for aid from another source. I will ask my friends if we can trade baby-sitting with each other.
Individual	
I'm really afraid that I can't do this math. I think I'm too old to learn it now.	I want to try for the supervisor job so I need to try to get over my fears. I have never been good at math, but I have to try hard because I must improve my math skills to get the job. I have to start thinking more positively about the future.

As you can see, Alice has some issues that are more easily handled than others. She can ask her family and friends to help her with her institutional and circumstantial barriers. She is going to have to really work hard to get over her fear of not being able to succeed in math. Alice must take responsibility for that. Once she gets started, an instructor can help her develop more self-confidence. Now try this exercise yourself.

1. List the institutional, circumstantial, and individual barriers you might face. Use the descriptions on page 8 to help you identify the different barriers. Write these in the spaces provided on the left side of the form below.

2. Match possible sources of support that you might use to help you overcome the barriers you have listed. Write these on the right side of the form.

Balancing Barriers and Supports Worksheet

Barriers	Supports
Institutional	Family, Friends, Neighbors, Community
_____	_____
_____	_____
_____	_____

Circumstantial

_____   _____

_____   _____

_____   _____

Individual

_____   _____

_____   _____

_____   _____

Notes to Myself:

_____   _____

_____   _____

_____   _____

Make Time for Learning

A common complaint of adult learners is that they lack time for studying and other learning activities. This section will help you document and analyze how you currently spend your time. It will also help you develop a plan to include your learning activities. Notice how Alice filled out her calendar: She used an X to indicate fixed activities—such as work. She used a ◊ to indicate flexible activities that could be scheduled at another time.

Alice filled her calendar out this way:

	Mon	Tues	Wed	Thurs	Fri	Sat	Sun
6:00 AM							
	XXXX	XXXX	XXXX	XXXX	XXXX		
7:00	XXXX	XXXX	XXXX	XXXX	XXXX		
	XXXX	XXXX	XXXX	XXXX	XXXX		
8:00	XXXX	XXXX	XXXX	XXXX	XXXX	Children's	
	XXXX	XXXX	XXXX	XXXX	XXXX	Sports	
9:00	XXXX	XXXX	XXXX	XXXX	XXXX	Events	
10:00	XXXX	XXXX	XXXX	XXXX	XXXX	XXXX	XXXX
	XXXX	XXXX	XXXX	XXXX	XXXX	XXXX	XXXX
11:00	XXXX	XXXX	XXXX	XXXX	XXXX	XXXX	XXXX
	XXXX	XXXX	XXXX	XXXX	XXXX		
12:00 PM	XXXX	XXXX	XXXX	XXXX	XXXX		
	XXXX	XXXX	XXXX	XXXX	XXXX		

	Mon	Tues	Wed	Thurs	Fri	Sat	Sun
1:00	XXXX	XXXX	XXXX	XXXX	XXXX		
	XXXX	XXXX	XXXX	XXXX	XXXX		
2:00	XXXX	XXXX	XXXX	XXXX	XXXX		
	XXXX	XXXX	XXXX	XXXX	XXXX		
3:00	XXXX	XXXX	XXXX	XXXX	XXXX		
4:00	Library						
	with						
	children						
5:00							
6:00	◊◊◊	◊◊◊	◊◊◊	◊◊◊		◊◊◊	◊◊◊
7:00	◊◊◊	Weekly Food	◊◊◊	◊◊◊	◊◊◊	◊◊◊	◊◊◊
		Shopping	◊◊◊	◊◊◊	◊◊◊	◊◊◊	◊◊◊
8:00					XXXX		
9:00					XXXX		
					XXXX		
10:00					XXXX		
					XXXX		
11:00					XXXX		
12:00 AM							

Step One: Look at this weeklong calendar. Place an *X* indicating the days and times when you know you have fixed activities, such as job hours, family meal times, and other activities that cannot be changed.

My Weekly Calendar

	Mon	Tues	Wed	Thurs	Fri	Sat	Sun
6:00 AM							
7:00							
8:00							
9:00							
10:00							
11:00							
12:00 PM							
1:00							
2:00							
3:00							
4:00							
5:00							
6:00							

My Weekly Calendar

	Mon	Tues	Wed	Thurs	Fri	Sat	Sun
7:00 8:00 9:00 10:00 11:00 12:00 AM							

Step Two: You have identified time slots that are *not* available for learning. Now ask yourself the critical questions below to help you plan your best times for learning during the week. Use the information you recorded about yourself on the Learner Preference Statement, page 7, to help you.

Here are Alice's responses:

When do I learn best? _Early morning_

How much time do I need during the day/week to study? _At least 3 hrs a week_

Are there any times available when I will be able to study without interruption?
Before 7 am or at night weekdays. Weekend mornings.

Write *your* conclusions here:

When do I learn best? _____

How much time do I need during the day/week to study? _____

Are there any times available when I will be able to study without interruption?

_____

Step Three: Use the answers to the preceding questions to help identify the best times for you to study. If there is a conflict, use your Barriers and Supports Worksheet to help you identify your supports. Make time in your schedule for studying by calling on your supports for help with tasks that must be done daily or weekly.

Write these times in on your preceding weekly schedule and on the lines that follow:

_____

_____

_____

_____

Create a Personal Learning Plan

Now that you (and Alice) have reflected on your situation, put all this information to work for you. Complete this learning plan as directed. Next, photo copy it, and put it in a place where you will see it every day. The refrigerator is a good location.

My Learning Plan

Goal/s (page 1): _____

Timeline (page 2): _____

Supports I need to reach my goals (page 9): _____

_____

_____

My Promises

I will study at the times, and in the ways, I learn best.

Write your Learner Preference Statement (page 8) here:

I will refer often to my Barriers and Supports Worksheet (pages 10–11).

I will continue to try to find and use the supports I need to overcome obstacles.

I will consult my weekly calendar (page 12) and use the study time I have scheduled.

I WILL SUCCEED.

LESSON 1 **The Challenge**

In Lesson 1, you will join Mike Rinaldi on a new and challenging journey. Mike graduated from high school not knowing how he would use his considerable computer skills. Mike changed jobs twice in two years, but he was still unsatisfied with the work he was doing. Then a friend told Mike about an ad for a job that required computer skills.

Mike was in for some surprises, both good and not so good, as he pursued employment at Ace Computer Chip Company.

Words to Know

Human Resources Manager	A business title for a manager of people in the workplace
Non-exempt employees	Hourly workers who are entitled to overtime pay
Mentor	Advisor, coach

Job Hunting

After Mike Rinaldi graduated from high school, he immediately started looking for a job. Mike wanted to do something with his computer skills. The jobs he found, including his current job, were not good "fits" for him. Mike had two goals. He wanted to learn much more about the computer programs used in business. He also wanted to earn enough to live on his own.

Mike had been looking for a new job for weeks, using the newspaper as well as the Internet. Then a friend told Mike about an opening he had seen posted on the Internet. Ace Computer Chip Company was advertising for entry-level employees who would be trained to handle information storage tasks.

Certain that he, undoubtedly, could handle the entry-level assignment, Mike immediately called about the job. He was invited to come in for an interview with Sue Mendez, the Human Resources Manager. Mike learned that the job required some computer skills that he had mastered and some that he had not. The new employee would enter data on new customers into the information system using a program Mike was familiar with.

During the interview, Sue asked Mike a lot of questions. She included questions about his favorite subjects in high school (Mike's were math and computer science). She also wanted to know about his least favorite subjects (English, especially writing). Mike wondered why Sue wanted to know so much about what he liked and didn't like. He soon found out.

Sue asked Mike if he wanted to fill out a complete application, and Mike replied, "Yes, absolutely. When can I start working?" Sue smiled and told him he needed to take one step at a time. Ace required all new non-exempt employees to take the TABE, Tests of Adult Basic Education. Sue watched as Mike grimaced. She said, "We need to know more about your reading, language, and math skills." Mike thought to himself, "I hate taking tests. I'm terrible at taking tests! I'll never get this job!" Sue explained that Mike needed to demonstrate more about his English, math, and reading skills. She said, "Mike, don't worry about the test right now. We'll provide you with a mentor—we do this for all new employees. The mentor will tell you what to expect and how to prepare for the TABE. Also, you can take one test at a time, starting with the reading test." Mike sat quietly for a while, thinking about what he should do. He knew one thing: He had two important goals, and he needed to do whatever was necessary to achieve them.

Sue followed through on her promises to Mike. She introduced Mike to Alicia Buchanan, her assistant. Alicia explained all the steps Mike would take as he went through the hiring process. Alicia knew that Mike was very concerned about taking the TABE, so she immediately introduced him to his mentor, Dave Elliot. Over a cup of coffee, Dave assured Mike that he could accomplish his goals. Dave would make another appointment with Mike after Mike taken some time to think about his goals, strengths, and weaknesses. Dave took Mike back to Alicia's office, where he started the onboarding process.

If you think about what you read in Chapter 1, you can relate to all that Mike did to evaluate himself as a learner and new employee. Mike eventually took a test very much like the one you, the reader, are about to take. First, think about your own reading habits and skills.

Reflection: Reading in My Daily Life

I read approximately _____ hrs a day/ _____ hrs a week to keep informed of current events and other issues that concern me.

I read approximately _____ hrs a day/ _____ hrs a week for workplace tasks.

I enjoy reading (what kind of subject matter) _____.

I would like to improve my ability to read _____.

Comprehension

I am able to understand, analyze, and use these types of materials:

Newspapers	___Yes	___No	___Need practice	___I don't know
Instructions	___Yes	___No	___Need practice	___I don't know
Maps, charts, and graphs	___Yes	___No	___Need practice	___I don't know
Stories and novels	___Yes	___No	___Need practice	___I don't know
Business letters	___Yes	___No	___Need practice	___I don't know
Manuals, handbooks	___Yes	___No	___Need practice	___I don't know
Standardized forms	___Yes	___No	___Need practice	___I don't know
Indexes, tables of contents	___Yes	___No	___Need practice	___I don't know

Vocabulary Knowledge

I know how to figure out the meanings of words from their *context* (the way they are used in a passage).

___Yes   ___No   ___Need practice   ___I don't know

I know how to identify the meanings of words by analyzing their *structure* (roots, prefixes, and suffixes).

___Yes   ___No   ___Need practice   ___I don't know

 TEST TIP

Before you start this test (and any test):

- Breathe. You probably think that you do this without thinking, and most of the time you do. However, when you are in a stressful situation (as tests are for Mike), you tend to hold your breath. So, start this test-taking opportunity by taking and releasing four deep breaths. Breathe in through your nose and out slowly with a slightly open mouth.
- Read the directions, noting any time limitations.
- Don't linger on any one question. You can always return to a question later.
- Use the process of elimination to check multiple-choice answers.
- Use any time left at the end to check your work.

Reading Skills Assessment

Take a look at this chart. Use it to answer Questions 1–5.

Calories Burned in 5 Minutes According to Body Weight

Locate the activity in which you are interested. Then find the body weight that corresponds most closely to your body weight. The number listed under the body weight is the number of calories you burn if you perform the activity for 5 minutes. If you perform the activity for 10 minutes, multiply the calories listed by 2. If you perform the activity for 15 minutes, multiply the calories listed by 3, and so on.

Activity	110 lb	130 lb	150 lb	170 lb	190 lb	210 lb
Badminton	25	28	33	37	41	46
Basketball	35	41	47	53	60	65
Carpentry, general	13	15	18	20	22	24
Cleaning, general	15	17	20	23	26	29
Cooking, general	12	14	17	19	21	23
Cycling, 5.5 mph	16	19	22	25	28	30
9.4 mph	25	30	34	38	43	47
Dancing, ballroom	13	15	17	19	22	24
Fishing	15	18	21	24	26	29
Food Shopping	15	17	21	24	25	28
Football	33	39	45	51	57	62
Gardening, digging	31	39	43	48	54	60
planting seeds	17	20	24	27	30	33
Golf	21	25	29	32	36	40
Horseback Riding, walking	10	12	14	16	18	20
trotting	27	32	37	42	47	52
Ironing	12	14	16	18	20	22
Judo	49	57	66	75	84	92
Jumping Rope, 70/min	40	48	55	62	69	77
125/min	44	52	60	67	76	84
Lawn Mowing	28	33	38	43	48	53
Mopping Floors	15	17	20	23	26	28
Music Playing, conducting	10	12	14	16	18	20
piano, sitting	10	12	14	16	18	20
brass, standing	8	9	10	11	12	14
string, sitting	11	13	15	17	19	21
Painting, inside	8	10	11	12	14	16
outside	19	22	26	27	34	36
Raking	13	16	18	21	23	25
Racquetball	44	52	60	68	76	84
Running, 11 min/mile	34	40	46	52	58	64
9 min/mile	48	57	65	74	83	91
Scrubbing Floors	27	32	37	42	47	52
Skiing, downhill	26	31	36	43	46	50
cross-country, moderate	36	42	48	55	61	68
cross-country, slow	30	35	40	45	50	55
Snowshoeing	41	49	56	64	71	79
Stairs, walking upstairs	65	76	87	99	110	122
Step Aerobics Class	42	46	51	57	64	70
Swimming, back stroke	42	50	57	65	72	80
breast stroke	40	48	55	62	72	77
crawl, slow	32	38	43	49	55	61
Table Tennis (ping pong)	17	20	23	26	29	32
Tennis	27	32	37	42	47	52
Vacuuming	12	14	17	19	21	23
Walking, slow (2.0 mph)	11	13	15	17	19	21
fast (4.0 mph)	20	26	31	37	42	48
Window Cleaning	15	17	20	22	25	28
Wood Chopping, slow	21	25	29	34	36	40

1. Find the word *corresponds* in the directions at the top of the chart. In this context, corresponds means

    A   writes to.

    B   is correct.

    C   is closest to.

    D   is less than.

2. The main reason for reading this chart is to discover

    A   which exercises are best for you if you weigh less than 110 lb.

    B   how much you should weigh at any particular height.

    C   your body mass index.

    D   the connection between calories, exercise, and body weight.

3. According to the directions for reading this chart, the first thing you should do is

    A   locate your weight.

    B   choose an activity.

    C   multiply your weight by 2.

    D   divide your weight by 2.

4. You can conclude from the information in the chart that

    A   skiing slowly or moderately uses the same number of calories.

    B   golf and judo use the same number of calories.

    C   painting outside uses fewer calories than painting inside.

    D   the longer you do an activity, the more calories you will use.

5. If you weigh 150 lb and it takes you 5 min to walk upstairs, how many more calories will you use than your 110-lb child?

    A   22

    B   11

    C   The same number of calories

    D   None of the above

Here is an excerpt from a work procedure at a manufacturing firm. Read the document and then answer Questions 6–10.

ABC Inc.

Manufacturing Engineering Procedures

The **purpose of this procedure is to document methods ABC Inc. uses to control manufacturing processes.** The procedure applies to ABC Inc. documents used at any of ABC Inc.'s facilities.

Responsibility

The **industrial engineering supervisor is responsible for the maintenance, interpretation, and implementation of this policy/procedure.** It is the **responsibility of all ABC Inc. supervisors and managers to enforce the use of this policy/procedure.**

Procedure

Location—Shop Floor

1.1   **Product drawings will be filed in a centrally located cabinet.** Prior to running the job, the machine operator will ensure that the drawing number and revisions match the shop order. **If a new drawing is required, the operator shall notify the department supervisor.**

1.2   **Process, test, inspection, and set-up instructions** will be available to production either **electronically via the ABC Inc. Intranet or through paper documents** kept in binders in the department they are used in.

1.3   **The supervisor or lead person can print out electronic documents from their local printer or paper documents may be removed from the binder they are stored in.** Under no circumstances should documentation remain at workstations after the process defined in the documents has been completed. **Paper documents must be returned to their proper location and any electronic document should be destroyed after it has been used.**

1.4   **Any drawings used on the manufacturing floor must be logged out at the central file, identifying the drawing, revision, and location of the document.**

It is the **department supervisor's responsibility to ensure that the most up-to-date revisions of all documents are available.**

---

6.   The purpose of this document is to

   A   provide general information about engineering.

   B   explain ABC Inc.'s sales procedures.

   C   outline the methods used to control ABC Inc.'s manufacturing processes.

   D   explain where company documents are kept.

7.   In the purpose statement at the beginning of this document, the word *processes* means

   A   policies.

   B   products.

   C   operations.

   D   inspections.

8. Who is responsible for enforcing this policy/procedure?

   A   The department supervisor

   B   The industrial engineering supervisor

   C   All ABC Inc. employees

   D   All managers and supervisors

9. After workers finish using electronic documents they should

   A   print them out.

   B   remove them from the binder.

   C   destroy them.

   D   leave them at the workstation.

10. Who should make sure the drawings are kept current?

   A   The ABC Inc. president

   B   The supervisors and managers

   C   The department supervisor

   D   The industrial engineering supervisor

Read this advertisement and answer Questions 11–14.

Receptionist Wanted: Busy Event Planning Office

Must be able to create and update files using Microsoft Word Excel. Important: The successful candidate must know how to greet and direct clients and handle inquiries and incoming phone calls and email requests. Go to topparties.com to submit your resume, attention Hiring Manager.

---

11. Which of the following is a correct inference based on the job advertisement?

   A   The new employee will have time to take computer courses.

   B   The new employee must know Excel but not Microsoft Word.

   C   The new employee must be comfortable handling more than one task at a time.

   D   The new employee can plan on a one-week vacation after the first year's employment.

12. In this advertisement, the word *inquiries* means

   A   data processing.

   B   questions

   C   orders.

   D   calendar invites

13. One of the computer software applications the new employee must know is

   A   PowerPoint.

   B   Algebra.

   C   Photoshop.

   D   Microsoft Word.

14. You can find out the main idea of this advertisement by

    A   Looking at the heading.

    B   reading the first half of the first sentence.

    C   calling the phone number provided.

    D   Submitting a cover letter.

Read this letter and answer Questions 15–19.

Cal Meinhard, President
Insurance Services of America
10 Afton Boulevard
Hartford, CT 00000

Dear Senator Ross:

A vote is coming up on increasing the funds for worksite training, and I am writing to ask you to cast a positive vote. Many factors, including economic, social, and technological, argue in favor of increased worksite training. We are now in an information age characterized by ever-changing technology, global competition, and a multicultural workforce. All of these changes require upgraded employee skills.

Although we are still concerned with graduating students who can read and write, and who have math skills, we know now that there are job-/work-specific skills that need to be addressed. We need to work together to define those skills and implement the necessary training. As a start, we should concern ourselves with employees' ability to value different cultures in the workplace. Inherent here are implications for teamwork as well. In addition, because of automation technology, our entry-level workers must make informed decisions, use critical thinking skills, and work with much less supervision. Finally, Senator, we must do a better job of bringing the workplace together with the schools—public, technical, and advanced—to ensure that our newest employees benefit from our experience. Please vote for the bill.

Very truly yours,
Cal Meinhard

15. The reader can tell what this letter is going to be about because

   A   the writer states in the first sentence that he needs better educated workers for his company.

   B   the writer states in the first sentence that he will also vote to increase worksite training funding.

   C   the writer states in the first sentence that he teaches worksite training.

   D   the writer asks the senator in the first sentence to vote for increasing worksite training funding.

16. The opposite of the word *inherent* in the second paragraph of this letter is

   A   included.

   B   inherited.

   C   excluded.

   D   invited.

17. You can infer from what you have read that Mr. Meinhard needs employees who can

   A   work a longer workweek.

   B   work independently.

   C   use technology in their jobs.

   D   Both B and C.

18. According to this letter, employees need to work on

   A   getting to their jobs on time.

   B   their communication skills.

   C   valuing different cultures.

   D   thinking less, doing more.

19. The purpose of this letter is to

   A   entertain.

   B   persuade.

   C   interrogate.

   D   insult.

Telephone message forms may appear to be simple. In fact, they may include essential ideas, details, and inferences that require careful reading skills.

Read the two messages below and answer Questions 20 to 25.

Message 1

To _Jason Chou_ ☐ URGENT
Date _6/23/15_ Time _10:00_ A.M. P.M.
WHILE YOU WERE OUT
From _Eli Blum_
of _Accurate Prints Corp_
Phone _999_ - _111-2222_ _196_
　　Area Code　　Number　　Ext.
Fax _Do Not Fax - Send email confirmation_
　　Area Code　　Number _Along @AccPrint.com_

Telephoned	✓	Please call	
Came to see you		Wants to see you	✓
Returned your call		Will call again	

Message _He says it is essential he show you the changes on the plan. Needs your OK on additions + documentation. He'll be in until 6 PM today. Can you meet over lunch._
Signed _April Lang_

Message 2

To _Jason Chou_ ☑ URGENT
Date _6/23/15_ Time _11:30_ A.M. P.M.
WHILE YOU WERE OUT
From _Eli Blum_
of _Accurate Prints_
Phone _999_ - _111-2222_ _196_
　　Area Code　　Number　　Ext.
Fax ____
　　Area Code　　Number

Telephoned	✓	Please call	✓
Came to see you		Wants to see you	
Returned your call		Will call again	

Message _His schedule has changed. He'll leave office at 4 PM sharp. Hopes you'll be able to see him at 1 PM._
Signed _April Lang_

20. The words "send email confirmation" in the "Fax" line of Message 1 mean

   A   say yes by e-mail.

   B   phone me if you can come.

   C   please reply by fax.

   D   phone April if you can't come.

21. Jason Chou has two messages from Eli Blum. Which one is more urgent?

   A   Message 1 is more urgent because Jason's boss will attend the meeting.

   B   Message 1 is more urgent because it requests lunch at 12 noon sharp.

   C   Message 2 is more urgent because the caller will not be able to meet for lunch at all.

   D   Message 2 is more urgent because the caller will be leaving earlier than he first said.

22. What is the first clue to the urgency of Message 2?

   A   The caller's name

   B   The time of the call

   C   The Urgent box is checked

   D   The date of the call

23. You can conclude that Eli Blum would prefer to

   A   meet and work with Jason over lunch.

   B   meet Jason at 4 P.M.

   C   meet Jason at 6 P.M.

   D   meet Jason tomorrow.

24. In Message 1, the caller asks Jason

    A   to fax him some information.

    B   to call him and email him.

    C   to fax, call, and e-mail him.

    D   to call him on his cell phone number.

25. You can infer from the two messages that Eli wants to see Jason

    A   no later than a week from now. There's plenty of time.

    B   no earlier than 9:30 A.M. He has a breakfast meeting.

    C   no later than today. He needs Jason's input in order to go forward.

    D   in 6 months. He wants to delay the project for as long as possible.

To the Student: As you check your answers, record the results in this chart. Use the three columns next to the Answer Key to mark your answers as *Correct, Incorrect,* or *Skipped.* Use the other columns to record additional information you want to remember about the individual questions. Total the number of your responses in each column at the bottom of the chart. Then read the recommendations that follow.

Reading Skills Assessment: Answers and Skills Analysis

Item Answers	Correct ✓	Incorrect X	Skipped O	I have a question.	I need instruction.	Refer to these lessons.	Reading Skill Categories*
1 C						4	2
2 D						2	4
3 B						4	1
4 D						5	4
5 A						3	5
6 C						6	5
7 C						4	2
8 D						2	3
9 C						2	3
10 C						2	3
11 C						6	5
12 B						4	2
13 D						2	3
14 A						2	4
15 D						2	3
16 C						4	2
17 D						5	4
18 C						2	3
19 B						6	5

Item Answers	Correct ✓	Incorrect X	Skipped O	I have a question.	I need instruction.	Refer to these lessons.	Reading Skill Categories*
20 A						4	2
21 D						6	4
22 C						3	5
23 A						5	4
24 D						2	3
25 C						5	4
Totals	Correct	Errors	Skipped	Questions	Instruction	Lessons	Skills

* Key to Reading Skill Categories
1. Interpret Graphic Information
2. Words in Context
3. Recall Information
4. Construct Meaning
5. Evaluate/Extend Meaning

Note: These broad categories of reading skills are broken down into subcategories. Question numbers are aligned with the subcategories as well as the lessons to which you can return for a review.

Reading Skills Analysis

Interpret Graphic Information

Reference Sources

LIBRARY CATALOG CARD DISPLAY

Maps

Forms   3   (See Lesson 4)

WORDS IN CONTEXT

Same Meaning   1, 7, 12, 20   (See Lesson 4)

Opposite Meaning   16

RECALL INFORMATION

Details   8, 10, 13, 18, 24   (See Lesson 2)

Sequence   9   (See Lesson 2)

Stated Concepts   15   (See Lesson 2)

CONSTRUCT MEANING

Character Aspects		
Main Ideas	2, 14	(See Lesson 2)
Summary/Paraphrase		
Cause/Effect		
Compare/Contrast	21	(See Lesson 6)
Conclusion	4, 17, 23, 25	(See Lesson 5)
Supporting Evidence		

EVALUATE/EXTEND MEANING

Fact/Opinion	22	(See Lesson 3)
Predict Outcomes		
Apply Passage Element	5	(See Lesson 3)
Generalizations		
Effect/Intentions	11	(See Lesson 6)
Author Purpose	6, 19	(See Lesson 6)
Point of View		
Style Techniques		
Genre		

RECOMMENDATIONS

To identify the areas where you need improvement in the Reading Section, do three things:

1. Total your number of correct answers out of the 25 possible answers. To score a passing grade, you should have 90 to 95 percent correct (or 23 to 24 correct answers).
2. Total the correct answers in each subcategory of skills. For example, in the subcategory *Recall Information,* there are seven correct answers. To score a passing grade, you should have 95 percent correct (or 6 correct answers).
3. Wherever your score is below 95 percent, go back to that lesson (indicated in parentheses) and review the skill.

In Lesson 2, you will follow Mike through his first weeks at Ace Computer Chip. He has taken the TABE reading pretest, just like you have. He has also participated in the self-study exercises you learned about in Section 1. You will see the results of Mike's work. Perhaps his experience will help you evaluate your own self-study.

You will also have the opportunity to think about important reading skills: reading to understand the main idea and supporting details.

Words to Know

Alliance	An association
Distinguish	Tell one from another
Preferences	Favorites
Confirmed	Found correct

Down to Work

During his interview with Sue Mendez, Mike learned that Ace Computer Chip Company had a training program. Training would increase Mike's knowledge of computer programs. In addition, through the training program, Mike would also explore many different jobs in the company. As a matter of fact, all employees at Ace were required to take six credits of training per year. Ace had good reasons for this. Ace hoped to promote employees from within the company. The courses offered employees a chance to learn about all the departments. Each department required different education and training.

The company also had an alliance with a nearby community college. Mike would be encouraged to take advantage of the college's more advanced computer courses. Before he interviewed at Ace, Mike had not known about financial aid. He learned that taking the TABE was a way to qualify for Ability to Benefit federal financial aid. This was another reason to do as well as possible on the tests.

TARGET: Reading for Main Ideas and Reading for Details

Reading for Main Ideas: Why is this always one of the first reading skills taught in any reading improvement course? You are probably saying, "The answer to that question is simple: If I don't get the main idea of what I'm reading, what is the point of wasting my time?" You would be right! That is why we will take the time to review this important skill.

Warming Up for the Event

A reader should prepare for reading just as an athlete prepares for an athletic event. Athletes need to warm up before a practice session, and readers need to warm up before a reading session. Your warm-up involves getting your brain "warmed up to" or familiar with the subject matter. How do you do that?

STUDY TIP

- Look at the title of the article, chapter, or other informational material. Does it give clues to the main idea?
- If you need more clues, read the first sentences of a few paragraphs. Then read the entire last paragraph, a summary of main ideas. Any of these may hold strong main idea clues.
- Before you read the entire article, ask yourself, whether you already know something about the topic. You may be able to predict what it is about.
- Ask yourself what you can expect to learn from the reading. After you finish reading, go back and check to see if you were right.
- Look for graphic information and pictures for clues to the main idea before you start reading.
- As you read, *actively* look for the main idea.

We hope we can convince you that this warm-up will take very little time. The more often you go through the steps listed above, the faster you will become. The time spent is well worth it. At the end of a reading, you won't hear yourself saying, "I just read two pages and I have no idea what they were about!"

When you read for a main idea, you actively look for the most important thought in the passage. You ask yourself what idea the writer wanted you to know after reading the passage. For example, on page 28, paragraph 1, under "Down to Work," what is the main idea? Look for the sentence that tells what the paragraph is about.

Write your answer here:_____

If you said that the paragraph is about Ace Computer Chip Company's ongoing learning program, you were right. Notice that the main idea is in the first sentence. Writers often (but not always) state the main idea in the first sentence. By doing this, the writer helps readers quickly establish a new train of thought. The readers do not have to wait to find out the most important idea. Their thinking is set in the correct direction to understand the details that follow.

If the main idea is not in the first sentence, where might it be? Sometimes a writer starts a paragraph with a transitional sentence. A transitional sentence ties the first sentence to the previous paragraph. You will read more about that later. Or, the writer might start by building evidence about the main idea in the paragraph. In that case, the writer might start with supporting ideas and work up to the main idea, stating it in the last sentence. The main idea is most often found in the first sentence.

Try to distinguish between the main idea and supporting details. Start by asking yourself a question: Which sentence is the sum of all the supporting details? That sentence is the main idea. Now you are ready to look at the details.

Reading for Supporting Details: Now go back to page 28. How do sentences 2, 3, 4, and 5 of paragraph 1 of "Down to Work" add detail and support to the main idea?

Write your answer here: _____

_____

You probably said that sentences 2, 3, 4, and 5 add meaning to the main idea by

- Stating that Mike would increase his knowledge of computers
- Explaining that the training program encourages employees to explore other job possibilities at Ace
- Stating that all employees must take six credits of training per year
- Specifying that the training program offered opportunities to learn about the job requirements of all departments

Target Practice: More Reading for Main Ideas

Now you know that when you search for a main idea in a paragraph, there is a very good chance that you will find it in the first sentence. Are main ideas found in other kinds of writing? Absolutely. Charts, graphs, and worksheets, for example, all have a main idea or a primary topic.

Look at Mike's Learner Preference Worksheet below. What would you say is the main idea or topic of the worksheet? Write your answer here:

_____

You probably realized that the main idea or primary topic of the worksheet is a person's learning preferences. How did you know that? The answer is simple, of course: You read the title and probably skimmed the worksheet to see if, in fact, preferences were explored, as the worksheet title indicated. Reading the title and skimming the worksheet are good examples of a reading warm-up.

Read Mike's Learner Preference Worksheet carefully.

Learner Preference Worksheet
Name: Mike Rinaldi

1. *What time(s) of day or night do you feel better able to study/work/read/write?*
   Early morning ____ Afternoon _✓_ Early evening ____ Late night ____

2. *Do you prefer to study or learn by yourself or with others?*
   I like learning about new things with a study group. ____
   I like learning about new things by myself. _✓_
   I like learning something new with one other person to help me. ____
   It depends on the subject matter. _✓_

---

3. *Do you learn best by: (Check all that apply)*
   Reading about something? ✓
   Looking at a picture or graph? ✓
   Listening to someone explain something? ____
   Doing what you are learning about? ____
   Writing it down? ✓
   Talking about it with or without someone else? ____

4. *What length of time do you prefer to spend studying?*
   I prefer to work for periods of 2 hours or more. ____
   I prefer to work for shorter periods of time (less than an hour). ____
   I can work whenever time permits. ✓

5. *How's your concentration?*
   I need complete quiet when I study or read. ____
   I can study or read with some background noise. ✓
   I can study or read in any environment, quiet or noisy. ____

Mike completed his Learner Preference Worksheet. He met again with the Sue. Together they reviewed the worksheet. Mike thought that he knew what it would reveal. He was right about one item: listening. He confirmed that he did prefer to learn or receive instructions by reading, not by listening. Mike told Sue that when he followed verbal instructions, he often made mistakes. In fact, Mike remembered many such experiences. He had failed or done poorly on tests because instructions had been given verbally instead of in print. Mike recalled, with some embarrassment, that he had actually been fired from one of his first part-time jobs because of this. He did not follow verbal directions on the use of a potentially dangerous machine.

Before you look back at the supporting details revealed in the worksheet, remember what Mike already knew about himself as a learner. He knew that he did not prefer listening as a learning tool. The Learner Preference Worksheet gave Mike an opportunity to explore many different aspects of his preferences.

STUDY TIP: SKIMMING AND SCANNING
When a question asks you to find a detail, be sure you are clear on what to look for. Then scan all the material for that word or number or phrase. That means that you should run your eyes down the middle of the reading passage, looking only for the item in question. You are not reading for meaning; you are reading to find a specific number, word, or phrase. When you find the detail, read the words around it to be absolutely sure you have the right answer. Remember, the same number, word, or phrase may appear more than once.

Now answer this detail question.

Find three supporting facts that Mike discovered by working on the Learner Preference Worksheet.

_____

_____

_____

Did you find the following facts?

1 There was one preference Mike had never thought about before. That was the fact that he liked to learn from graphs or pictures or other visual representations of instructions.

2 Mike had never thought about studying or learning with others. He thought that most often he would want to study alone. Now, for the first time, he considered that he might work with others—depending upon the subject.

3 Mike had never considered the time of day he studied. He had never thought that his ability to concentrate was important.

After Mike finished working on his Learning Preference Worksheet, he talked it over with Sue. More than ever, he was concerned about his listening skills. Sue agreed with his self-evaluation. Mike should definitely try to get instructions in writing whenever possible. She mentioned that one of the company's training courses, "Communication Skills: Listening, Speaking, and Writing," would be an excellent course for Mike. Mike could work on both of his areas of concern: listening and writing.

More About Main Ideas

You will recall that a main idea may be found somewhere other than in the first sentence. The paragraph immediately above is a good example. Look at the paragraph that follows right after details 1, 2, and 3. The paragraph begins, "After Mike finished working on his Learner Preference Worksheet, he talked it over with Sue." Look back at that paragraph. Do you think of the first sentence as the main idea sentence? Is the entire paragraph about Mike's finishing the worksheet?

Your answer is probably, "No." In fact, that sentence is the bridge between the worksheet and what Mike really wants to discuss. His real concern is his inability to follow verbal instruction. The first sentence is a good example of a transitional sentence. It ties the Learner Preference Worksheet to the new topic, Mike's concern about his listening ability.

Let's apply the test of a main idea. If, in fact, the second sentence is the main idea sentence, then all sentences that follow should support the main idea. Sentences 3, 4, and 5 strongly support Mike's concern.

Sue agreed with Mike's self-evaluation and suggested that he do two things:

1. When possible, ask for written instructions in the workplace.
2. Take the training course, "Communication Skills: Listening, Speaking, and Writing."

Target Practice: Reading for Main Ideas and Supporting Details

The following is a paragraph from Ace Computer Chip Company's Drug-Free Workplace Policy. All new employees must sign the statement. Read the paragraph and answer the question that follows.

> Employees and management of Ace Computer Chip Company wrote the Drug-Free Workplace Policy together. The policy hopes to create and maintain a healthy and productive work environment. We believe that this policy will ensure the good health of the new employee who signs it. The rest of our workforce is also positively affected by the policy. Without a doubt, one employee's use of drugs or alcohol affects the safety and security of our entire staff. We believe that substance abuse negatively impacts the workplace by increasing absenteeism. It also lowers productivity and undermines, or weakens, the safety of all employees.

1. What is the main idea of the paragraph?
  A The Drug-Free Policy was created because the company's health insurance required it.
  B The Drug-Free Policy was created because use of drugs and alcohol was widespread in the company.
  C The Drug-Free Policy was created because of the increase in absenteeism and accidents in the workplace.
  D The Drug-Free Policy was created to keep the working environment healthy and productive.

The following is a portion of the employment application that Mike completed after his first interview with Sue. After you read it, answer the supporting detail questions that follow.

Application for Employment

Date _____ Name: First _____ Middle _____ Last _____

Social Security Number _____

Date of Birth _____

Present Address _____ Previous Address _____

City _____ State _____ Zip _____

Home Telephone _____ Cell Phone _____

When are you available? Days? Evenings? Both?

Do you have any relatives employed at Ace Computer Chip Company? If yes, please list their names.

Please list your relative's/relatives' dates of employment?

How did you learn about the job at Ace?

What position are you applying for? Salary desired?

Do you have a legal right to work in the United States?

Have you ever been convicted of a criminal offense?

If yes, please describe, including dates.

2. Complete this statement: The applicant may have a relative employed at Ace Computer
   A but only within the past five years.
   B at any time present or past.
   C but not in the same department in which the applicant wants to work.
   D but the relative may not live at the same address as the applicant.

3. True or False: The applicant has little or no choice in the time of day he will work. _____

4. This application asks a potential employee if he/she has thought about
   A moving to another state where the company has a larger facility.
   B the salary he/she wants.
   C getting a college degree.
   D working overseas.

Use Reading Skills to Comprehend Graphs and Tables

 STUDY TIP: FINDING MAIN IDEAS
You can find main ideas and details in graphic—or picture—materials. Look at the bar graph that follows. Use the skills you learned on page 29 to "warm up" before reading the graph. The technique works with other materials as well. Try this with charts, graphs, maps, tables, diagrams, and so forth.

Study the graph below. Use the three questions that follow to start your thinking process.

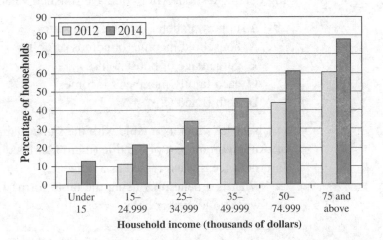

The Warm-Up

5. Where did you find the main idea of the graph?_____

6. What one thing did you probably already know about the topic?

_____

7. What can you expect to learn from reading the graph?_____

Answers to these questions will vary somewhat. Check the Answer Key to see if you are on the right track.
Now answer the following question. Then check the Answer Key.

8. What is the main idea of the graph?
   A The years 2012 and 2014 in U.S. households
   B Internet access in the United States
   C Internet access in U.S. households by income in 2012 and 2014
   D Household income (thousands of dollars)

Supporting details can usually be found in several places on a graph. To warm up, do this:

- Look at the left, right, and bottom margins of the graph.
- Write down any information you may have found there, e.g., Household Income.
- How do you think these details are related?
- Look at the graph itself. Are there any distinctive ways the information is presented—for instance, different colors, bar heights, and so on?

Now review the skimming and scanning skills above. Then answer the following detail question. After you have finished, check the Answer Key.

9. A supporting detail in the graph states
   A household income (hundreds of dollars).
   B percentage of households.
   C each family member's income.
   D both B and C.

Now let's look at a table with the same main idea as the graph we just looked at. An important part of the title (main idea) is that the number of households with Internet access is expressed as a percent.

What is a benefit of using the table form? Look at the table carefully before you write your answer below.

_____

The answer, of course, is that in the table the reader can see the specific listed. In the bar graph the reader has to "read" all the information and find the answer based on what he or she sees.

U.S. households with Internet access, by income: 2000 and 2011 (Percent)

| Year | Household income (thousands of dollars) | | | |
	Under 30	30–49.999	50–74.999	75 and above
2000	28%	50%	67%	79%
2011	62%	83%	90%	97%

Source: The Pew Research Center's Internet American Life Project, 2000–2011.

10. What percentage of households earning under $30,000 had access to the Internet in 2000?
   A 12.4 percent
   B 11.0 percent
   C 34.0 percent
   D 28 percent

What reading skills did you use to answer this question? You probably used clue words from the question: *2000* and *Under 30*. You skimmed the table, looking for those clue words and numbers. There you found a number that was the percentage. Compare your answer with the Answer Key.

Think About This

11. In your opinion, is the table or the graph better for communicating the main idea?_____

12. Which one communicates specific details better?_____

Answers to these questions may vary. Look at the Answer Key for some ideas. In the Math Section you will learn about working with the numbers in a table.

Answer Key

1. D

2. B

3. False

4. B

5. The main idea is found in the title, U.S. households with Internet access, by income: 2012 and 2014.

6. Answers will vary. You may have already known that Internet access increases with income.

7. Answers will vary. You may expect to learn how percentage of households at your income level increased over these years.

8. C. Answer C is the only answer that includes all parts of the main idea.

9. B. Answer B is the only correct answer. Answer A is an incorrect detail because income is stated in thousands; answer C is an incorrect detail because the graph deals with entire households; answer D is an incorrect answer because answer B is not correct.

10. D

11. You looked at the title in both the graph and the table in order to find the main idea. However, for many readers, there is a "picture" quality to the graph that provides meaning. The fact that the bars go from low to high suggests growth. Darker and lighter bars present a clear picture of the different years.

12. Clearly, the table communicates specific details better. The percentages of households, for example, 28% and 62%, provide immediate knowledge of the numbers involved.

In Lesson 3, Mike will learn much more about his choices for the future. The steps he has already taken have helped him think about what he really wanted of himself and the workplace. Now we follow Mike to the local community college where he and other new students start the admissions process.

Words to Know

Admissions process	Steps for getting into a program
Expand	Enlarge
Prerequisite	Requirement or precondition

Looking into the Future

Mike set some goals for himself after he graduated from high school and started working. You probably recall that Mike said he wanted to (1) learn much more about the computer programs used in business and (2) earn enough to live on his own. Completing the Where Are You Headed? worksheet and going through the interviewing process at Ace Computer helped Mike expand his thinking about his future. Read his worksheet below and think about where his answers might lead him.

> **Where Are You Headed?**
> Prospective Employee: Mike Rinaldi
>
> I am studying to do well on the TABE to
>
> (✓ all that apply):
>
> ✓ Qualify for "Ability to Benefit" federal financial aid
>
> ✓ Enroll in credit courses at a community college
>
> ✓ Enter a program of job training or career advancement
>
> ✓ Qualify for a promotion to the next level at my workplace
>
> ✓ Become more independent in handling my affairs
>
> ✓ Upgrade my basic skills for personal satisfaction
>
> ____ Enter a technical school
>
> ____ Help family members with their schooling
>
> ✓ Become proficient in Excel

TARGET: Reading for Inferences

Have you ever thought about what it means to "read between the lines"? Obviously, there is nothing written between the lines, but there is *unwritten meaning* for the savvy reader to interpret. When you read to find inference, you are *not* looking for stated facts. You are, instead, trying to figure out what the writer meant, but did not say. How do you do this? You look at the stated facts, but then you add your own knowledge to what you have just read. When you take these two steps, you are reading between the lines (reading for inferences).

One note about this reading skill: Inferences can be found in most kinds of reading material. You can even use this skill for reading worksheets. Later in this chapter you will use this skill to read a nutrition label. But for now, look back to the worksheet, Where Are You Headed? Answer this question:

1. You can infer from the worksheet that
    A Mike will never qualify for a promotion at Ace Computer.
    B Mike thinks becoming more independent is his most important goal.
    C Mike expanded his thinking about what he could accomplish at Ace Computer.
    D Mike decided that a technical school would provide him with the education he needed.

Write your answer here. _____

Did you choose answer C? If you did, you were right. Answer A is not correct. You have no way of knowing if or when Mike will qualify for a promotion. What you do know is that he wants to learn more about the use of computers in business. Answer B is not a correct inference because the worksheet asks for "all that apply," not the most important goal. Answer C is correct. The goals that Mike talked about when you first met him were (1) to learn more about computer programs in business and (2) to earn enough to live on his own. You can see from his choices on the worksheet that he's thinking about applying for financial aid, enrolling in a community college, and upgrading his personal and work. These choices imply that his knowledge of available resources has expanded and that his thinking has broadened to include many different choices.

Just ahead, you will have the opportunity to use this skill to read a catalog of courses.

Going for the Goal

Mike was eager to find out what courses were offered at the community college. He went there to pick up a catalog of courses that would be given in the next semester. Mike found out that he could have accessed the courses just by going online. The community college had its own Web site. As he looked through the catalog he saw a woman who was doing the same thing, but she looked very puzzled and worried. Mike asked her if she, too, was planning to take computer courses. She said, "Yes, I am, but I'm really nervous because I know nothing about computers."

Mike introduced himself and said, "Maybe I can help. Why do you need to use a computer?"

"I'm Michelle Gordon. I'm starting coursework to become a registered nurse. I haven't been in school since I became a Certified Nursing Assistant (CNA) years ago. I just found out that I must use a computer. Most courses require that assignments be emailed to the instructor. I don't know how to do that!"

Mike asked, "Can someone help you?"

"Well, my children are young and I want to be able to supervise their use of e-mail."

"It's not as hard as you might think. If you want me to, I'll look at the catalog with you and maybe we can figure out which course will help. I have to find a course, too, so I don't mind looking for both of us."

Mike opened the catalog to the section on computer courses. He found the following:

Brightwater Community College
Catalog of Courses, Spring Semester

- **Introduction to Computers,** CT001, 4 credits, prerequisites: none, Professor Cabral, Tuesday, Thursday, 5 P.M.

  Description: Students will gain a basic understanding of computers and procedures used in a work and/or study environment. This class focuses on hands-on experience with word processing, setting up e-mail accounts, and report writing and presentation.

- **Computer Business Applications,** CBA003 and IE005, 3 credits, prerequisites: CT001, Professor Mintz, Monday, Wednesday, 6 P.M.

  Description: This is a hands-on computer lab course using software for managing numerical, text, or graphic data in real-life business simulations.

- **Introduction to the Internet,** II002, 1 credit, prerequisite: CT001, Professor Santos, Saturday, 9 A.M.

  Description: This course is for individuals totally inexperienced in using the Internet. You will learn the tools needed to navigate and search the Internet. Included is information on search engines, email, and access to many useful Internet resources.

- **Introduction to Microsoft Word,** IMW004, 3 credits, prerequisite: CT001 or permission of the instructor, Professor Davidson, Tuesday, Thursday, 6:30 P.M.

Description: This is a basic course for people with little computer experience, using the current version of Microsoft Word. Participants will learn all of the main elements of the program, Word for Windows, toolbars, inserting and deleting text, scrolling, and much more.

- **Introduction to Excel,** IE005, 3 credits, prerequisite: CT001, Professor Cabral, Monday, Wednesday, 6 P.M.

    Description: If you need to use a spreadsheet for business, family expenses, or any other numerical data management, this is the course for you. Learn to navigate a worksheet, enter text, edit cells, and produce clear reports.

- **Topics in Computers,** TC006, 2 credits, prerequisite: CT001, Professor David Dudley, Monday, 6 P.M. to 8 P.M.

    Description: Students will learn about various software used in the business environment, with a focus on presentation software.

Target Practice: More Reading for Inferences

2. From what you know about Michelle's educational needs, you can infer that she will choose which of the following courses?
    A Introduction to Microsoft Word
    B Computer Business Applications
    C Introduction to Computers
    D Introduction to Excel

3. Considering what you know about Mike's goals for the future, what course would you say that Mike will choose?
    A Introduction to Microsoft Word
    B Computer Business Applications
    C Introduction to Computers
    D Introduction to Excel

4. After reading the course information, you can infer that a new student with no background in computer use would be allowed to take which of the following courses?
    A Introduction to Excel
    B Computer Business Applications
    C All of the above
    D None of the above

Review Reading for Supporting Details (Important! Review the skimming and scanning skills presented in Lesson 2.)

5. A course that will teach Michelle how to use electronic mail (e-mail) is
   A Introduction to the Internet
   B Introduction to Excel
   C Introduction to Microsoft Word
   D Topics in Computers

6. Which one of the following courses does not require students to take a prerequisite?
   A Computer Business Applications
   B Introduction to Excel
   C Introduction to Computers
   D Topics in Computers

7. Which course teaches the use of a computer spreadsheet?
   A Introduction to Computers
   B Introduction to Excel
   C Introduction to the Internet
   D Introduction to Microsoft Word

8. Which course teaches the student how to use presentation software?
   A Introduction to Computers
   B Topics in Computers
   C Introduction to Microsoft Word
   D Computer Business Applications

Reading for Inferences in Nutrition Labels

Study the two nutrition labels below. Both are based on information from cereal boxes.

FRUIT AND BRAN CEREAL

Nutrition Facts

Serving Size 1¼ cups (55 g)
Servings Per Container About 8

Amount Per Serving	Cereal	Cereal with ½ cup skim milk
Calories	190	230
Calories from Fat	0	0
		% Daily Value**
Total Fat 0g*	0%	0%
Saturated Fat 0g	0%	0%
Cholesterol 0mg	0%	0%
Sodium 90mg	4%	7%
Total Carbohydrate 47g	16%	18%
Dietary Fiber 6g	24%	24%

Amount Per Serving	Cereal	Cereal with ½ cup skim milk
Sugars 13g		
Protein 5g		
Iron	6%	6%

Not a significant source of Vitamin A, Vitamin C, or Calcium.

* Amount in cereal. One half cup skim milk contributes an additional 40 calories, 65mg sodium, 6g total carbohydrate (6g sugars), and 4g protein.

** Percent Daily Values are based on a 2,000 calorie diet. Your daily values may be higher or lower depending on your calorie needs:

	Calories	2,000	2,500
Total Fat	Less than	65g	80g
Saturated Fat	Less than	20g	25g
Cholesterol	Less than	300mg	300mg
Sodium	Less than	2,400mg	2,400mg
Total Carbohydrate		300g	375g
Dietary Fiber		25g	30g
Calories per gram:			
Fat 9	Carbohydrate 4	Protein 4	

NATURAL OAT CEREAL

Nutrition Facts

Serving Size: ½ cup dry (40g)
Servings Per Container 13
Amount Per Serving

Calories	150
Calories from Fat	25
	% Daily Value*
Total Fat 3g	5%
Saturated Fat 0.5g	2%
Polyunsaturated Fat 1g	
Monounsaturated Fat 1g	
Cholesterol 0mg	0%
Sodium 0mg	0%
Total Carbohydrate 27g	9%
Dietary Fiber 4g	15%
Soluble Fiber 4g	
Insoluble Fiber 2g	
Sugars 1g	
Protein 5g	
Vitamin A	0%
Vitamin C	0%

Calories	150
Calcium	0%
Iron	15%

* Percent Daily Values are based on a 2,000 calorie diet. Your daily values may be higher or lower depending on your calorie needs:

Calories		2,000	2,500
Total Fat	Less than	65g	80g
Saturated Fat	Less than	20g	25g
Cholesterol	Less than	300g	300g
Sodium	Less than	2,400mg	2,400m
Total Carbohydrate		300g	
Dietary Fiber		25g	30g

Target Practice: Reading for Inferences

Now that you have read the nutrition facts on both labels, you can answer the inference questions that follow. Apply the two steps you have already learned to use in reading for inferences: (1) Look for the facts presented and (2) add *your* knowledge to the facts in order to read between the lines.

For example, suppose your doctor, Dr. Wylie, has advised you to lower your caloric intake to 2,000 calories per day. Dr. Wylie has also advised you to keep your sodium as close as possible to 0 mg per day.

9. You can infer from the nutrition facts for both cereals that
   A Fruit and Bran Cereal is your better choice.
   B Natural Oat Cereal is your better choice.
   C you can eat either cereal; the nutrition information is practically the same for both.
   D you should not eat either cereal; both are very bad for you.

Suppose Dr. Wylie also wants you to lose weight. She advises you to choose foods that are as low as possible in fat.

10. You can infer from the additional facts above that
   A Fruit and Bran Cereal is the better choice.
   B Natural Oat Cereal is the better choice.
   C you may eat either cereal.
   D you should not eat either cereal.

11. Another of Dr. Wylie's patients has been diagnosed with a mild case of diabetes. That patient
   A should eat Fruit and Bran Cereal.
   B should eat Natural Oat Cereal.
   C may eat either cereal.
   D should not eat any kind of cereal.

Review Main Ideas and Details in Labels

12. Which of the following is the main idea of these labels?
  A Every food contains certain nutrients and those facts are listed on the label.
  B Everyone should avoid all fat and calories.
  C It is possible to get large quantities of vitamins A and C from eating Fruit and Bran Cereal.
  D Cereal provides all nutritional needs.

13. A detail on the Fruit and Bran Cereal label tells you that you increase your total calorie intake by
  A increasing the amount of sodium.
  B increasing the amount of Vitamin C.
  C adding Vitamin A.
  D adding ½ cup skim milk.

14. The two kinds of dietary fiber listed on the food label are
  A cholesterol and sodium.
  B insoluble and polyunsaturated.
  C soluble and insoluble.
  D soluble and saturated.

Once again, you found that you needed to apply reading skills to fully understand the labels. You needed something else as well: special math skills. Look for information on grams (*g,* as in *3 g*) and milligrams (*mg,* as in *300 mg*) on page 128 in Section 3, Lesson 10. You will study percents (%) in Section 3, Lesson 3.

Answer Key

1. C	**8.** B	**12.** A
2. C	**9.** D	**13.** D
3. D	**10.** A	**14.** C
4. D	**11.** B (To answer this question, you needed to know that people	
5. A	diagnosed with diabetes generally avoid foods that contain	
6. C	sugar.)	
7. B		

LESSON 4 **Getting Information**

In this lesson, Michelle and Mike pool their information and their resources. They have an opportunity to discuss their personal situations. You will have an opportunity to practice this skill: understanding the meaning of words in context.

Words to Know

Literate	To be educated about, and skillful in using, something; for example, if you are computer-literate, you know about computers and are skillful in using them
User-friendly	An expression used to describe a computer program that is easy to use
ISP (Internet Service Provider)	A company that connects you directly to the Internet

Networking

"Why does a nursing student have to take a computer class?" Mike asked Michelle.

"That's just what I asked!" Michelle exclaimed. "My very first nursing course requires me to get weekly assignments through the Internet. I also have to turn in my homework by e-mail. What a shock! Between raising a family and holding a part-time job, it took me eight years to complete the coursework I needed for acceptance into the Registered Nursing Program. Now I find out that I actually need another prerequisite—computer skills. I barely know how to turn on a computer, let alone use it for schoolwork. I never dreamed it would be such a large part of my training as an RN.

"My advisor said not to worry because the computer program I need to learn is 'user-friendly.' She also informed me that being computer-literate is essential in today's workplace, no matter what your profession. Look here on top of the syllabus that outlines what we will study. She wrote down my username and password. I'm supposed to use these when I connect with the community college computer network. I'm not even sure which is which! Computer talk is like a foreign language to me."

"Whoa, slow down," Mike said. "Don't you have a friend who can help you?"

"Not really, my friends are as computer-challenged as I am. I did buy a second-hand computer for my kids, since they are starting to use one in school. They are way ahead of me but are too young to use the Internet. As a matter of fact, we're not even connected. Someone told me I had better choose an ISP and get connected quickly. What is an ISP and where do I get one?"

"Hey, I love computers; they are my world. Let me help. I can give you a couple of hands-on lessons using the computers in the library. You will be e-mailing in no time. Hands-on practice will help you so that computer talk like ISP is user-friendly and will start to make sense to you."

TARGET: Understanding Words in Context

We don't always know the exact meaning of all the words that we read (or hear). Of course, it is not practical to carry a dictionary all the time. However, there are techniques that good readers (and listeners) use to figure out what is being said. In fact, there is a helpful procedure to figure out the meaning of a word. That is, you examine the *context,* or situation, in which it is used. You check for clues in the words and sentences that surround the unknown word. Checking the main idea and tone of the whole article will also provide clues to word meanings.

STUDY TIP 1

Look at the word or words *immediately following* the word that you don't understand. Are commas or parentheses setting off those words? If so, the words within those punctuation marks may explain what the unknown word means. If not, look for clues in the sentences *just before or after* the word.

Example: Reread the paragraph that precedes Study Tip 1. Find the word *context.* Now look at the words *or situation* that follows. What do you think? If you are thinking that *situation* is another way to say *context,* you are correct. These two words are synonyms, words that mean more or less the same thing. Writers will often place synonyms that are more familiar words immediately before or after difficult words. Notice that the word *synonym* is defined, or explained, in the sixth sentence of this example.

Complete these sentences:

1. Synonyms are _____.
2. Another word for *defined* is _____.

You should have completed sentence 1 with *words that mean more or less the same thing.* You should have completed sentence 2 with *explained.*

Now use Study Tip 1 to identify the meaning of the words in *italics* in the following sentences:

1. In response to the stress of tiring exercise, the human body produces chemicals called *endorphins,* the body's natural pain relievers.
   Endorphins are
   A a reaction to emotional stress.
   B safe medication for humans.
   C pain killers produced by the body.
   D chemicals also known as dorphins.

2. The professor wrote her name and email address on the top of my copy of the course *syllabus* that lists topics she will cover in her class.
   A syllabus is
   A a list of dates for quizzes, tests, and exams.
   B a password to access study materials.
   C a list of websites where students can purchase used books.
   D an outline of what will be studied.

STUDY TIP 2

Look for patterns in the sentences that surround the unknown word. Do you see a group of words that is repeated two or more times? Are these groups of words also next to or near the unknown word? Writers sometimes structure the way they say things in order to help the reader get the message. They may purposely repeat groups of words in a sentence or paragraph for emphasis.

Example: Look back at the first paragraph under the heading, "Target: Understanding Words in Context." Locate and <u>underline</u> the group of words that is repeated in sentences three and four.

Did you underline the phrase *figure out* twice? Now circle the words that come before each of those phrases. Notice that these words—*technique* and *procedure*—have a similar meaning: They are both *a system, or a way,* to accomplish something—in this case, *a system to figure out the meaning* of words.

Now it's your turn to use Study Tip 2. In the sentences that follow, look for the similar word patterns that help define the words in *italics*.

3. Teaching about *morphemes* is an effective way to improve students' reading comprehension. Teaching about word parts that have meaning—prefixes, suffixes and roots—helps students improve their understanding of what they read.

    Morphemes are

    A vocabulary lists.

    B parts of words that have meaning.

    C special dictionaries.

    D study guides.

4. It took Michelle eight years to complete the coursework she needed before she could start the Registered Nursing Program. Then she discovered there was another kind of *prerequisite* she needed before she started: basic computer skills.

    Prerequisite means

    A a technical skill.

    B an internship for nurses and doctors.

    C an entrance exam.

    D something required before you can do something else.

5. *Consumption* of *legumes* in the U.S. is quite low. The average *per capita* consumption is about one pound per person each year. That means the average person eats just over one ounce of beans a month.

    Complete the sentences below using context clues given in the sentences above.

    A Legumes are _____

    B Consumption means _____

    C Per capita means _____

STUDY TIP 3

Many words have more than one meaning. Sometimes you need to see a word used in a specific situation to know what it means. Often, the topic or the main idea of the passage will help you interpret the meanings of individual words.

Example: (1) I was *down* for three days in bed with the flu. A friend unknowingly gave me the invisible *virus* when she sneezed.

(2) My computer system was *down* for three days after my friend unknowingly sent me e-mail that was infected by a *virus*.

In both sentences, the word *down* means "not working as usual." However, in the first sentence *down* means "in poor health." In the second sentence, it refers to "mechanical failure." Likewise, the word *virus* has two different meanings in the context of these sentences. In both cases, *virus* refers to something that has caused trouble. The system has stopped functioning normally. However, in the first sentence, *virus* means a biological organism that causes an illness. In the second sentence, *virus* means a piece of programming code that can cause damage to computer files.

Now it is your turn. Choose the correct meanings of the words in the context of these sentences.

6. The *mouse* rolled across the smooth top of the computer desk and fell with a crash on the tile floor.

Mouse means

A a small rodent with a long tail.

B a small stuffed animal.

C a small facial bruise, usually around the eyes.

D a small device used to make selections on a computer screen.

7. The suspect's testimony provided the detective with the missing *link* he needed to solve the crime.

Link means

A an association of detectives.

B one of the connecting parts of a metal chain.

C a word or icon connecting websites.

D information needed to connect other information.

Target Practice: Understanding Words in Context

Read the following selection. Pay special attention to the words in *italics*. Then answer the questions that follow.

The World Wide Web (WWW) is a system that uses the Internet to link information to the world. The Web offers many different resources: Libraries, newspapers, shopping malls, telephone directories, and more are available on a *global* scale. The Web is constantly changing and expanding, an enormous *repository* of human culture. The Web is a storage area for information about different ways of life.

Why is the Web so widely used? First, it is a user-friendly information access tool. Second, it is fast and as accessible as the nearest computer. The Web is the research tool of choice. Today's students can *readily* obtain information that took their parents and grandparents lots of time and energy to find. Indeed, even very small children seem to know *intuitively* how to use the Web without having to ask. Learning opportunities are available to users of all ages, providing unlimited education at a distance. There are many irritatingly commercial, money-seeking sites, but there are also many other sites that are wonderfully *altruistic*. Many sites offer information, services, and products free of charge.

Use the context clues in the paragraphs above to select the correct meanings of these words:

8. altruistic
   A Wonderful
   B Generous
   C Old-fashioned
   D Expensive

9. global
   A On a small scale
   B Shaped like a globe
   C Worldwide
   D Electronically

10. repository
    A A safe place
    B A large container
    C A deposit box
    D A main storage area

11. readily
    A Gathering
    B Easily
    C Prepared
    D Steady

12. intuitively
    A Naturally
    B Bravely
    C Cheaply
    D Quickly

More (or Less) about Michelle

Michelle wanted to stop talking about herself so she asked Mike, "How about you? Why are you looking at computer courses?"

He replied, "I can't wait to get my own place and get a better job that will pay my bills and more. After high school, I just wanted to get a job. I was so happy to be done with school. Now, my new job with Ace has opened my eyes to possibilities I hadn't considered. So funny enough I am looking at going back to school so

I can improve my future. I know I want a career in computers. I know I want to earn a good salary. I am trying to find out how to get started."

"Well," Michelle offered, "I think the library is a great place to begin. My guidance counselor gave me some handouts today about job market trends for registered nurses. There is a great demand for registered nurses and that is likely to continue and even increase. She told us to check out the reference section of the college library for more of the same. I'll bet you could find something like this for computer jobs."

Occupation Report

Occupation: Registered Nurses

State: (Your State)

Typical Educational Level: Associate degree

Licenses: This is a licensed occupation in (Your State). *Click here* to view licensing requirements.

Description: Administer nursing care to ill or injured persons. Licensing or registration required. Include administrative, public health, industrial, private duty, and surgical nurses.

Wages

	Registered Nurse Wages			
Location	Median, 2014		Midrange, 2014	
	Hourly	Annual	Hourly	Annual
United States	$45.84	$95,300	$39.77–54.55	$82,700–113,500
(Your State)	$48.27	$100,400	$40.39–55.61	$84,000–115,700

Source: *Bureau of Labor Statistics, Occupational Employment Statistics Survey; Labor Market Information, Rhode Island Department of Labor and Training.*

Mike was excited. "This is good stuff. The future job market looks promising for you. Where did these numbers come from? Looks like a printout from the Internet . . . oh yes, see these letters and symbols? (http://www.acinet.org/acinet/occ_rep.htm?oescode=32502&stfips=44/ . . .) That's the address of the Web site where your instructor found this chart."

"I will use this same address to search for data on computer jobs. Maybe the library *is* a good place to look for career information. I'm going to head for their computer lab right now. If you have time to come along, I can show you how easy it is to find this page on the Internet."

When Mike and Michelle reached the library, Mike said, "It's amazing how getting information has changed." As they passed the library's card catalog, Mike couldn't resist pulling out a drawer to show Michelle an entry card. "Remember these?"

HF	
5600	Duffy, Malvern C.
W437	The Quality Revolution in Business / Malvern C. Duffy
1998	400 p
HF 5600 W425	1998
Library of Congress	

(Note: The above is a model only.)

"Many people don't even use the card catalog in the library anymore. Now we can use the college library's website to see all of the titles in the library."

Michelle was amazed.

Mike continued, "But that's not all. You can use this computer to write your college papers or you could start using your kids' computer home! Look at this book," Mike said as he pointed to the reference shelf. He opened *Roget's Thesaurus* (a book of synonyms), and they looked at one example in it:

encourage, *v.* cheer, hearten, reassure . . .

(Partial entry, *The New American Roget's College Thesaurus in Dictionary Form,* Third Revised Edition, 2002.)

"Microsoft Word has a thesaurus in it—and a spell check, too. As Ms. Santos said, we have no more excuses for spelling and word choice mistakes!"

"Actually, I should show you the library's home page first. I can also show you how easily you can link, or connect, from the home page to the website you showed me. You can find tons of information about registered nursing."

"That sounds good to me," said Michelle. "I have a couple hours before the school bus drops my kids off. The sooner I get into this computer stuff, the better. Let's go."

Review: Reading for Main Ideas, Supporting Details, Inferences, and Conclusions

Look at the home page Mike accessed at the college library. Use the information to answer the questions that follow.

Bridgewater College Library
10 College Road
Anywhere, USA 00000
Phone: 000-000-0000 Fax: 000-000-0000

Library Online Catalog Library Hours & General Information

Online Research

Selected Web Sites

Reference Desk

Fiction

Local Newspaper

Newspapers Worldwide

Ask a Reference Question by E-Mail Help! I don't know which link to click.

Access other libraries in this state.

13. You can conclude that students use the library home page
   A to sign up for classes.
   B only to read the local newspapers.
   C to link to whatever information they need.
   D to apply for financial aid.

14. You can use this home page to
   A get your advisor's signature.
   B ask a question via e-mail.
   C pay your bills.
   D buy the college newspaper.

15. If the book you need is not available at this library,

    A it is not available anywhere.

    B you have to buy it.

    C you should inform your instructor.

    D you should click on Access other libraries in this state.

16. Michelle and Mike are likely most interested in which link on this home page?

    A Online Research

    B Reference Desk

    C Fiction

    D Newspapers Worldwide

Reread the Occupation Report that Michelle showed Mike (see page 51). Use the information found there to answer the following questions.

17. What is the topic of this chart?

    A Registered Nursing in Your State

    B Median Wages for RNs Worldwide

    C Registered Nurses' Hourly Wages

    D Wages and Trends for the Occupation of Registered Nurses

18. In 2014, the median hourly wage for a registered nurse in the United States was

    A $16.55–23.59

    B $21.95

    C $45.84

    D $34,400

19. If you click on the words "click here"

    A you can view licensing requirements.

    B you can view wages for the past 10 years.

    C you can register for the courses you'll need.

    D you can see the occupation trends for the 20th century.

20. Look at the section of the chart on Wages. You can infer that *annual* means

    A hourly.

    B yearly.

    C weekly.

    D monthly.

21. True or False? A registered nurse does private duty only. _____

22. From this chart, Michelle and her fellow nursing students can conclude that

    A nursing is a respected profession.

    B the need for registered nurses is declining.

    C licensing requirements are the same in every state.

    D the future for registered nurses is promising.

Answer Key

1. C
2. D
3. B
4. D
5. beans, eating, per person
6. D
7. D
8. B
9. C
10. D
11. B
12. A
13. C
14. B
15. D
16. A
17. C
18. C
19. A
20. B
21. False
22. D

LESSON 5   A Continuing Search

In Lesson 5, Michelle continues her search for information about college nursing courses. She was able to get lesson samples from Sally, another nursing student. Sally gave Michelle the following lesson samples from two of her first-year nursing classes. These were readings from patient treatment texts. Sally advised Michelle not to be concerned about the unfamiliar words used in the lesson samples. She should, however, definitely look at the Words to Know list first as part of her reading warm-up. Michelle should read the lesson samples to see if she understood the content. She can then decide if she can handle required courses like these.

Words to Know

Paraplegia	Complete inability to move the lower half of the body
Vena cava	A large vein that empties blood into the right atrium of the heart
Extremities	Body limbs (arms, legs)
Catheter	A flexible tube inserted into a vein or other hollow body space

Intravenous	Within a vein or veins
Edema	Swelling of tissue

Read the following two samples from a case study textbook for nursing students. Six of the medical terms used in the readings are defined in Words to Know immediately above. Remember: Don't let new and unfamiliar words frighten you. Read to get a general understanding of the case study.

Sample I, Patient History, Juan Pallo

Juan Pallo is a 23-year-old man who was injured in an automobile accident last spring. As a result of blood loss from the trauma, he suffered a spinal cord injury. The spinal cord injury led to paraplegia (i.e., paralysis of the lower extremities). Juan had a filter inserted in his inferior vena cava. It was placed there because of the high risk of complications from blood pooling in the lower extremities. The filter was to prevent blood clots from traveling to his lungs. However, approximately six months after his injury, he was readmitted to the hospital. He had developed blood clots in both legs.

Juan has been unable to work. Instead, he watches his three-year-old daughter while his spouse works. Juan and his family live in an apartment in his mother's home. Juan does not receive physical therapy in his home or at an outpatient facility. He does not have a whirlpool or a gym set up in his home, and finances are tight. During the admission history, the nurse learned that Juan does his own passive range of motion exercises. He lifts and lowers his thighs as he sits in his wheelchair.

Sample II, Medical Procedure
Parenteral Hyperalimentation

Some patients are unable to take food orally. Part of their care is to provide the total caloric needs by intravenous route. Although this is extremely difficult, patients have been maintained in a healthy state for prolonged periods. Nutrients are provided through a catheter extending through the subclavian vein to the superior vena cava.

The daily feeding of 2,500–3,000 kcal for an adult includes the following:

- 2,500–3,000 ml of water, 100–130 gm.
- Protein hydrolysate (amino acids).
- 525–625 gm dextrose; 125–150 mEq sodium, 75–120 mEq potassium; 4–8 mEq magnesium; vitamins A, D, E, C; thiamine; niacin; pantothenic acid.

- Calcium, phosphorus, and iron are given as required.
- Vitamin B12, folic acid, and vitamin K are given intramuscularly as needed.
- Trace elements are required after one month of continuous feeding.

Nursing Implications:

- Explain the procedure to the patient.
- Obtain a nutritional assessment of the patient.
- Monitor and record intake and output.
- Assist with the catheter insertion. Observe for adverse effects.
- Document procedure and initial fluid administration.
- Monitor fluid flow with mechanical device and record observations.
- Inspect and re-dress catheter site every 24 to 48 hours using strict aseptic technique.
- Document condition of site and position of catheter. Evaluate for catheter leakage and report to any leakage physician immediately.
- Monitor electrolytes. Administer (I.M.) weekly vitamin supplements as prescribed.
- Observe for presence of edema or dehydration.
- Provide discharge teaching for patient and those in the household who will be caring for the patient.

(Adapted from *Taber's Cyclopedic Medical Dictionary*, Philadelphia: Davis, 1954.)

TARGET: Reading to Draw Conclusions

The two samples are filled with words and information that are probably unfamiliar to you. However, keywords and phrases help explain the patient history and the medical procedure. You can draw conclusions about the meanings of unfamiliar words. You can figure out their meanings by reading more familiar words and phrases that are found nearby the unfamiliar words. Go back to Juan's case history and answer the following questions by looking for keywords and phrases in the text.

1. From which keywords can you draw a conclusion about how Juan's injury occurred?
   A Automobile accident
   B Spinal cord
   C Blood loss
   D Blood pooling

If you answered A, *automobile accident,* you are correct. You knew the answer because the keywords are familiar to you; they are used in the same sentence as the word *injury.* Sometimes, however, you must search harder for the keywords in the text. Go back to Sample I, Juan's patient history, and answer Question 2.

2. What can you conclude about Juan's current situation?
   A Juan has made a full recovery and needs no further treatment of any kind.
   B Juan will be able to go back to his full-time job.
   C Juan can afford to have a nurse come to his home for therapy.
   D Juan is on his own when it comes to his physical therapy.

If you answered D, you are correct. Look at keywords and phrases, "finances are tight," "does not receive physical therapy," "does the key his own . . . exercises," and "does not have a whirlpool or gym." You are able to draw the conclusion from these facts that Juan is on his own when it comes to his physical therapy. None of these words or phrases support answers A through C.

Michelle was nervous when she saw so many unfamiliar words in the two nursing textbook samples. However, after trying to answer the first two questions, she felt better about her ability to figure out the meaning of what she was reading. She found that her training and experience as a Certified Nursing Assistant made it a little easier for her to understand some of the words in the samples.

Use the keyword and phrase technique when you draw conclusions, and you too will find it easier to understand unfamiliar text. Try this technique now when answering questions about Sample II above.

3. Parenteral Hyperalimentation refers to
   A parental duties.
   B vitamin deficiency.
   C intravenous feeding of a patient.
   D documentation procedures.

If you answered C, *intravenous feeding of a patient*, you are correct. Keywords and phrases in the first paragraph, "unable to take food orally" and "daily feeding for an adult," help you draw the correct conclusion. *Parenteral hyperalimentation* refers to intravenous feeding of a patient. Even though the term may be unfamiliar, the keywords and phrases in the paragraph assist you in drawing the correct conclusion about the meaning. Let's try the next question.

4. What conclusion can you draw from reading the Nursing Implications?
   A Intravenous feeding of a patient is not a complicated procedure.
   B Once the patient is discharged, he or she cannot be fed intravenously.
   C A patient who is being fed intravenously must be monitored regularly.
   D Patients can feed themselves intravenously.

If you answered C, you are correct. The keywords "assist," "observe," "document," "inspect," and "evaluate" all lead you to draw that conclusion. A patient being fed intravenously must be monitored regularly. None of the other statements can be made based on the information presented in Sample II.

Review: Reading for Details and Conclusions

5. According to Sample II, Medical Procedure, nutrients flow through a catheter
   A extending through the subclavian vein to the superior vena cava.
   B extending through the vena cava to the subclavian vein.
   C folic acid and vitamin K.
   D only if the patient is able to walk.

6. You can infer from the information in Sample I that
   A Juan will return to full activity in one week.
   B Juan will not be able to work in the near future.
   C Juan's wife must give up her job to care for him.
   D Juan's child will care for him.

7. One of the nursing implications in Sample II, Medical Procedure is the importance of
   A keeping Juan's wheelchair in excellent working order.
   B obtaining a nutritional assessment of the patient.
   C explaining the procedure to the doctor.
   D leaving the room while the catheter is inserted.

Drawing Conclusions from a Chart

When she was nursing assistant, Michelle learned to take a patient's vital signs. Vital signs are the important signs of life. These signs indicate the health of the body in four main ways. The main vital signs include:

- Temperature—The measure of the balance between heat loss and heat produced
- Pulse—The pressure of the blood felt against the wall of an artery
- Respiration—Breathing in and breathing out
- Blood pressure—The force exerted by the heart against arterial walls when the heart contracts or relaxes

Reading a patient's chart requires many skills. The chart that follows gives you many facts. You can also use those facts to draw conclusions. Start by reading the title; it tells you the main idea or topic of the chart. Go on to read the supporting details such as Day in Hospital, Date, Hour, and so forth.

Study this portion of a vital signs chart. Then answer the questions.

Chart of Vital Signs

Patient's Name: Doe, Felix/Doctor's Name: Dr. John Smith Room No. 206 Patient ID907.

Date:	12/1/15	12/2/15	12/3/15	12/4/15	12/5/15	12/6/15
Day in Hospital:	1	2	3	4	5	6

Hour:	AM PM	AM PM	AM PM	AM PM	AM PM	AM PM
	4 8 12 4 8 12	4 8 12 4 8 12	4 8 12 4 8 12	4 8 12 4 8 12	4 8 12 4 8 12	4 8 12

T E M P E R A T U R E   A D M I T T E D

102°   100° 101°   99.8° 99.6°   98.6° 98.6°

8. According to the chart, Felix's temperature became normal
   A on the third day after admission to the hospital.
   B at the same time each day.
   C two days after Felix went home.
   D only in the morning.

9. After he was admitted, Felix remained in the hospital for a total of how many days?
   A One
   B Two
   C Three
   D Four

10. If normal temperature is just below 99°, Felix's temperature was normal on day

A one.

B two.

C three.

D four.

11. You can also conclude that Felix's temperature was higher in the

A evening.

B admitting room.

C morning.

D in the operating room.

Michelle knew that all children were supposed to be immunized, or protected against diseases. She knew that the immunizations would keep her children safe from serious diseases. Her children were up-to-date with their immunizations and other shots. But Michelle had never seen an actual chart of immunizations until now. Read along with Michelle to see the immunizations that children must have.

There are many facts in this chart and even a conclusion that you can draw from these facts. Warm up for the activity by reading the title and the explanation below it.

Recommended Childhood Immunization Schedule, United States

Vaccines are listed under recommended ages they should be given. Bars indicate the range of recommended ages for immunization. Any dose not given at the recommended age should be given as a "catch-up" immunization at a later doctor's visit as shown. Ovals indicate vaccines to be given if the recommended doses were missed or given earlier than the recommended minimum age.

Recommended Childhood Immunization Schedule–United States, 2015

Vaccine	Birth	1 mo	2 mos	4 mos	6 mos	12 mos	15 mos	18 mos	24 mos	4–6 yrs	11–12 yrs	14–18 yrs
Hepatitis B	Hep B #1											
Rota virus X		Hep B #2			Hep B #3						Hep B	
Diphtheria-tetanus toxoids-pertussis			RV DTaP	RV DTaP	RV DTaP		DTaP			DTaP	TD	
Haemophilus Influenzae type b			Hib	Hib	Hib	Hib						
Inactivated poliomyelitis			IPV	IPV	IPV				IPV			
Pneumococcal conjugate			PCV	PCV	PCV	PCV						
Measles-mumps-rubella						MMR			MMR		MMR	
Varicella						VAR					VAR	
Hepatitis A									Hep A in selected areas			

☐ Range of recommended ages for vaccination.

⬭ Vaccines to be given if previously recommended doses were missed or were given earlier than the recommended minimum age.

▨ Recommended in selected states and/or regions.

Source: Centers for Disease Control and Prevention.

http://www.cdc.gov/mmwr/preview/mmwrhtml/mm5001a3.htm

12. The bars and oval in the chart are used to indicate
A where and when the children were born.
B the names of two diseases only.
C age ranges and missed doses.
D the names of doctors you need to see.

13. The Hepatitis B #1 immunization is given
A After Hepatitis B #2
B between birth and age two months.
C after DTaP3.
D to adults only.

14. You can conclude from information in the chart that
   A immunizations are never given to anyone after age 18.
   B all children receive their shots and doses at exactly the same ages.
   C if an immunization is missed, it can always be given later.
   D there is only one hepatitis vaccine.

Answer Key

1. A	**4.** C	**7.** B	**10.** C	**13.** B
2. D	**5.** A	**8.** A	**11.** A	**14.** C
3. C	**6.** B	**9.** D	**12.** C	

LESSON 6 Back to School

In Lesson 6, you will follow Michelle as she experiences the trials and tribulations of going back to school as an adult. She has been to her first class and has returned home, thinking about the commitment she has made.

In this lesson, you will have an opportunity to practice the reading skills associated with essays, autobiography, and fiction. You will consider the author's purpose, style, and technique.

Words to Know

Metaphor	A symbol used for something else, usually something abstract
Empathizes	Identifies with
Eligible	Entitled

The First Class

Michelle drove home after her first class, amazed that she had not only learned and understood her first class of Introduction to Computers, but also that she had really enjoyed it. She couldn't wait to demonstrate her new skills to her children. She feared that the course would not continue to be so clear and easy. Fortunately, she could add Mike Rinaldi to her list of supports. He would help her if she asked him for help. She thought he was a great person and that he would achieve his goals.

Michelle also felt fortunate to have met another woman her age, perhaps a little older, who was starting her second semester at the community college. She confided her worst fears of failure to Ruth.

As they left class together that first day, Ruth told Michelle a friend of hers had given her something to read. Ruth had placed it on her refrigerator door six months ago. Whenever Ruth felt unsure of herself, it helped to know that others had been through the same experiences and survived. Ruth reread the statements many times. She wanted to share them with Michelle, so she promised to bring them to their next class.

True to her word, Ruth arrived at the next class with two personal statements, one written by a student and the other by a well-known comedian. Michelle read them and smiled. Here were two people who knew exactly how she felt.

Read the passages and answer the questions that follow.

Passage I

I find that life can be compared to a gigantic roller coaster, with a never-ending track, boasting extremely dangerous curves. Sometimes you can be moving so fast that it feels like the brakes have been torn out from under you. I find that when you start in a downward motion, your roller coaster car can be hard to steer on your own.

But sometimes in the roller coaster nightmare you are going so fast that it becomes difficult to get off and you begin to feel like there is nobody who is willing or capable of helping you slow down that roller coaster car, or even help you negotiate those tight and narrow turns.

Sometimes there are other people's roller coaster cars that are more skilled at traveling that track, and they are so concerned to reach the end of their journey that they forget about other people's roller coaster cars. When you are traveling that track, your body and soul become worn down and eventually you end up falling off one of those tight and narrow turns.

Is there anybody on that track who is willing to slow down and help you travel that twisty, windy path?

I hope that type of individual exists on our track of life today, for you and me.

If this individual does exist, I hope I can find him or her before I hit the wall and end up burning in a ball of flames. I hope society is able to realize the importance of those types of people and the gifts they offer society, before society destroys all the tracks by traveling too rapidly.

—Cindy Hedrick, "The Roller Coaster," *Voices: New Writers for New Readers* Issue 10, Vol. 4, No. 1, Fall 1991.

Passage II

Life is truly a ride. We're all strapped in and no one can stop it. When the doctor slaps your behind, he's ripping your ticket and away you go. As you make each passage from youth to adulthood to maturity, sometimes you put your arms up and scream; sometimes you just hang on to that bar in front of you. But the ride is the thing. I think the most you can hope for at the end of life is that your hair's messed, you're out of breath, and you didn't throw up.

—Jerry Seinfeld, excerpt from *SeinLanguage,* p. 153.

TARGET: Reading to Recognize Literary Techniques

Two very different people wrote these passages. A student wrote the first one. A well-known comedian wrote the second one. Both used the same technique. Both used similar metaphors, or symbols, for life. What are those symbols? Write your answer here: _____

One writer used a ride and the other one used a roller coaster as a symbol for what happens in life. The reader easily empathizes with the image of the rider hurled through space. You know or can vividly imagine the feeling of being flung through space (life) as you hang on with all your strength and try to cope.

What else can you tell about the two writers from these passages? Can you tell something about their moods? What is the overall tone—that is, the outlook or feelings they express?

Answer the following questions that explore the writers' motivations, tone, and meaning.

1. The conclusion that Jerry Seinfeld has reached is that
   A if you don't want to ride, just get off.
   B everyone knows exactly what life will bring them.
   C the ride is the important thing.
   D you're a baby if you scream.

2. The tone of the first passage tells you that the writer's life has
   A been very easy and predictable.
   B been easy to steer, especially the tight turns.
   C been as frantic and scary as a roller coaster ride.
   D been all of the above.

3. The student's passage ends
   A in complete despair.
   B on a hopeful note.
   C with a definite plan.
   D very happily.

4. In the Seinfeld passage, what does the final sentence mean?
   A Don't go on the roller coaster if you don't like getting your hair messed up in the wind.
   B Don't go on the roller coaster if you're afraid of getting sick or if you have a hard time breathing.
   C Don't go on the roller coaster if you have a cold and have a hard time breathing.
   D If your hair's messed, you're out of breath, and you didn't throw up, you've probably taken part in and succeeded in life.

5. The second and third paragraphs of Passage I express

    A a real cry for help.

    B her despair because she is worn down in body and soul.

    C the fear that she will fall off the track.

    D all of the above.

6. What is the Passage I author's hope for society?

    A Society will realize the importance of people who help others.

    B Everyone will leave her alone so that she can get on with her life.

    C She can get her children to school on time with the help of others.

    D Both A and B.

7. Compare the two passages. Which of the following statements is true about the passages?

    A Seinfeld's is true for everyone, while Cindy's is true for no one.

    B Seinfeld's is resigned but positive, while Cindy's is fearful but willing to go forward.

    C Seinfeld's is without humor, while Cindy's humorous throughout.

    D Cindy writes about other people's lives, while Seinfeld writes only about himself.

The Star Thrower Story

From the story by Joel Barker, inspired by Loren Eiseley (www.starthrower.com/aboutbody.html#4).

There's a story I would like to share with you. It was inspired by the writing of Loren Eiseley. Eiseley was . . . a scientist and a poet. And from those two perspectives he wrote insightfully and beautifully about the world and our role in it.

Once upon a time, there was a wise man, much like Eiseley himself, who used to go to the ocean to do his writing. He had a habit of walking on the beach before he began his work. One day he was walking along the shore. As he looked down the beach, he saw a human figure moving like a dancer. He smiled to himself to think of someone who would dance to the day. So he began to walk faster to catch up. As he got closer, he saw that it was a young man and the young man wasn't dancing, but instead he was reaching down to the shore, picking up something and very gently throwing it into the ocean.

As he got closer, he called out, "Good morning! What are you doing?"

The young man paused, looked up and replied, "Throwing starfish into the ocean."

"I guess I should have asked, Why are you throwing starfish into the ocean?"

"The sun is up and the tide is going out. And if I don't throw them in they'll die."

"But young man, don't you realize that there are miles and miles of beach and starfish all along it. You can't possibly make a difference!"

The young man listened politely. Then bent down, picked up another starfish and threw it into the sea, past the breaking waves. "It made a difference for that one!"

> His response surprised the man. He was upset. He didn't know how to reply. So instead, he turned away and walked back to the cottage to begin his writings.
>
> All day long as he wrote, the image of the young man haunted him. . . .

8. The author's purpose in writing this story is to remind the reader that
   A the tide goes out once a day.
   B we have to find time to relax.
   C the beach is no place for serious work.
   D each of us has the ability to make a difference in the world.

9. You can conclude that Eiseley used his writing ability as well as his knowledge of science to
   A help people better understand and live in their environment.
   B make people understand that throwing one starfish in the ocean is no help at all.
   C comment on different things people notice when they walk the beach.
   D help people decide what kind of job best suits them.

10. How do you think this story ends?
   A The writer in the story goes home and spends the day thinking angrily about the young man.
   B The young man stops throwing the starfish after he talks with the writer because he realizes that he alone cannot make a difference.
   C When the writer in the story goes home, he realizes that the young man was someone who had decided to make a difference.
   D When the story ends, only two starfish have been saved.

Now let's look at the work of the writer Maya Angelou, whose autobiography, *I Know Why the Caged Bird Sings*, was published in 1970. The book was nominated for the National Book Award.

When Maya and her brother were three and four years old, respectively, father sent them to live with their grandmother. As you will see, Maya's name was Marguerite Johnson before she changed it. The following has been adapted from the original.

> When I was three and Bailey four, we had arrived in the musty little town, wearing tags on our wrists which instructed—"To Whom It May Concern"—that we were Marguerite and Bailey Johnson Jr., from Long Beach California, en route to Stamps, Arkansas, c/o Mrs. Annie Henderson.
>
> Our parents had decided to put an end to their calamitous marriage. Father shipped us home to his mother. A porter had been charged with our welfare—he got off the train the next day in Arizona—and our tickets were pinned to my brother's inside coat pocket.

I don't remember much of the trip. But after we reached the segregated southern part of the journey, things must have looked up. Negro passengers, who always traveled with loaded lunch boxes, felt sorry for "the poor little motherless darlings" and plied us with cold fried chicken and potato salad . . .

The town reacted to us as its inhabitants had reacted to all things new before our coming. It regarded us a while without curiosity but with caution. After that we were seen to be harmless (and children). The town closed in around us, as a real mother embraces a stranger's child. Warmly, but not too familiarly.

We lived with our grandmother and uncle in the rear of the Store (it was always spoken of with a capital s). She had owned it for some twenty-five years.

Early in the century, Momma (we soon stopped calling her Grandmother) sold lunches. She sold to the sawmen in the lumberyard (east Stamps) and the seedmen at the cotton gin (west Stamps). Her crisp meat pies and cool lemonade, when joined to her miraculous ability to be in two places at the same time, assured her business success. From being a mobile lunch counter, she set up a stand between the two points of fiscal interest. She supplied the workers' needs for a few years. Then she had the Store built in the heart of the Negro area. Over the years, it became the lay center of activities in town.

The formal name of the Store was the Wm. Johnson General Merchandise Store. Customers could find food staples, a good variety of thread, mash for hogs, corn for chickens, coal oil for lamps, light bulbs for the wealthy . . . Anything not visible had only to be ordered.

11. In the first paragraph, you can conclude that the word *calamitous* means
  A loving.
  B disastrous.
  C enduring.
  D bright.

12. According to the passage, Marguerite and Bailey did not go hungry on the train; they
  A ordered all the food they could eat in the dining car; money was not a problem.
  B carried enough food with them for a three-day trip.
  C were fed very well by other Negro passengers once they reached the southern part of the trip.
  D offered some of their very large food supply to other people on the trip.

13. After a while, the children referred to their grandmother as
  A their best friend.
  B their aunt.
  C their teacher.
  D their mother.

14. If you met Marguerite's grandmother today, you might think of her as

    A a very mean and unfeeling woman.

    B a busybody who spent little time with her grandchildren.

    C a lazy person with no ambition.

    D a very talented businesswoman.

Review Reading Skills

Read the following paragraph adapted from a nonfiction book called *Coping with Difficult People*. Answer the questions that follow the paragraph.

Introduction to *Coping with Difficult People*, by Robert M. Bramson, Ph.D.

This is a book about impossible people and how to cope with them. Your life may be free from hostile customers and co-workers. You may not have an indecisive, vacillating boss. The people who work for you may not be overagreeable (but do-nothing). If you work with none of those who deserve to be called Difficult People, read no further. Consider yourself extraordinarily lucky and move on to pleasanter fare. If, however, those constant headaches have intruded, read on. The purpose of this book is to show you how to identify, understand, and cope with the Difficult People who come into your life. It is directed primarily to those who must work with others to accomplish common tasks. The methods described here, however, are applicable in many different settings . . .

---

15. You can see that the main idea of the paragraph

    A tells the reader the main theme of the book.

    B is stated in the first sentence.

    C immediately prepares the reader for what is to come.

    D all of the above.

16. The paragraph talks about a serious subject, but the author.

    A does not expect many people to agree with him.

    B feels that all readers have all the answers to the problem.

    C has adopted a light tone.

    D believes the topic is too difficult for most people to understand.

17. Read the word *vacillating* in its context. What other word helps you understand it?

    A Indecisive

    B Hostile

    C Do-nothing

    D Subordinates

18. The writer says that those who are "free from hostile customers and coworkers . . ." should "read no further." You can conclude that

A the author expects you to close the book immediately.

B the author believes that everyone must read this book.

C the author himself has never had experiences with difficult people.

D the author is certain that many people have had experiences with difficult people in different settings.

Answer Key

1. C	**5.** D	**9.** A	**13.** D	**17.** A
2. C	**6.** A	**10.** C	**14.** D	**18.** D
3. B	**7.** B	**11.** B	**15.** D	
4. D	**8.** D	**12.** C	**16.** C	

Mathematics

This section begins with survey-length assessments for both math computation and applied math. These will give you a chance to see how well you remember the math you took in high school and what your strengths and weaknesses are. There are also two survey-length math posttests at the end of the book.

On the actual TABE A test, each survey-length test consists of 25 multiple-choice questions. The problems on the computational skills test have five answer choices, one of which is "none of these," and calculators may *not* be used. The problems on the applied math test have four answer choices and a calculator may be used. Both tests are timed—15 minutes for computational skills and 25 minutes for applied math.

There are six lessons on math computation:

- Decimals
- Fractions
- Integers
- Percent
- Order of Operations
- Algebraic Operations

There are nine lessons on applied math:

- Numbers and Number Operations
- Computation in Context
- Estimation
- Measurement
- Geometry
- Data Analysis
- Statistics and Probability
- Patterns, Functions, Algebra
- Problem Solving and Reasoning

Since you should be proficient in adding, subtracting, multiplying, and dividing whole numbers (0, 1, 2, 3, and so forth), there are no lessons on these topics in this book. There are practice problems in each lesson. Most of the practice problems in the math computation lessons are not in multiple-choice format, while most in the applied math lessons are. You should try all of these practice problems. Answers are given at the end of Section 3.

Math Skills Assessment

Choose Your Time and Place   Take this assessment when you have the time and the energy to focus on the questions. Take it in a place where you will be undisturbed. If you get interrupted, and cannot concentrate, finish it at another time.

Set Your Own Pace   This is *not* a timed test. Its purpose is to help you sort out what you know and don't know. *If you don't know how to work a problem, put a ? beside it and move on.* You will have a chance to learn about that type of math question in the lessons that follow.

 FYI
This two-part assessment is the same length, and covers the same type of math, as the Survey Edition of the TABE 9 & 10 Level A test. The posttest at the *end* of this book will be timed in the same manner as the TABE. For now, make a note of your start and stop times in order to get an idea of how long it takes you to complete your math work *at this point in time.*

Math Skills Assessment

Part I: Computation
Note: No calculator permitted.

Date: _____ Location: _____ Start time: _____

1 $5.065 + 25 + 1.3 =$

   A 31.365

   B 5.215

   C 5.315

   D 5,315

   E None of these

2 $44 \times 10.60 =$

   A 848.0

   B 4,664

   C 46.64

   D 466

   E None of these

3 $7.50 \div 2.5 =$

   A 3.0

   B 2.30

   C 0.34

   D 30.00

   E None of these

4 $2\frac{3}{4} \times \frac{1}{2} =$

   A $1\frac{3}{8}$

   B $5\frac{1}{2}$

   C $3\frac{5}{8}$

   D $1\frac{1}{2}$

   E None of these

5 $12\frac{1}{4} - 9\frac{3}{4} =$

   A $3\frac{1}{2}$

   B $3\frac{1}{4}$

   C $21\frac{1}{4}$

   D $2\frac{1}{2}$

   E None of these

6 $|-30| + |8| =$

   A -22

   B 38

   C -24

   D 22

   E None of these

7 (−7) + 3 =

A 10

B −4

C +4

D 21

E None of these

8. 6 − (−9) =

A −3

B −15

C 15

D 3

E None of these

9 25% of 40 =

A 65

B ¼

C 10

D 15

E None of these

10 $6.00 is what percent of $8.00?

A 50%

B 0.75%

C 48%

D 75%

E None of these

11 5% of $100 =

A $5.25

B $20.25

C $5

D $52.25

E None of these

12 $80^2 + 8^2 =$

A 176

B 6,416

C 640^2

D 6,464

E None of these

13 7a − 2a =

A −5

B $7a^2$

C 5a

D 5 + 2a

E None of these

14 $8a + a − 3b^2 =$

A $9a^2 − 3b^2$

B $6a^2b^2$

C $9a − 3b^2$

D $8a^2 − 3b^2$

E None of these

15 $10^6 ÷ 10^2 =$

A 10^4

B 1^4

C 100^4

D 100^3

E None of these

16. $4 + 6^2 ÷ 3 =$

A 7

B $13\frac{1}{3}$

C 16

D $33\frac{1}{3}$

E None of these

17. $|3-8| =$

    A   −5

    B   5

    C   11

    D   −11

    E   None of these

18. $-8-15 =$

    A   −7

    B   7

    C   23

    D   −23

    E   None of these

19. $(5-2)^2 =$

    A   9

    B   29

    C   21

    D   3

    E   None of these

20. $5\frac{1}{4} - 3\frac{1}{2} =$

    A $2\frac{1}{4}$

    B $2\frac{3}{4}$

    C $1\frac{1}{4}$

    D $1\frac{3}{4}$

    E   None of these

21. 18% of 45 =

    A   7

    B   9

    C   12

    D   12.3

    E   None of these

22. $2^3 + 2^4 =$

    A   14

    B   16

    C   20

    D   24

    E   None of these

23. The number 6 is 5% of what number?

    A   0.3

    B   30

    C   60

    D   120

    E   None of these

24. $\frac{2}{3} \div \frac{1}{2} =$

    A $\frac{1}{3}$

    B   3

    C $\frac{4}{3}$

    D $\frac{3}{4}$

    E   None of these

25. $12x - 5x =$

    A $7x^2$

    B $-60x^2$

    C   7

    D $7x$

    E   None of these

Stop time:

Math Skills Assessment

Part II: Applied Math
Note: Calculator permitted.

You may use a calculator to solve the problems in Part II, but you may find that some questions are solved just as easily without one. Have scratch paper handy to help you work through the problems.

Date: _____ Location: _____ Start time: _____

Questions 1–3 refer to the following information.

> ### Recycling
> The Parent Group of the local Head Start promoted recycling in their neighborhood one Saturday in March by distributing sets of blue and green recycling bins to grocery shoppers at Central Marketplace. Out of the 248 shoppers who stopped by Head Start's Recycling Information Table, 168 took home a set of bins. "We are pleased," said Rosa Torres. "That's a pretty good percentage. Some of them said they had never recycled before."

1. What percentage of shoppers stopping by the table took home bins? Round your answer to the nearest whole percent.

   A 50%

   B 80%

   C 68%

   D 34%

2. The recycling bins came in sets of two: blue for paper; green for glass, plastics, and metal. Which expression can be used to find the total number of bins given out?

   A $2(168 + 248)$

   B 168×2

   C $2(248 - 168)$

   D $416/2$

3. The ratio of shoppers who took bins to the total number of shoppers who stopped at the Information Table is approximately

   A 1 out of 2.

   B 2 out of 3.

   C 3 out of 4.

   D 5 out of 8.

Questions 4 and 5 refer to the following information.

The U.S. Environmental Protection Agency collects data yearly on the estimated amounts and types of solid waste generated in this country. It also keeps records on the amount of waste that is recovered (reused) through recycling. The waste measured comes from residential, commercial, institutional, and industrial sources.

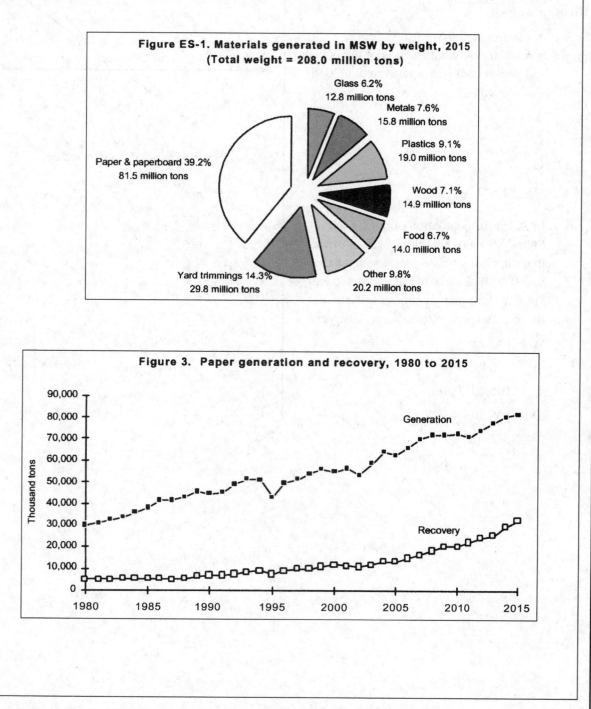

Figure ES-1. Materials generated in MSW by weight, 2015 (Total weight = 208.0 million tons)

Glass 6.2%
12.8 million tons

Metals 7.6%
15.8 million tons

Plastics 9.1%
19.0 million tons

Wood 7.1%
14.9 million tons

Food 6.7%
14.0 million tons

Other 9.8%
20.2 million tons

Yard trimmings 14.3%
29.8 million tons

Paper & paperboard 39.2%
81.5 million tons

Figure 3. Paper generation and recovery, 1980 to 2015

4 How many tons of paper and paperboard waste were generated in 2015?

    A 81.5 tons

    B 39.2 tons

    C 81,500,000 tons

    D 81,500 tons

5 According to the line graph above, approximately what fraction of the paper and paperboard waste generated in 2015 was recovered?

    A ¼

    B ½

    C ⅙

    D ⅜

6 In 2015, the population of the United States was 300,000,000. It was estimated that the plastic waste per person per day was 0.40 lb. Based on this estimated daily amount, how many pounds of plastic did the average person throw away that year?

    A 14.6 lb

    B 146 lb

    C 105,102,000 lb

    D 105,102 lb

7 Two straight roads intersect at point A. The highway surveyor measured the angles formed at that intersection. If the measurement of ∠WAX is 120°, what is the measurement in degrees of ∠YAX?

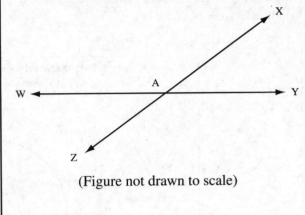

(Figure not drawn to scale)

    A 90°

    B 45°

    C 60°

    D 30°

> **Prices at the Pump**
>
> Premium: 1.659; Super: 1.599; Regular: 1.499
>
> Carol had just begun her drive to work when the dashboard's warning light flashed. It signaled an almost-empty tank. She knew she would run out of gas before she reached work, so she pulled into the nearest gas station. She had a $5 bill in her wallet. Under the car floor mats, she found 6 quarters. She estimated the total amount of money she had would buy her enough regular gas to last for her driving needs for that day.

8 Carol watched the numbers fly by on the gas pump window. She put in exactly the number of gallons that her money would buy. How many gallons of gas was she able to put into her gas tank? Round your answer to the nearest tenth of a gallon.

  A 9.7 gallons

  B 17 gallons

  C 4.3 gallons

  D 4.16 gallons

9 Carol's car traveled an average of 28 miles per gallon. At that rate, *approximately* how many miles could she travel on the gas she bought that morning?

  A A little over 100 miles

  B A little under 100 miles

  C Between 130 and 150 miles

  D Between 150 and 200 miles

Was $2.91! SALE: $1.89 / SF!

Laminate Blowout!
RED OAK
Price: Was $70.08! SALE: 45.56
Per Carton (24.11 SF)

Installation Type: Click Together
Dimensions: 7.75″ × 50.5″
Board Thickness: .25″
Pieces per Unit: 9
Unit Weight: 38 lb
(SF = square feet)

```
              ↑  Entertainment Center
                      12 ft × 3 ft
                 ┌─────────────────┐
                 │                 │
                 │   FAMILY ROOM   │
       20 ft     │                 │
                 │                 │
              ↓  └─────────────────┘
                   ←──── 12 ft ────→
```

Home Remodeling

Diana and Robert Green decided to rip out the worn wall-to-wall carpeting in their family room and replace it with oak laminate flooring. The local building supply store was running a special on do-it-yourself flooring. Diana and Rob looked at the laminate samples. They liked the Red Oak, but their final choice would be made based on the total cost. They agreed that $500.00 was their limit. Above is a diagram of their family room and the sales information for the Red Oak laminate.

10 The family room is in the shape of a

    A   quadrilateral.

    B   polygon.

    C   parallelogram.

    D   All of the above

11 According to the specifications mentioned in the sales ad above, approximately how much will each board of Red Oak laminate weigh?

    A   4 lb

    B   7 lb

    C   9 lb

    D   38 lb

12 The space taken up by the built-in entertainment center in the family room does not require new flooring. Which expression below answers the question, "How many square feet of Red Oak laminate will be needed for the family room?"

    A $2(20) + 2(12)$

    B 12×20

    C $12(20 - 3)$

    D $[2(20) + 2(12)] - (3 \times 12)$

13 How many cartons of Red Oak laminate will the Greens need to purchase for their flooring project?

   A   8 cartons

   B   9 cartons

   C   10 cartons

   D   9½ cartons

14 What is the price for each carton during this sale?

   A $1.89

   B $24.11

   C $70.08

   D $45.56

15 Diana put all the figures into her calculator and found that the flooring would cost them $410.04 before the sales tax was added.

On that basis, Diana and Rob decided

   A   they could buy what they needed for the family room and have enough money left over to buy three additional cartons to redo their 8- × 12-ft kitchen floor.

   B   they could afford to buy the flooring itself, but not the added 7% sales tax.

   C   they could not afford the Red Oak at the discounted sale price.

   D   they could afford to cover their family room floor with the Red Oak.

16 Solve the equation for x: $3x + 2 = x - 8$.

   A $x = -5$

   B $x = 5$

   C $x = -2.5$

   D $x = 2.5$

U.S. Postal Rates Rising Again New Rates Recommended by Postal Rate Commission			
	Current	**Recommended**	**% Increase**
First-class letter (1 oz)	.49	.5	2.0%
Additional ounce	.22	.23	4.5%
Priority Mail (1 lb)	$6.45	$7.00	?
Express Mail (½ lb)	$22.95	$24.00	4.5%

17 If a one-pound Priority Mail package and 20 first-class stamps were purchased at the "current" price, what change would be received from a twenty dollar bill?

   A $11.25

   B $3.75

   C $8.75

   D $10.30

18 By what percent did the cost of Priority Mail (1 lb) rise?

   A   8.52%

   B   12%

   C   3.5%

   D   9.1%

19 Which of the following notations is another way to express the 4 billion dollars that might be raised the next year by the higher rates?

   A $4,000,000,000,000

   B 4×10^9

   C $4,000,000

   D 4×10^6

20 While on a vacation in Australia, Bob spiked a fever. By the time he got to the emergency room, the nurse told him he had a temperature of 40°C (Celsius.) How high was Bob's temperature in degrees Fahrenheit (F)? Use this formula to convert Fahrenheit to Celsius: $F = 1.8C + 32$.

   A   102.8°F

   B   104°F

   C   103.8°F

   D   105°F

Questions 21–23 refer to the following situation.

21 A pair of skates cost $139.79 plus 7% tax. What is the total cost of buying the skates?

    A $149.79

    B $139.79

    C $149.58

    D $140.77

A waitress earned $10.90, $9.25, $8.10, $11.75, $9.55 in tips for one five-day period. She found the average by dividing the total tip amount by the number of days it took to earn the tips.

22 Choose the expression that shows the average daily tip.

    A $10.90 + 9.25 + 8.10 + 11.75 + 9.55 \div 5$

    B $0.07 (10.90 + 9.25 + 8.10 + 11.75 + 9.55)$

    C $139.70 - (10.90 + 9.25 + 8.10 + 11.75 + 9.55) \div 5$

    D $(10.90 + 9.25 + 8.10 + 11.75 + 9.55) \div 5$

23 If Tom can save $9.25 per day, how long would it take to save $148?

    A 14 days

    B 15 days

    C 16 days

    D 17 days

Questions 24 and 25 refer to the following table of information.

TABE 7 & 8 Levels E, M, D, and A: Item Counts and Time Limits

Subtest	Complete Battery		Survey	
	No. Items	Testing Time (minutes)	No. Items	Testing Time (minutes)
Reading	50	50	25	25
Math Computation	40	124	25	15
Applied Math	50	50	25	25
Language	55	55	25	25
Spelling	20	10	20	10
Language Mech	20	14	20	14
Vocabulary	20	14	20	14
Total				

24 To answer the questions on the Applied Math Subtest of the Complete Battery of the TABE, examinees

   A are given 9 minutes to complete their work.

   B have an average of one-half minute to spend on each question.

   C may use a calculator to solve the problems.

   D have an average of one minute to spend on each question.

25 What is the total testing time for the Complete Battery Form of the TABE?

   A 128 minutes

   B 1 hour and 64 minutes

   C 3 hours and 37 minutes

   D 247 minutes

Stop time: _____

Answer Key to Math Skills Assessment
Part I: Computation

To the Student: As you check your answers, record the results in this chart. Use the three columns next to the Item Answers to mark your answers as *Correct, Incorrect,* or *Skipped*. Total the number of your responses in each column at the bottom of the chart.

Answer Key and Skills Analysis Chart

Item Answers	Correct	Incorrect	Skipped	Refer to these lessons.
1 A				1
2 E				1
3 A				1
4 A				2
5 D				2
6 B				6
7 B				3
8 A				3
9 C				4
10 D				4
11 C				4
12 D				6
13 C				6
14 C				6
15 A				6
16 C				5
17 B				6
18 D				3
19 A				5
20 D				2
21 E				4
22 D				5
23 D				4
24 C				2
25 D				6

Answer Key to Math Skills Assessment
Part II: Applied Math

To the Student: As you check your answers, record the results in this chart. Use the three columns next to the Item Answers to mark your answers as *Correct*, *Incorrect*, or *Skipped*. Use the other columns to record additional information you want to remember about the individual math problems. Total the number of responses you marked in each column. Then read the recommendations that follow.

Answer Key and Skills Analysis Chart

Item Answers	Correct	Incorrect	Skipped	Refer to these lessons.
1 C				8
2 B				8
3 B				8
4 C				12
5 D				12
6 B				8
7 C				11
8 C				12
9 A				12
10 D				11
11 A				12
12 C				11
13 B				12
14 D				12
15 D				12
16 A				14
17 C				12
18 A				12
19 B				12,1
20 B				12
21 C				12
22 D				13
23 C				12
24 D				12
25 C				10

Analyze Your Results

Write the number of items you answered correctly for Parts I and II in the spaces provided below.

Divide your score for each part by the total number of questions asked. The result of each division will be a decimal fraction, such as 0.875 or 0.72. Record it.

Move the decimal point two spaces to the right and add the % sign. Record your percentage.

Math Assessment, Part I—*Correct Answers* ÷ 25 = _____ = _____%

Math Assessment, Part II—*Correct Answers* ÷ 25 = _____ = _____%

Plan Your Course of Study

This assessment gives you a good idea of the types of items you will find on Math Parts I and II of the TABE, Level A. To be confident of doing well on the math section of the exam, a score of 90 percent or better is recommended. That means answering 23 or more correctly on each part.

Recommendation:

For each item you answered incorrectly, skipped, or did correctly but still have questions about, study the pages of the lessons indicated. At this point, don't worry if it seems you have a long way to go. The lessons that follow are designed to improve your skills and boost your confidence.

Mathematics Computation

The Mathematics Computation section includes lesson on decimals, fractions, percent, and integers. The Order of Operations lesson describes the convention that mathematicians have adopted to carry out more complex computations. Before we begin, let's review some basic terminology:

- When you add numbers, the answer is called a **sum**.
- When you subtract one number from another, the answer is called a **difference**.
- When you multiply numbers, called **factors**, the answer is called a **product**.
- When you divide one number by another, the answer is called a **quotient**. The number being divided is called the **dividend**, and the number doing the dividing is called the **divisor**. A quantity that is left over after division is called the **remainder**.

LESSON 1   Decimals

Decimal Numbers

A decimal is a *form* of a number that is based on **place value**. It is not a *type* of number. In order to understand place value, we need to review the idea of an exponent. An **exponent** is a small raised number that indicates how many times the **base** number is to be multiplied. The symbol 2^3 means $2 \times 2 \times 2$. The **base** 2 is factor 3 times. An exponent is also called a **power**. Read the symbols 2^3 as "two to the third power."

Positive powers of 10 tell you how many zeros follow the digit 1: $10^0 = 1$ (no zeros), $10^1 = 10$ (one zero), $10^2 = 100$ (two zeros), $10^3 = 1000$ (three zeros), and so forth. *Negative* powers of 10 indicate division: 10^{-1} means divide by 10^1, 10^{-2} means divide by 10^2, and so forth. Therefore, negative powers tell you how many places to the right of the decimal point to put the digit 1: $10^{-1} = 0.1$, $10^{-2} = 0.01$, $10^{-3} = 0.001$.

The table below summarizes place value names and corresponding powers of 10.

Place Values

Whole Numbers												Decimals				
Billions			Millions			Thousands			Units							
10^{11}	10^{10}	10^9	10^8	10^7	10^6	10^5	10^4	10^3	10^2	10^1	10^0	10^{-1}	10^{-2}	10^{-3}	10^{-4}	10^{-5}
Hundred Billions	Ten Billions	Billions	Hundred Millions	Ten Millions	Millions	Hundred Thousands	Ten Thousands	Thousands	Hundreds	Tens	Units	Tenths	Hundredths	Thousandths	Ten Thousandths	Hundred Thousandths

We can now see how place value is based on powers of 10. The number 4396 is

$$4\times1000+3\times100+9\times10+6\times1$$
$$=4\times10^3+3\times10^2+9\times10^1+6\times10^0$$

We can reverse this procedure to determine that the number

$$7\times10^2+3\times10^1+6\times10^0+4\times10^{-1}$$

is 736.4 in decimal form.

A missing power of 10 means that there is a 0 in the place value.

Example A. Write $7\times10^1+3\times10^{-2}$ as a decimal.

The powers of 10 that are "missing" are 0 and −1. Therefore, 70.03 is the decimal number.

Having place values based on powers of 10 makes it easy to multiply or divide a number by a power of 10 (10, 100, 1000, and so forth.).

Example B. Multiply 98.6 by 1000.

Since $1000=10^3$, move the decimal point three places to the right, adding zeros where there is no place value: $98.6\times1000=98,600$.

When you divide by a positive power of 10, move the decimal point to the left, adding zeros where there is no place value.

Example C. Divide 98.6 by 100.

Since $100=10^2$, move the decimal point two places to the left: $98.6\div100=.986$.

Place Value Practice

Write each number as a decimal.

1. $7\times10^2+3\times10^1+8\times10^0$
2. $5\times10^0+3\times10^{-1}+7\times10^{-2}$

3. $1\times10^4 + 5\times10^2 + 2\times10^1 + 9\times10^0$

4. $8\times10^1 + 2\times10^0 + 4\times10^{-2}$

5. $9\times10^7 + 2\times10^3 + 7\times10^1$

6. $3\times10^0 + 1\times10^{-1} + 4\times10^{-2}$

7. Divide 0.745 by 100.

8. Multiply 46 by 10,000.

9. Multiply 12 by 20.

10. Divide 0.16 by 200.

Scientific Notation

Powers of 10 are also used to write numbers in **scientific notation**. This method of writing numbers is used for very large numbers (such as those used in astronomy) and numbers that are very close to zero (which are used in many branches of science). A number written in scientific notation has two factors. The first factor is a number between 1 and 10. The second factor is a power of 10. When a number is larger than 10, the power of 10 is positive. When a number is smaller than 1, the power of 10 is negative. When a number is between 1 and 10, the power of 10 is 0.

Example D. Write 3,562,300,000 in scientific notation.

Place the decimal point so there is only one digit to its left and drop the "trailing" zeros: 3.5623. This is the first factor. The number is bigger than 1, and there are nine digits to the right of the decimal. Therefore, the second factor is 10^9. In scientific notation, $3,562,300,000 = 3.5623\times10^9$.

Example E. Write 0.0000000124 in scientific notation.

Place the decimal point so there is one *non-zero* digit to its left and write the resulting number: 1.24. This is the first factor. The original number is smaller than 1, and the 1 is the eighth digit. The second factor is 10^{-8}. In scientific notation, $0.0000000124 = 1.24\times10^{-8}$.

Example F. Write 8.34×10^6 as a decimal.

The number is greater than 1, and the first digit is 8. The 10^6 indicates that the decimal number has six more places to the left of the decimal point. The first two are 3 and 4; the rest are all 0. The decimal number is 8,340,000.

Example G. Write 1.24×10^{-5} as a decimal.

The number is less than 1, and the first non-zero digit is 1. The exponent -5 indicates that the 1 is the fifth digit to the right of the decimal. The decimal number is 0.0000124.

Scientific Notation Practice

Write each decimal number in scientific notation.
1. 5,345,862
2. 0.000000634
3. 56,130,000,000
4. 0.0000000039

Write each number as a decimal.

5. 4.44×10^6
6. 3.528×10^9
7. 9.05×10^{-6}
8. 6.3×10^{-7}

Decimal Arithmetic

Adding and **subtracting** decimals is just like adding and subtracting whole numbers. Just make sure you line up the decimal points vertically.

Example H. 23.5+53.95.

Arrange the numbers vertically with the decimal points lined up. Put a 0 after the 5 in 23.5 so that both numbers have the same number of places to the right of the decimal point. Then add.

$$
\begin{array}{r}
23.50 \\
+53.95 \\
\hline
77.45
\end{array}
$$

Example I. 46.28−18.354.

Arrange the numbers vertically with the decimal points lined up. Put a 0 after the 8 in 46.28, again so both numbers have the same place values to the right of the decimal point. Then subtract.

$$
\begin{array}{r}
46.280 \\
-18.354 \\
\hline
27.926
\end{array}
$$

To **multiply** decimals, first count the total number of places to the right of the decimal in both numbers. Then multiply the two numbers as if they were whole numbers and move the decimal point this many places from the right of the answer.

Example J. 2.3×1.02. There are three places to the right of the decimal in the two numbers.

Multiply 23 by 102. You get 2346. The decimal point is three places to the left, between the 2 and the 3 in 2346. The answer is 2.346.

To **divide** one decimal by another, first identify the number with the larger number of places to the right of the decimal point. Move the decimal point this number of places to the right in both numbers, adding zeros where necessary. Then divide the resulting numbers.

Example K. $1.8 \div 0.09$.

The number 0.09 has the larger number of places to the right of the decimal. Move both decimal points two places to the right, adding a 0 to 1.8: $180 \div 9$. The answer is 20.

Decimal Arithmetic Practice

Add, subtract, multiply, or divide as indicated.

1. $4.3 + 6.67$
2. $8.39 - 4.63$
3. 1.8×2.3
4. $6.4 \div .2$
5. $12.1 + 4.93$
6. $9.07 - 1.5$
7. 8.9×25
8. $1.5 \div 0.3$
9. $17.4 + 158.36$
10. $14.26 - 6.9$
11. 5.6×13.2
12. $0.24 \div 0.08$

Rounding to a Place Value

Call the digit in the place value that you are rounding the **rounding digit**. Look at the digit to the right of the rounding digit. If that digit is less than 5, leave the rounding digit as it is. If the digit to the right of the rounding digit is 5 or more, increase the rounding digit by 1 and make the remaining digits to the right zeros.

Example L. Round 2456 to the nearest hundred.

The rounding digit 4 is in the hundreds place, and the digit to its right is 5. Therefore, change the 4 to 5 and make both the 5 and 6 zeros. The rounded number is 2500.

When the rounding digit is to the right of the decimal point, you don't need to replace the digits to the right of the rounding digit by zeros.

Example M. Round 7.314 to the nearest tenth.

The rounding digit 3 is in the tenths place, and the digit to its right is 1. Since 1 is less than 5, leave the 3 as is: 7.3 is the rounded number.

Practice Rounding to a Place Value

Round each number to the indicated place value.

1. 9.653 to the nearest tenth
2. 84.3 to the nearest unit (whole number)
3. 57,308 to the nearest hundred
4. 0.016 to the nearest hundredth
5. 2.3454 to the nearest thousandth
6. 85.68 to the nearest tenth
7. 346.258 to the nearest ten
8. 0.000765 to the nearest thousandth
9. 5.016 to the nearest hundredth
10. 4093 to the nearest hundred

LESSON 2 Fractions

A **fraction** is a number that is the result of dividing two whole numbers. In the fraction $\frac{2}{5}$, 2 is called the **numerator**, and 5 is called the **denominator**. The line between them indicates division and is called the **division bar**. The division symbol ÷ is a fraction with dots in the numerator and denominator.

When the numerator is smaller than the denominator, the fraction is called a **proper fraction**.

When the numerator is larger than the denominator, the fraction is called an **improper fraction**. And when the numerator and denominator are equal, the fraction equals 1.

A proper fraction represents part (the numerator) of a whole (the denominator). You can think of the fraction $\frac{2}{5}$ as 2 out of 5. Two out of five bananas are rotten, or two-fifths of the bananas are rotten.

Improper fractions cannot be interpreted as part of a whole since the numerator is larger than the denominator, and a part can't be larger than the whole. You can think of an improper fraction as an actual division. For instance, you can split $500 among four people, and each person gets $\frac{500}{4}$ dollars, or $125. It is also useful to think of an improper fraction as a ratio—a way of comparing two numbers.

For instance, the fraction $\frac{47}{23}$ could represent the ratio of strikes to balls a pitcher throws in a game. Improper fractions can also be changed to mixed numbers. When you divide 23 into 47, you get 2 with a remainder of 1. This result can be written as the mixed number $2\frac{1}{23}$. You can change the mixed number $2\frac{1}{23}$ back to the improper fraction by doing the following calculation: $\frac{2 \times 23 + 1}{23} = \frac{47}{23}$.

Reducing Fractions

You can reduce proper or improper fractions. Divide the numerator and denominator by the largest number that divides into both. The original fraction and the reduced fraction are called **equivalent**. They have the same value. You should always reduce fractions as you work with them, even if they're not the final answer.

Example A. Reduce the fraction $\frac{12}{15}$.

Both 12 and 15 are divisible by 3. Therefore, $\frac{12}{15}$ reduces to $\frac{4}{5}$.

Example B. Reduce the fraction $\frac{30}{18}$.

Both 30 and 18 are divisible by 3. But both are also divisible by 6, which is larger than 3. Therefore, $\frac{30}{18}$ reduces to $\frac{5}{3}$. You could do this in two steps. First divide by 3 to reduce to $\frac{10}{6}$. Then divide by 2 to reduce to $\frac{5}{3}$. Not all fractions can be reduced. If 1 is the largest number that divides into both numerator and denominator, the fraction is already in lowest terms. An example of a fraction that cannot be reduced is $\frac{4}{7}$.

If the denominator is 1 after you reduce a fraction, the original denominator divided evenly into the original numerator, and the result is a whole number.

Example C. Reduce $\frac{20}{4}$.

Divide the numerator and denominator by 4 to get $\frac{5}{1}$. This reduces further to just 5, which you would get if you divided 4 into 20 to begin with.

Reducing Fractions Practice

Reduce each fraction to lowest terms.

1. $\frac{5}{10}$

2. $\frac{6}{16}$

3. $\dfrac{24}{18}$

4. $\dfrac{3}{9}$

5. $\dfrac{20}{12}$

6, $\dfrac{5}{12}$

7. $\dfrac{8}{12}$

8. $\dfrac{21}{28}$

9. $\dfrac{15}{5}$

10. $\dfrac{24}{36}$

Multiplying Fractions

To multiply fractions, just multiply the numerators and multiply the denominators. It doesn't matter whether the fractions are proper or improper.

Example D. Find the product $\dfrac{3}{5}\times\dfrac{7}{4}$.

$\dfrac{3}{5}\times\dfrac{7}{4}=\dfrac{3\times7}{5\times4}=\dfrac{21}{20}$. In this example, you could also write the answer as the mixed number $1\dfrac{1}{20}$.

Example E. Find the product $5\times\dfrac{2}{3}$.

The number 5 is equal to $\dfrac{5}{1}$. So $5\times\dfrac{2}{3}=\dfrac{5}{1}\times\dfrac{2}{3}=\dfrac{10}{3}$. As a mixed number, $\dfrac{10}{3}=3\dfrac{1}{3}$.

Example F. Find the product $\dfrac{1}{5}\times1\dfrac{1}{2}$.

Change the mixed number $1\dfrac{1}{2}$ to $\dfrac{3}{2}$ as explained earlier. Then multiply $\dfrac{1}{5}\times\dfrac{3}{2}=\dfrac{3}{10}$.

When you multiply fractions, you may get a fraction that can be reduced. For instance, when you multiply $\dfrac{3}{4}\times\dfrac{8}{7}$, you get $\dfrac{24}{28}$, which can be reduced to $\dfrac{6}{7}$ by dividing the numerator and denominator by 4. A more efficient method is to divide by 4 first; then multiply the result: $\dfrac{3}{\cancel{4}_1} \times \dfrac{\cancel{8}^2}{7} = \dfrac{3 \times 2}{1 \times 7} = \dfrac{6}{7}$.

Multiplying Fractions Practice

Find each product and reduce the answer to lowest terms. Write improper fraction answers as mixed numbers.

1. $\dfrac{3}{5} \times \dfrac{4}{7}$

2. $\dfrac{1}{8} \times \dfrac{3}{4}$

3. $\dfrac{2}{7} \times \dfrac{28}{3}$

4. $\dfrac{2}{3} \times \dfrac{6}{7}$

5. $4 \times \dfrac{3}{5}$

6. $\dfrac{3}{8} \times 1\dfrac{1}{4}$

7. $\dfrac{1}{3} \times \dfrac{12}{7}$

8. $3 \times \dfrac{5}{12}$

9. $1\dfrac{1}{3} \times 1\dfrac{3}{4}$

10. $\dfrac{13}{9} \times \dfrac{9}{13}$

Dividing Fractions

First we need to review another vocabulary word. The **reciprocal** of a fraction is the number you get by switching the numerator and denominator. For example, the reciprocal of $\dfrac{2}{3}$ is $\dfrac{3}{2}$. Since a whole number is equal to that number over 1, the reciprocal of a whole number is just 1 divided by the number. Since $7 = \dfrac{7}{1}$, for example, the reciprocal of 7 is $\dfrac{1}{7}$. Notice that a number times, its reciprocal is always equal to 1.

To divide one fraction by another, multiply the first fraction by the reciprocal of the other.

Example G. Find the quotient $\dfrac{2}{3} \div \dfrac{5}{6}$.

$$\frac{2}{3} \div \frac{5}{6} = \frac{2}{\underset{1}{\cancel{3}}} \times \frac{\cancel{6}^{2}}{5} = \frac{4}{5}.$$

Example H. Find the quotient $6 \div \dfrac{1}{4}$.

$$6 \div \frac{1}{4} = 6 \times \frac{4}{1} = 6 \times 4 = 24.$$

Example I. Find the quotient $\dfrac{3}{4} \div 2$.

$$\frac{3}{4} \div 2 = \frac{3}{4} \div \frac{2}{1} = \frac{3}{4} \times \frac{1}{2} = \frac{3}{8}.$$

Example J. Find the quotient $1\dfrac{2}{3} \div 6$.

$$1\frac{2}{3} \div 6 = \frac{5}{3} \div \frac{6}{1} = \frac{5}{3} \times \frac{1}{6} = \frac{5}{18}.$$

Dividing Fractions Practice

Find each quotient and reduce the answer to lowest terms. Write improper fraction answers as mixed numbers.

1. $\dfrac{3}{5} \div \dfrac{2}{3}$

2. $\dfrac{1}{2} \div \dfrac{3}{4}$

3. $\dfrac{5}{6} \div \dfrac{2}{3}$

4. $8 \div \dfrac{1}{2}$

5. $\dfrac{9}{4} \div \dfrac{9}{2}$

6. $\dfrac{7}{3} \div \dfrac{1}{6}$

7. $1\dfrac{1}{4} \div \dfrac{2}{3}$

8. $3\dfrac{1}{3} \div 1\dfrac{2}{3}$

9. $\dfrac{5}{8} \div 2$

10. $1\dfrac{1}{2} \div 3\dfrac{1}{3}$

Adding and Subtracting Fractions

Fractions can be added or subtracted only when they have the same denominator. In this case, find the sum or difference of the numerators and put that over the common denominator. Then reduce and change to a mixed number, if possible.

Example K. Find the sum of $\dfrac{2}{5} + \dfrac{1}{5}$.

Both denominators are 5, and the sum of the numerators is 3, so the answer is $\dfrac{3}{5}$.

Example L. Find the difference of $\dfrac{11}{12} - \dfrac{5}{12}$.

Both denominators are 12, and the difference of the numerators is 6, so the answer is $\dfrac{6}{12}$, which reduces to $\dfrac{1}{2}$.

If the denominators are different, one or both fractions must be changed to equivalent fractions that have the same denominators. Making such a change is the reverse of reducing a fraction. Basically, you must find the smallest number that both denominators divide into. This is called the **least common denominator**, or **LCD**.

Example M. What is the LCD of 12 and 6?

The smallest number that 12 and 6 divide evenly into is 12, so 12 is the LCD.

Example N. What is the LCD of 4 and 5?

The smallest number that both 4 and 5 divide evenly into is 20 (and no smaller number), so 20 is the LCD.

Example O. What is the LCD of 8 and 12?

The smallest number both 8 and 12 divide evenly into is 24, so 24 is the LCD.

Example P. Find the sum of $\dfrac{7}{10} + \dfrac{1}{5}$.

The LCD of 10 and 5 is 10. Multiply the numerator and denominator of $\dfrac{1}{5}$ by 2 to get $\dfrac{2}{10}$. Then add $\dfrac{7}{10} + \dfrac{2}{10}$ to get the sum $\dfrac{9}{10}$.

Example Q. Find the difference of $\dfrac{2}{3} - \dfrac{1}{4}$.

The LCD of 3 and 4 is 12. Multiply the numerator and denominator of $\dfrac{2}{3}$ by 4 to get $\dfrac{8}{12}$. Multiply the numerator and denominator of $\dfrac{1}{4}$ by 3 to get $\dfrac{3}{12}$. Then subtract $\dfrac{8}{12} - \dfrac{3}{12}$ to get the difference $\dfrac{5}{12}$.

Example R. Find the sum of $\frac{2}{9}+\frac{5}{12}$.

The LCD of 9 and 12 is 36. Multiply the numerator and denominator of $\frac{2}{9}$ by 4 to get $\frac{8}{36}$. Multiply the numerator and denominator of $\frac{5}{12}$ by 3 to get $\frac{15}{36}$. Then add $\frac{8}{36}+\frac{15}{36}$ to get the sum $\frac{23}{36}$.

Example S. Find the difference of $\frac{7}{12}-\frac{1}{4}$.

The LCD of 12 and 4 is 12. Multiply the numerator and denominator of $\frac{1}{4}$ by 3 to get $\frac{3}{12}$. Then subtract $\frac{7}{12}-\frac{3}{12}$ to get the difference $\frac{4}{12}$, which reduces to $\frac{1}{3}$. In summary, $\frac{7}{12}-\frac{1}{4}=\frac{1}{3}$.

Example T. Find the sum of $2\frac{1}{3}+1\frac{1}{2}$.

First change the mixed numbers to improper fractions: $\frac{7}{3}+\frac{3}{2}$. The LCD of 3 and 2 is 6. Multiply the numerator and denominator of $\frac{7}{3}$ by 2 to get $\frac{14}{6}$ and multiply the numerator and denominator of $\frac{3}{2}$ by 3 to get $\frac{9}{6}$. Then add $\frac{14}{6}+\frac{9}{6}$ to get $\frac{23}{6}$. Change $\frac{23}{6}$ to the mixed number $3\frac{5}{6}$. In summary, $2\frac{1}{3}+1\frac{1}{2}=3\frac{5}{6}$.

Adding and Subtracting Fractions Practice

1. $\frac{2}{7}+\frac{8}{7}$

2. $\frac{9}{11}-\frac{7}{11}$

3. $\frac{1}{3}+\frac{3}{4}$

4. $\frac{11}{12}-\frac{5}{6}$

5. $\frac{3}{10}+\frac{7}{15}$

6. $\frac{3}{4}-\frac{1}{6}$

7. $6\frac{1}{3}+4\frac{1}{3}$

8. $3\dfrac{5}{8} - 2\dfrac{1}{3}$

9. $2\dfrac{1}{3} + \dfrac{3}{5}$

10. $1\dfrac{1}{2} - \dfrac{3}{5}$

Converting Between Fractions and Decimals

To change a fraction to a decimal, divide the numerator of the fraction by its denominator. The fraction $\dfrac{5}{8}$, for example, means 5 divided by 8. When you do this division, you get $0.6250\cdots$, where the $\cdots$ means the rest of the digits are zeros. Such a decimal is called a **terminating decimal**.

Sometimes division results in a never-ending **repeating decimal**. For example, $\dfrac{1}{3} = 0.333\cdots$. The repeat can be indicated by writing it once and putting a line over it: $\dfrac{1}{3} = 0.\overline{3}$. Repeats can have more than one digit. For example, $\dfrac{10}{11} = 0.\overline{90}$.

The decimal form of any fraction, defined as one whole number divided by another, is either terminating or repeating.

For the TABE A, it is only necessary to be able to convert a terminating decimal to a fraction. This conversion is based on place value and a correct reading of the decimal.

Example U. Convert 0.567 to a fraction.
Read 0.567 as 567 thousandths. This would be written as $\dfrac{567}{1000}$, the fraction form of 0.567.

Example V. Convert 0.0025 to a fraction.
Read 0.0025 as 25 ten thousandths. This would be written as $\dfrac{25}{10000}$, the fraction form of 0.0025.

Ratio and Proportion

A **ratio** compares two numbers by division. Suppose you are 32 years old and your sister is 28 years old. You are 4 years older than your sister, but the ratio of your ages is $\dfrac{32}{28} = \dfrac{8}{7}$. You have lived 8 years for every 7 your sister has. Or you are $1\dfrac{1}{7}$ times older than your sister. You will always be 4 years older than your sister, but the ratio of your ages changes each year. For instance, she will be 60 when you are 64. At that time, the ratio of your ages will be $\dfrac{64}{60} = \dfrac{16}{15}$. At that point, you will be only $1\dfrac{1}{15}$ times older than your sister.

The equality of two ratios is called a **proportion**, and the two ratios are called proportional. Every proportion has four numbers: two numerators and two denominators. If you know three of the four numbers, you can determine the fourth one. This is called **solving a proportion**.

Example W. Solve the proportion $\dfrac{5}{8} = \dfrac{15}{x}$.

Since this is a proportion, it must be true that $5 \times x = 8 \times 15$. This is called **cross multiplication**. Divide both sides by 5, and you get $x = 24$.

Example X. Suppose a doctor says that a healthy 6-foot-tall man should weigh 180 pounds. What should a healthy man who is 5 feet 8 inches tall weigh?

A 5-foot-8-inch man is 68 inches tall, and a 6-foot man is 72 inches tall. If the height/weight ratio is the same for the two men and if we call the weight of the shorter man x, we have the proportion $\dfrac{72}{180} = \dfrac{68}{x}$. Cross multiply to get $72 \times x = 68 \times 180$. Use a calculator to compute $68 \times 180 \div 72$. The shorter man should weigh 170 pounds.

Example Y. Cherie believes her garden is most attractive when the ratio of red to yellow tulips is 5 to 2. This year she decides to plant 20 yellow tulip bulbs. How many red tulip bulbs should she plant?

Solve the proportion $\dfrac{5}{2} = \dfrac{x}{20}$. Cross multiply to get $2 \times x = 5 \times 20$. Then divide both sides of the equation by 2 to get $x = 50$. Cherie should plant 50 red tulip bulbs.

Ratio and Proportion Practice

Note: Some of the answer choices have been rounded.

1. A map has a scale of 1 inch = 5 miles. How far is it from Barnesville to Carlton if the map distance between them is 3 inches?
    a. 15 miles
    b. 7 miles
    c. 9 miles
    d. 8 miles

2. A 12-ounce can of soda costs $1.25. How much would you expect a 15-ounce bottle to cost?
    a. $1.40
    b. $1.56
    c. $1.62
    d. $1.75

3. Debra is planning to paint a picture of a photograph that is 4 inches wide by 6 inches high. If her painting must be 16 inches wide, how high should it be?

    a. 18 inches

    b. 20 inches

    c. 24 inches

    d. 28 inches

4. George took a 20-question math test, and he got 16 problems right. How many problems could he expect to get right on a 50-question test covering the same topics?

    a. 32

    b. 38

    c. 40

    d. 46

5. A 16-ounce package of frozen vegetables costs $2.10. How much would you expect a 12-ounce package to cost?

    a. $1.05

    b. $1.25

    c. $1.45

    d. $1.58

6. A small package of 230 colored candies contains 10 red pieces. How many red pieces would you expect to find in a large package containing 450 pieces?

    a. 15

    b. 20

    c. 25

    d. 30

7. Last week, five of six cameras sold in the Camera Mart store were digital cameras. This week they sold 72 cameras. How many of these would you have expected to be digital cameras?

    a. 36

    b. 40

    c. 45

    d. 60

8. The hair color of 500 members of the high school senior class was classified as brunette, blonde, or redhead. The results are shown in the table below.

Hair Color	Number of Students
Brunette	230
Blonde	180
Redhead	90

If there were 2000 students in the high school, how many brunettes would you expect to find?
   a. 800
   b. 850
   c. 920
   d. 1010

9. Last year, Carlos got 120 hits in 400 times at bat. He got 150 hits this year. How many times would you expect Carlos to have been at bat?
   a. 430
   b. 450
   c. 480
   d. 500

10. Ray made 10 two-point shots and 6 three-point shots in a basketball game. How many three-point shots would you expect Ray to make if he makes 15 two-point shots?
   a. 7
   b. 8
   c. 9
   d. 10

LESSON 3 Percent

A **percent** (%) is a fraction whose denominator is 100. The word "percent" means "out of 100." To write a fraction as a percent, divide the numerator of the fraction by its denominator and multiply the result by 100 (move the decimal point two places to the right).

Example A. Write $\frac{1}{4}$ as a percent.

Divide 4 into 1 to get 0.25. Multiply 0.25 by 100 to get 25%.

Any fraction whose denominator is a power of 10 is easy to write as a decimal and therefore a percent. First write the fraction as a decimal. Then move the decimal point two places to the right (multiply by 100).

Example B. Write $\frac{3}{10}$ as a decimal and a percent.

Divide 3 by 10 to get 0.3, the decimal. In order to move the decimal point two places to the right, you must add a 0 after the 0.3. This gives you 30%.

Example C. Write $\dfrac{7}{1000}$ as a decimal and a percent.

Divide 7 by 1000 to get 0.007, the decimal. Then move the decimal point two places to the right to get 0.7%.

The table below shows equivalent fraction, decimal, and percent values that you should know for the TABE A.

Fraction	Decimal	Percent
$\dfrac{1}{2}$	0.5	50%
$\dfrac{1}{4}$	0.25	25%
$\dfrac{3}{4}$	0.75	75%
$\dfrac{1}{3}$	$0.\overline{3}$	$33\dfrac{1}{3}\%$
$\dfrac{2}{3}$	$0.\overline{6}$	$66\dfrac{2}{3}\%$

Percent is probably the most frequently used mathematics concept in everyday life. Percents appear as discounts and markups in retail scenarios, they are used to summarize all kinds of sports results, they are used to measure proficiency on tests, and you see them in political polls. These applications will be described in the Applied Mathematics part of this book. This lesson deals strictly with three computational problems:

- Find the percent, knowing the part and the whole
- Find the part, knowing the percent and the whole
- Find the whole, knowing the part and the percent

While there are several methods to accomplish these three tasks, the most direct is to solve the proportion $\dfrac{\text{percent}}{100} = \dfrac{\text{part}}{\text{whole}}$. In any problem, we will know two of the three values (part, whole, or percent) and be asked to find the third.

Example D. What percent of 8 is 5?

The problem says the part is 5 and the whole is 8. Find the percent.

1. Set up the proportion: $\dfrac{\text{percent}}{100} = \dfrac{5}{8}$

2. Cross multiply: $8 \times \text{percent} = 500$

3. Divide by 8: $\text{percent} = \dfrac{500}{8} = 62.5$

Five out of eight is 62.5%.

Example E. What is 15% of 60?

The problem says the percent is 15 and the whole is 60. Find the part.

1. Set up the proportion: $\dfrac{15}{100} = \dfrac{\text{part}}{60}$. Reduce $\dfrac{15}{100} = \dfrac{3}{20}$, so $\dfrac{3}{20} = \dfrac{\text{part}}{60}$
2. Cross multiply: $20 \times \text{part} = 180$
3. Divide by 20: $\text{part} = 9$

15% of 60 is 9.

Example F. Seven is 35% of what number?

The problem says the part is 7 and the percent is 35. Find the whole.

1. Set up the proportion: $\dfrac{35}{100} = \dfrac{7}{\text{whole}}$. Reduce $\dfrac{35}{100} = \dfrac{7}{20}$, so $\dfrac{7}{20} = \dfrac{7}{\text{whole}}$
2. Cross multiply: $7 \times \text{whole} = 140$
3. Divide by 7: $\text{whole} = 20$

7 is 35% of 20.

Percent Practice

1. What is 10% of 50?
2. What percent of 80 is 16?
3. 7 is 20% of what number?
4. 3 is what percent of 15?
5. 15 is 60% of what number?
6. What is 20% of 34.6?
7. What percent of 30 is 12?
8. What is 12% of 30?
9. 30 is 12% of what number?
10. 18 is 75% of what number?

LESSON 4 Integers

The numbers 0, 1, 2, 3, $\cdots$ are called **whole numbers**. The $\cdots$ means "and so on, forever." The **opposites** of these numbers are $-1, -2, -3 \cdots$ (read negative one, negative two, negative three, and so forth). Taken together, these numbers are called **integers**. While most of the numbers you use every day are positive numbers, there are many uses for negative numbers in real life. Yards lost by a football team are negative numbers, as are temperatures below zero and locations below sea level.

Positive and negative numbers can be pictured on a **number line**. This is a horizontal line extending forever in both directions. As shown below, positive and negative numbers are mirror images of each other around 0 on a number line. When a number is positive, it does not need a + sign, but when a number is negative, it must have a – sign in front of it.

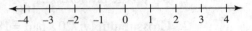

Numbers get larger as you move from left to right on the number line. Note, for example, that –2 is larger than –3.

Adding Integers

If two integers have the same signs, ignore the signs and add. The sign of the sum is the common sign. The sum of opposites is zero. For instance, $3+(-3)=0$.

Example A. Find the sum $4+7$.
   Both numbers are positive, so the sum $4+7=11$.

Example B. Find the sum $(-4)+(-7)$.
   Both numbers are negative, so the sum $(-4)+(-7)=-11$.
   When adding two integers with different signs, ignore the signs and subtract the smaller number from the larger number. The sign of the sum is the same as the sign of the larger number (with signs ignored).

Example C. Find the sum $-4+7$.
   If we ignore the signs, the two numbers are 4 and 7; $7-4=3$. Since the larger number (with signs ignored) is 7, which is positive, the sum $-4+7=3$.

Example D. Find the sum $4+(-7)$.
   If we ignore the signs, the two numbers are 4 and 7, and $7-4=3$. Since the larger number (with signs ignored) is 7, the sum $4+(-7)=-3$.

Adding Integers Practice

Find each sum.

   1. $-5+8$
   2. $8+(-3)$
   3. $9+13$
   4. $7+(-15)$
   5. $-6+(-12)$
   6. $2+(-15)$
   7. $5+12$
   8. $-8+(-11)$

9. $(-2)+(-2)$

10. $17+(-12)$

Subtracting Integers

To subtract one integer from another, *add* the opposite. Since you already know how to add, you don't need to learn anything new to subtract integers. This is best illustrated by examples.

Example E. Find the difference $6-2$.
Instead of subtracting 2, add -2: $6+(-2)=4$. The difference $6-2=4$.

Example F. Find the difference $6-(-2)$.
Instead of subtracting -2, add 2: $6+2=8$. The difference $6-(-2)=8$.

Example G. Find the difference $-6-2$.
Instead of subtracting 2, add -2 : $-6+(-2)=-8$. The difference $-6-2=-8$.

Example H. Find the difference $-6-(-2)$.
Instead of subtracting -2, add 2: $-6+2=-4$ The difference $-6-(-2)=-4$.

Subtracting Integers Practice

1. $12-(-3)$
2. $-5-8$
3. $-6-(-9)$
4. $13-7$
5. $-8-6$
6. $-3-(-10)$
7. $14-(-3)$
8. $19-17$
9. $7-(-14)$
10. $-1-4$

Multiplying and Dividing Integers

Multiplying and dividing integers is easier than adding and subtracting them. To find the product or quotient of two integers, multiply or divide without regard to sign. The product or quotient is positive if the two signs are the same and negative if the two signs are different.

Example I. Find the product 8×7.

Since both numbers have the same sign (+), the product is 56.

Example J. Find the product $(-8) \times (-7)$.

Since both numbers have the same sign (−), the product is 56.

Example K. Find the product $8 \times (-7)$.

Since the numbers have different signs, the product is −56.

Example L. Find the quotient $10 \div 2$.

Since both numbers have the same sign (+), the quotient is 5.

Example M. Find the quotient $25 \div (-5)$.

Since the two numbers have different signs, the quotient is −5.

Multiplying and Dividing Integers Practice

1. -8×3
2. $7 \times (-5)$
3. $(-27) \div (-3)$
4. 6×15
5. $(-12) \div 8$
6. $36 \div 12$
7. $52 \div (-13)$
8. $(-50) \div (-5)$
9. $60 \div 12$
10. $14 \div (-1)$

Mixed Integer Arithmetic Practice

1. $22 - (-3)$
2. -6×3
3. $-12 + (-5)$
4. $18 \div (-3)$
5. $9 + (-12)$
6. $(-35) \div (-7)$
7. $6 - 13$
8. $(-3) \times (-20)$
9. $-8 + 13$
10. $3 \times (-1)$

LESSON 5 Order of Operations

In math, an **operation** is doing something to a number or several numbers to get another (possible the same) number. Examples are the following:

- Adding two numbers
- Subtracting one number from another
- Multiplying two numbers
- Dividing one number by another
- Raising a number to a power
- Finding the square root of a number

When you perform any of these operations, alone or in combination, you evaluate an expression. If the problem consists of all numbers, the expression is called **numerical**. If there are variables (letters that stand for numbers), the expression is called **algebraic**.

What if more than one operation is required to complete a single problem? For example, suppose you are asked to evaluate $12 - 2 \times 4$. If you do the operations from left to right, your first calculation is $12 - 2$, which is 10. Then $10 \times 4 = 40$, and you would get the answer 40. If you went from right to left, you would first multiply 2×4, which is 8, and then subtract 8 from 12, which is 4. Which answer is correct? (As you will see shortly, 4 is the correct answer.)

Because we got two different answers for the same problem, mathematicians have agreed to follow a specific **order of operations**. First we need to describe symbols called **grouping symbols**. Parentheses ( ) are one grouping symbol. When you see $4(5 + 2)$, do the operation in parentheses first: $4(5 + 2) = 4(7) = 28$. A division bar — is also a grouping symbol. For example $\dfrac{2 + 8}{3 + 2} = \dfrac{10}{5} = 2$ because the operations in the numerator, then the denominator, are done first, then the division is done. Finally, the $\sqrt{}$ is also a grouping symbol. For example, $\sqrt{25 - 16} = \sqrt{9} = 3$. Subtract 16 from 25 before finding the square root. If you find the square roots before subtracting, you would get $\sqrt{25} - \sqrt{16} = 5 - 4 = 1$. *This also demonstrates that* $\sqrt{25 - 16} \neq \sqrt{25} - \sqrt{16}$.

The order of operations is as follows:

1. Do the operations within grouping symbols first. If there are multiple grouping symbols, work from the inside out.
2. Do exponents. An exponent applies to whatever expression immediately comes before it.
3. Do multiplication and division, left to right.
4. Do addition and subtraction, left to right.

Step 1 requires clarification. An expression may "nest" several sets of parentheses. For example, $3(4 - (8 + 12))$. According to step 1, you must work from the inside out. First add 8 and 12 to get 20. Then subtract 20 from 4 to get -16. Finally, multiply -16 by 3 to get -48. In short, $3(4 - (8 + 12)) = -48$.

In step 3, multiplication and division have the same "status." Don't do all the multiplications and then all the divisions. Do them as they occur, left to right. The same comment applies to addition and subtraction in step 4. An acronym to help you remember the order of operations is the following:

Please **E**xcuse **M**y **D**ear **A**unt **S**ally (PEMDAS): **p**arentheses, **e**xponents, **mu**ltiplication, **d**ivision, **a**ddition, and **s**ubtraction.

Example A. Evaluate $3^2 + 5$.

Apply the exponent 2 to the number 3 first to get 9. Then add $9 + 5$ to get 14.

Example B. Evaluate $3 + 2(4 - 1)$.

First, subtract 1 from 4 to get 3. The multiply 3 by 2 to get 6 and then add 3 to get 9.

Example C. Evaluate both $4^2 + 5^2$ and $(4 + 5)^2$.

In the first case, do 4^2, which is 16, and add to 5^2, which is 25, and add these to get 41. In the second case, add 4 and 5 to get 9 and then square 9 to get 81. These two are different: in general, $a^2 + b^2$ is *different from* $(a + b)^2$.

Example D. Evaluate $9 - 5 \div (8 - 3) + 2$.

First subtract 3 from 8 in the parentheses to get 5. Then divide 5 by 5 to get 1. Then do the additions and subtractions in order: $9 - 1 + 2$ to get 10.

You may also be asked to evaluate an algebraic expression given values of the variables. In these problems, substitute the numerical value or values in the expression and evaluate the resulting numerical expression. Since the value(s) to be substituted may be negative, *it is best to put the substituted value in parentheses.*

Example E. Evaluate $5a - b$ for $a = 3$ and $b = -4$.

Substituting, we get

$$5(3) - (-4)$$
$$= 15 - (-4)$$
$$= 15 + 4$$
$$= 19$$

Example F. Evaluate $\dfrac{a}{b^2} + a - b$ for $a = 8, b = -2$.

$$\frac{8}{(-2)^2} + 8 - (-2)$$
$$= \frac{8}{4} + 8 - (-2)$$
$$= 2 + 8 - (-2)$$
$$= 2 + 8 + 2$$
$$= 10 + 2$$
$$= 12$$

Example G. Evaluate $b^2 - 4ac$ for $a = 2, b = -1, c = -5$.

Substituting, we get

$$(-1)^2 - 4(2)(-5)$$
$$= 1 - (8(-5))$$
$$= 1 - (-40)$$
$$= 1 + 40$$
$$= 41$$

Order of Operations Practice

Evaluate each expression.

1. $7 + (3)(1 + 4)$
2. $10 \div 5 + \left(\dfrac{12}{3} \right)$
3. $6 + 4 \div 2 - 3^2$
4. $\sqrt{25 - 16}$
5. $1^2 + 2^2 + 3$
6. $\dfrac{3}{2^2} + \dfrac{9}{4}$
7. $a - (b + c)$ for $a = 2, b = -5, c = 8$
8. $x - 9(1 + y)$ for $x = 20, y = 2$
9. $-p^2 - (q + 1)^2$ for $p = -5, q = 1$
10. $5(u - v) + 3$ for $u = 2, v = 3$

LESSON 6 Algebraic Operations

This lesson describes methods of simplifying algebraic expressions and discusses techniques for solving equations. The lesson begins with a summary of important properties of numbers, stated algebraically.

Properties of Numbers

Use of letters in algebra makes it possible to state results that are true for *all* numbers. Numbers have several important properties that are typically taken for granted when we do arithmetic. These properties and their names are listed below:

Name	Property
Commutative Property of Addition	$a+b=b+a$
Commutative Property of Multiplication	$ab=ba$
Associative Property of Addition	$(a+b)+c=a+(b+c)$
Associative Property of Multiplication	$(ab)c=a(bc)$
Distributive Property for Addition	$a(b+c)=ab+ac$
Distributive Property for Subtraction	$a(b-c)=ab-ac$
Property of Zero (0 times any number equals 0)	$0a=0$
Property of 1 (1 times any number equals the number)	$1a=a$
Property of -1 (-1 times any number equals its opposite)	$-1a=-a$
Zero Product Property	$ab=0$ implies $a=0$ or $b=0$

The commutative properties say that it doesn't matter which order you add or multiply two numbers—you get the same answer. The associative properties say that if you add or multiply *three* numbers, it doesn't matter which two you add or multiply first. The distributive properties say that adding or subtracting two numbers and multiplying the result by a third gives you the same answer as multiplying each of the two numbers by the third and then adding or subtracting the results.

Example A. What property does $(6+3)+5=6+(3+5)$ illustrate?

This illustrates the Associative Property of Addition with $a=6, b=3, c=5$.

Example B. What property does $3(x+5)=3x+15$ illustrate?

This illustrates the Distributive Property for Addition with $a=3, b=x, c=5$.

Example C. What is the value of $(-1)(5)$?

$(-1)(5)=-5$, the opposite of 5.

Example D. If $5x=0$, then $x=0$. What property does this illustrate?

This illustrates the Zero Product Property with $a=5$ and $b=x$.

Absolute Value

The **absolute value** of a number is the "positive" of the number. For example, 3 is the absolute values of both 3 and -3. The absolute value of a number is also its distance from 0 on the number line. Both 3 and -3 are both 3 units away from zero. The notation in math for absolute value is a pair of vertical lines around the number. Using this notation, you would write $|3|$ for "the absolute value of 3" and $|-3|$ for the absolute value of -3. Using this notation, $|3|=3$ and $|-3|=3$.

Absolute value is also a grouping symbol. For example, when determining $|8-10|$, calculate $8-10=-2$ first and then $|-2|=2$.

The formal definition for absolute value is

$$|x| = \begin{cases} x & \text{if} \quad x \geq 0 \\ -x & \text{if} \quad x < 0 \end{cases}$$

In words, the absolute value of a number is just the number if the number is positive (or 0), and the absolute value of a number is its opposite if the number is negative.

Exponents and Their Properties

Recall that an exponent says how many times the base is a factor. For instance, $x^3 = (x)(x)(x)$. The base x is a factor (multiplied) 3 times. There are four important properties of exponents you should know. The variable b is the base, and m and n are integer exponents (positive or negative whole numbers). These properties don't have names, but they can be described in a useful way:

- $b^m b^n = b^{m+n}$ When multiplying, add the exponents.
- $\dfrac{b^m}{b^n} = b^{m-n}$ When dividing, subtract the exponents.
- $(b^m)^n = b^{mn}$ When raising a power to a power, multiply the exponents (powers).
- $(ab)^m = a^m b^m$ The power of a product is equal to the product of the powers.
- $b^0 = 1$ Any number (except 0) to the 0 power equals 1; 0^0 is not a number.
- $b^{-n} = \dfrac{1}{b^n}$ A negative power means the reciprocal of the positive power.

Example E. Simplify $b^5 b^3$.

$b^5 b^3$ means multiply b^5 and b^3, so *add* the exponents:

$$b^5 b^3 = b^{5+3}$$
$$= b^8$$

$b^5 b^3$ simplifies to b^8.

Example F. Simplify $\dfrac{b^5}{b^3}$.

$\dfrac{b^5}{b^3}$ means divide b^5 by b^3, so *subtract* the exponents:

$$\frac{b^5}{b^3} = b^{5-3}$$
$$= b^2$$

$\dfrac{b^5}{b^3}$ simplifies to b^2.

Example G. Simplify $(b^5)^3$.

$(b^5)^3$ means raise b^5 to the third power. This is a power (5) to a power (3), so *multiply* the exponents:

$$(b^5)^3 = b^{(5)(3)}$$
$$= b^{15}$$

$(b^5)^3$ simplifies to b^{15}.

Example H. Simplify $(5b)^2$.

$(5b)^2$ means find the product $(5b)(5b)$. It is the second power of the product of 5b with itself. According to the commutative and associative properties of multiplication, the four factors (2 fives and 2 b's) can be multiplied in any order: $(5)(5) = 25$ and $(b)(b) = b^2$. The product of these powers is $25b^2$. Therefore, $(5b)^2$ simplifies to $25b^2$.

Example I. $10^0 = 1$.

Example J. $3^{-1} = \dfrac{1}{3}$.

Example K. $\left(\dfrac{1}{3}\right)^{-2} = 9$.

Properties of Exponents Practice

Use the properties of exponents to simplify each expression.

1. $x^2 x^8$
2. $\dfrac{x^{10}}{x^2}$
3. $(2z)^3$
4. $(x^3)^4$
5. $x^3 x^{-2}$
6. $\dfrac{x^5}{x^{-3}}$
7. $(y^{-3})^{-2}$
8. $(2r)^{-2}$
9. 6^{-2}
10. $(12x)^0$
11. $(u^2)^{-1}$
12. 8^0

Simplifying Algebraic Expressions

There are a few additional basic facts and conventions that you need to know before we discuss simplification of algebraic expressions:

- When a number that is represented by a variable is multiplied by a known number, write the known number first, for example, $5x$ instead of $x5$. The number is also called the **coefficient**.
- Number (or variables) that a multiplied are called **factors**.
- Numbers or variables that are added or subtracted are called **terms**.
- A particular number or a particular variable can be either a factor or a term, depending on context. For example, 5 and x are *factors* in the expression $5x$, but both 5 and x are *terms* in the expression $5 + x$.

You must be careful to distinguish between addition (or subtraction) and multiplication (or division) when working with algebraic expressions. You can multiply (or divide) *any* two expressions.

Example L. Find the product $(8x)(2x)$.

$$(8x)(2x) = (8)(2)(x)(x)$$
$$= 16x^2$$

The first step is based on both commutative and associative properties of multiplication. You can multiply the four factors in any order, and they can be grouped or not in any manner. The second step uses the facts $(8)(2) = 10$ and $(x)(x) = x^2$.

Example M. Find the quotient $\dfrac{8x}{2x}$.

$$\frac{8x}{2x} = \left(\frac{8}{2}\right)\left(\frac{x}{x}\right)$$
$$= (4)(1)$$
$$= 4$$

Example N. Find the product $(8x)(2y)$.

$$(8x)(2y) = (8)(2)(x)(y)$$
$$= 16xy$$

The first step reorders the factors, and the second step multiplies: $(8)(2) = 16$. The only shorter way of writing $(x)(y)$ is to drop the parentheses.

Example O. Find the quotient $\dfrac{8x}{2y}$.

$$\frac{8x}{2y} = \left(\frac{8}{2}\right)\left(\frac{x}{y}\right)$$
$$= 4\left(\frac{x}{y}\right)$$

Unlike multiplication or division, you may only add or subtract **like terms**. Two terms are called **like** when they have the same variables to the same powers.

Example P. Are $7x^2$ and $3x^2$ like terms? If so, find the sum.
Yes, $7x^2$ and $3x^2$ are like terms. The distributive property for addition applies:

$$7x^2 + 3x^2 = (7+3)x^2$$
$$= 10x^2$$

When two terms are like, just add the coefficients and leave x^2 alone.

Example Q. Find the difference $7x^2 - 3x^2$.
$7x^2 - 3x^2 = 4x^2$. The distributive property for subtraction applies:

$$7x^2 - 3x^2 = (7-3)x^2$$
$$= 4x^2$$

Just subtract the coefficients and leave x^2 alone.

Example R. Are $8x^2$ and $2x$ like terms? If so, find the sum.
The sum is $8x^2 + 2x$, and this cannot be simplified because $8x^2$ and $2x$ are not like terms.

Example S. Are $3x$ and $2y$ like terms? If so, find the sum.
The sum is $2x + 3y$, which cannot be simplified because $3x$ and $2y$ are not like terms.

Example T. Simplify $6a + a$ if possible.
These are like terms because the variable is a in both terms. Since $a = 1a$, use the distributive property to see that

$$6a + 1a = (6+1)a$$
$$= 7a$$

Example U. Simplify $6a + b$.
Since $6a$ and $1b$ are not like terms, $6a + b$ cannot be simplified.

Simplifying Algebraic Expressions Practice

Simplify each expression, if possible.

1. $8x + 5x$
2. $(4x)(3y)$
3. $\dfrac{10u}{5u}$

4. $\dfrac{14p}{7q}$

5. $6x + 5y$

6. $2x - 5x$

7. $\dfrac{12x^2}{3}$

8. $4u^3 - 10u^3$

9. $8p + 12p^2$

10. $\dfrac{9x}{3x}$

11. $a - 2a$

12. $8q - 3q$

13. $a^3 a^5$

14. $6x^2 + 5x^2$

15. $\dfrac{w^3}{w^5}$

16. $\dfrac{8x^5}{2x^3}$

17. $(5p)(-4q)$

18. $x - y^2$

19. $(y + x) + 2x$

20. $7x - x$

21. $(ab)^4$

Applied Mathematics

This section includes lessons on the following:

- Number and number operations
- Computation in context
- Estimation
- Measurement
- Geometry
- Data analysis
- Statistics and probability
- Patterns, functions, and algebra
- Problem solving and reasoning

You may be familiar with some of these topics from when you were in school. Even if you think you know the topic well, look at each lesson to see if there are any points that you may have forgotten.

LESSON 7 Number and Number Operations

The previous lessons have dealt with a variety of numbers. In this lesson, we will classify numbers and describe how numbers can be compared.

Number Classification

The **counting numbers** are numbers that are used to count: $1, 2, 3, \cdots$. These are the first kinds of numbers that you learned in elementary school. You also learned how to do arithmetic with these numbers: adding, subtracting, multiplying, and dividing them.

The **whole numbers** are the same as the counting numbers with 0 included. These are the numbers $0, 1, 2, 3 \cdots$. Although it's easy to think of 0 as "nothing," it is a very important number for the following reasons:

- Zero added to any number is equal to that number.
- Zero multiplied by any number is zero.
- You *cannot* divide by zero!

Every number that is a counting number is also a whole number. We say that the counting numbers are a **subset** of the whole numbers.

If you include the negative counting numbers with the whole numbers, you get the **integers**. You can think of the integers as "partners" for the counting numbers. They include pairs of opposites. Zero has no opposite.

Rational numbers are numbers that we previously defined as fractions: one integer divided by another (not zero). Since fractions with denominators equal to 1 are really whole numbers, every whole number is also a rational number. For instance, 5 is equal to $\frac{5}{1}$, so the whole number 5 can be seen as a rational number as well.

The counting numbers, whole numbers, integers, and rational numbers are "nested." Each set is contained in the next set. The decimal form of rational numbers either (a) has all zeros somewhere to the right of the decimal point (for example $\frac{72}{10} = 7.200\cdots$) or (b) has a repeating pattern following the decimal point (for example, $\frac{1}{3} = 0.\overline{3}$).

Square Root Numbers

Exponents were introduced in Lesson 1. An exponent is a raised number that tells you the number of times a base number is a factor. For instance, in 2^3, 2 is the base, 3 is the exponent, and 2^3 means $2\times2\times2$, which equals 8. A number raised to an exponent of 2 is called the **square** of the number. For example, $5^2 = 25$ is the square of 5. You already know the squares of 1 through 12 as special numbers in the multiplication table:

$1^2 = 1\times1 = 1$	$7^2 = 7\times7 = 49$
$2^2 = 2\times2 = 4$	$8^2 = 8\times8 = 64$
$3^2 = 3\times3 = 9$	$9^2 = 9\times9 = 81$
$4^2 = 4\times4 = 16$	$10^2 = 10\times10 = 100$
$5^2 = 5\times5 = 25$	$11^2 = 11\times11 = 121$
$6^2 = 6\times6 = 36$	$12^2 = 12\times12 = 144$

The numbers $1, 4, 9, 16, \cdots, 144$ are called **perfect squares**. When you see a number such as 49, you should recognize it as the square of 7.

Square root numbers are obtained by reversing the process of squaring. The symbol for square root is $\sqrt{}$. For example, $\sqrt{9} = 3$ because $3^2 = 9$. By recognizing the perfect squares in the table above, you will know the square roots of $1, 4, 9, 16, \cdots, 144$.

Once you have learned the square roots of perfect squares, you will be able to approximate square roots of numbers (up to 144) that are not perfect squares.

For example, suppose we want to approximate $\sqrt{12}$. Since 12 is between 9 and 16, $\sqrt{12}$ is between $\sqrt{9}$ and $\sqrt{16}$. This means that $\sqrt{12}$ is between 3 and 4 because $\sqrt{9} = 3$ and $\sqrt{16} = 4$. This approximation makes it possible to locate (approximately) $\sqrt{12}$ on a number line.

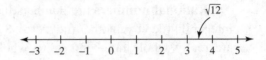

Square roots of numbers that are not perfect squares are examples of **irrational numbers**. The number π (pi) is also an irrational number. The decimal form of an irrational number is neither terminating (ends with all zeros) nor repeating (such as $0.333\cdots = 0.\overline{30}$). The decimal form of an irrational number goes forever without repeating. While irrational numbers have limited practical application, their **decimal approximations** of irrational numbers are used in several fields, such as carpentry and agriculture. For example, the decimal approximation of π is 3.14. Taken together, the rational and irrational numbers make up the **real numbers**. This name suggests that there are numbers that aren't real, and there are such numbers, but they are beyond the scope of the TABE A. The figure below shows the relationship among the various number sets.

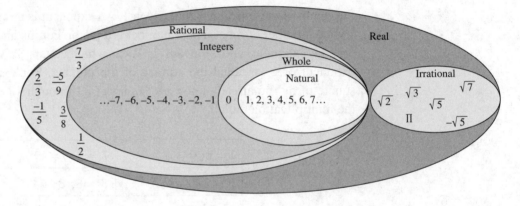

Comparing Numbers

There are six symbols used to compare the sizes of numbers. The meanings of these symbols are described below with examples:

Symbol	Meaning	Examples
=	same value	$5+3=8$
≠	different values	$5+3 \neq 10$
<	less than	$6<7$
≤	less than or equal to	$6 \leq 7, 7 \leq 7$
>	greater than	$9>8$
≥	greater than or equal to	$9 \geq 8, 9 \geq 9$

Any negative number is smaller than any positive number. If a and b are positive numbers with $a < b$, then $-a > -b$.

Example A. $6 < 10$, but $-6 > -10$.

This reflects the number line's mirror nature around 0 (both 6 and -6 are closer to 0 than are 10 and -10).

Compare decimals by comparing place value digits. Just to be clear, the digits are ordered from least to greatest as follows: 0, 1, 2, 3, 4, 5, 6, 7, 8, 9. When there are no digits to the right of the decimal point, the decimal numbers are whole numbers, which you already know how to compare. When there are digits to the right of the decimal point, first compare the tenths place. Whichever number has the larger digit is the larger number. If the digits in the tenths place are equal, move right to the hundredths place and compare the digits. Whichever number has the larger digit is the larger number. Continue this process, moving one place at a time to the right, until the larger number is determined.

Example B. Compare 12.067 and 12.0607.

The digits are the same until the thousandths place. At that point, the first number has the digit 7, while the second number has the digit 0. Since $7 > 0$, $12.067 > 12.0607$.

If the denominators are the same, fractions are easy to compare. Just compare the numerators.

Example C. Compare $\dfrac{5}{12}$ and $\dfrac{7}{12}$.

Since $5 < 7$, $\dfrac{5}{12} < \dfrac{7}{12}$.

If the numerators are the same, the larger number has the smaller denominator.

Example D. Compare $\dfrac{7}{9}$ and $\dfrac{7}{11}$.

Since $9 < 11$, $\dfrac{7}{9} > \dfrac{7}{11}$.

If the both numerators and denominators are different, you could always find a common denominator and change one or both fractions to fractions that have that common denominator. A second option is to change both fractions to decimals and compare the decimal forms. There is a shortcut, however. Multiply each numerator by the other fraction's denominator. The fraction with the numerator that produces the larger product is larger.

Example E. Compare $\dfrac{5}{9}$ and $\dfrac{7}{11}$.

$5 \times 11 = 55$ and $9 \times 7 = 63$. Since $63 > 55$ and since 63 was produced by the fraction with 7 in the numerator, that fraction is larger: $\dfrac{7}{11} > \dfrac{5}{9}$.

Example F. Compare 7 and $\sqrt{50}$.

Since $49 < 50$, $\sqrt{49} < \sqrt{50}$. But $\sqrt{49} = 7$, so $7 < \sqrt{50}$.

Number and Number Operations Practice

Classify each number by all names that apply.

1. 0

2. 17

3. −9

4. $\dfrac{7}{10}$

5. $\sqrt{2}$

6. .22

7. $5\dfrac{1}{2}$

8. −200

9. $-0.\overline{4}$

10. $\dfrac{5}{4}$

Write the numbers in order from smallest to largest.

11. $2.1, \dfrac{5}{2}, 2.09$

12. $\dfrac{8}{3}, \dfrac{9}{4}, 2$

13. $\dfrac{9}{16}, 0.5, \dfrac{7}{16}$

14. $-\dfrac{2}{3}, -0.6, .001$

15. $-0.34, -0.339, -.341$

16. $8, \sqrt{59}, -9$

17. $-1, -\sqrt{2}, 0$

18. $9.1, 9.01, \sqrt{80}$

LESSON 8 Computation in Context

This lesson deals with "story" problems that are solved using methods of the previous seven lessons. What makes story problems difficult is the fact that you must decide *which* method to use to answer the question and not simply perform a computation. The key is to read a problem carefully and be sure you know what the question is before choosing a method.

Several examples are given below.

Example A. A $75 pair of shoes is advertised at 35% off. What is the cost after this discount?

The whole is 75, and the percent is 35. We need to find the part. Set up a proportion:

$$\frac{\text{part}}{75} = \frac{35}{100}$$

Then cross multiply and divide:

$$100 \times \text{part} = 2625$$
$$\text{part} = 26.25$$

The savings from the discount is $26.25. Subtract this from $75 to get the answer, $48.75. A shortcut for this problem is to realize that if you get 35% off, you pay 65% (100% − 65%). This time, the part is the amount you pay, so no subtraction is necessary. Set up the proportion

$$\frac{\text{part}}{75} = \frac{65}{100}$$

Then cross multiply and divide:

$$100 \times \text{part} = 4875$$
$$\text{part} = 48.75$$

The amount you pay is $48.75.

Example B. A football team gains 23 yards, gains 14 yards, loses 18 yards, gains 3 yards, and loses 7 yards. How much did they gain or lose altogether?

In this problem you have to find the sum of five integers: $23 + 14 - 18 + 3 - 7 = 15$. Since the answer is positive, the team gained 15 yards altogether.

Example C. Paul got 15 problems right out of 20 problems altogether. How many would he have expected to get right if there had been 52 problems?

This is a proportion problem: $\frac{15}{20} = \frac{x}{52}$. Cross multiply and divide by 20:

$$20x = 780$$
$$\frac{20x}{20} = \frac{780}{20}$$
$$x = 39$$

He could have expected to get 39 right.

Example D. Laurie paid $4.08 for a bag of 12-cent candies. How many candies did she get?

First change 12 cents to 0.12 dollars. Then divide 4.08 by 0.12 to get 34 candies.

Example E. Robert bought a $150 coat on sale for 20% off. When he got to the store, they gave him $5 off. Given a choice, should he take the 20% off or the $5 off first?

Use the shortcut method for the 20%. He pays 80%. If he takes the 20% off first and then the $5, he would pay $(.8)(150)-5=115$. If he takes the $5 off first and then the 20%, he would pay $(.8)(150-5)=(.8)(145)=116$. He would save $1 by taking the 20% off first.

Example F. Randy averages 35.8 miles per hour on a 67-mile trip. How long did the trip take?

This problem uses the fact that distance equals speed times time ($d=rt$). This problem asks for time, which is distance divided by speed. Therefore, time $=\dfrac{67}{35.8}=$ 1.87 hours, or 1 hour and 52 minutes.

Computation in Context Practice

1. The local community college awarded 245 certificates and 1700 associate degrees to students this spring. Of the students receiving certificates and associate degrees, 238 were unable to attend the graduation ceremony. Which expression represents the number of graduates who did attend?
   a. $1700-(245+328)$
   b. $(238+1700)-245$
   c. $(1700+245)-238$
   d. $1700-238$

2. Suzanne paid $324.70 for a coat that was on sale at 15% off. What was the regular price of the coat?
   a. $339.70
   b. $373.40
   c. $382
   d. $412

3. When you woke up, the temperature was $-13°$ F. By noon, the temperature was $7°$ F. Which expression represents the difference in temperature between waking up and lunch?
   a. $-13+7$
   b. $-13-7$
   c. $7-13$
   d. $7-(-13)$

4. The population of the United States on December 31 was reported as 322,583,006. Round this to the nearest hundred thousand.
   a. 322,600,000
   b. 322,580,000
   c. 323,000,000
   d. 323,600,000

5. Last week, Grace worked her regular 40-hour week plus 10 hours overtime. She gets paid time and a half overtime, and her regular 40 hours pays her $800. What was her total pay last week?
   a. $810
   b. $1000
   c. $1100
   d. $1500

6. Four friends went to a restaurant for lunch. The bill, without tax, was $56, and they decided to each leave a $2 tip. What percent tip did they leave (rounded to the nearest whole percent)?
   a. 4%
   b. 7%
   c. 14%
   d. 18%

7. A certain recipe calls for $\frac{1}{4}$ cup of sugar to make enough for 6 people. Amanda has invited 15 guests for dinner and wants to use this recipe. How much sugar will she need?
   a. $\frac{1}{6}$ cup
   b. $\frac{1}{2}$ cup
   c. $\frac{5}{8}$ cup
   d. $\frac{3}{4}$ cup

8. Kathy drives an average speed of 35 miles per hour for 45 minutes. How far does she travel?
   a. 26.25 miles
   b. 31.25 miles
   c. 32.00 miles
   d. 34.75 miles

9. Paul bought shares of a certain stock for $9 per share. He sold 100 shares a year later for $1050. How much did the value of each share change during the year?
   a. down $1.50
   b. down $.75
   c. up $.75
   d. up $1.50

10. Richard has a 4:30 pm appointment in Center City, 15 miles away. He can average 25 miles per hour driving. By what time must he leave home to make it to his appointment on time?

    a. 3:36 pm

    b. 3:48 pm

    c. 3:54 pm

    d. 4:02 pm

LESSON 9 Estimation

It isn't always necessary to determine an exact value of something. For example, if you buy four items at $1.95 each, you could round $1.95 up to $2.00, multiply by 4, and get an estimate of $8.00 for the total. Since you rounded up, the actual total should be just under $8.00. Estimation means rounding numbers up or down to numbers that are easier to work with, such as $2.00 instead of $1.95. There is even a symbol that indicates that some value is an estimate. In our example, we would write $4 \times \$1.95 \approx \$8.00$, where the symbol $\approx$ is read "approximately equals." The examples that follow use a variety of "shortcuts" to estimate computations.

Example A. You want to plant a row of flowers, and the row is 75 inches long. The flowers should be planted about 7.5 inches apart. How many flowers will you need?

    To be safe, round the value 7.5 down to 7. You need to divide 75 by 7 and add 1 because you will want a flower at each end of the bed. If we want to be sure to have enough flowers, we should round 75 inches up to 77 inches, the nearest number bigger than 75 that is divisible by 7. You would need $11 + 1 = 12$ flowers.

Example B. You use a calculator to multiply 104×51, and the calculator displays the answer 714.

    Use an estimate to determine if you typed in the correct numbers for the problem.

    Round 104 to 100 and 51 to 50. We know that $50 \times 100 = 5000$ is an underestimate, so the displayed answer 714 cannot be correct. What was the error? The number 14 was typed into the calculator instead of 104.

Example C. Add $77 + 51 + 22 + 50$.

    Group the numbers so you can add mentally: $77 + 22 = 99$, which is one less than 100, and $50 + 51 = 101$, which is one more than 1100, so the total is 200.

Example D. What is 15% of 375?

    First round 375 to 380. The plan is to divide 15% into two parts: 10% and 5%. Taking 10% moves the decimal point one place to the left. The 5% is half of 38, which is 19. You can also add $38 + 19$ by adding 40 and 20, then subtracting 3 to get 57.

Estimation Practice

1. Estimate 45% of 700.
   a. 300
   b. 350
   c. 400
   d. 450

2. Estimate 3.07×59.
   a. 150
   b. 160
   c. 170
   d. 180

3. Estimate $397 \div 98$.
   a. 4
   b. 5
   c. 6
   d. 7

4. Joanne is buying a dress that is 25% off. The original cost of the dress is $51.95. Estimate how much would save if she were to buy this dress.
   a. $10
   b. $13
   c. $20
   d. $25

5. Mike and four friends buy a pizza for $19.50. Estimate how much each should pay.
   a. $3.00
   b. $3.50
   c. $4.00
   d. $4.50

6. Joe wants to estimate the number of words he wrote in an essay. The essay is four pages long, and he estimates about 18 words per line. Each page has about 32 lines. Which of the following is the best estimate for the number of words in the essay?
   a. 1600
   b. 2400
   c. 3000
   d. 3500

7. A watch costs $45 wholesale. The price is marked up 80% for sale in a store. Which of the following is the best estimate of the marked-up price?
   a. $53
   b. $65
   c. $70
   d. $80

This lesson on measurement covers the measurement of time, length, liquid volume, weight, and temperature. Of these, only time is measured the same way universally. The other quantities are measured using the customary system in the United States and using the metric system elsewhere in the world. You need to be able to convert these units within the customary or metric system from memory.

The metric system is based on powers of 10 and is more systematic than is the customary system. Each power of 10 corresponds to a prefix:

- $10^1 = 10 = \text{deca}$ $10^{-1} = 0.1 = \text{deci}$
- $10^2 = 100 = \text{hecto}$ $10^{-2} = 0.01 = \text{centi}$
- $10^3 = 1000 = \text{kilo}$ $10^{-3} = 0.001 = \text{milli}$

For example, a *kilo*meter is 1000 meters, while a *milli*meter is 0.001 meter.

There are two fundamental principles that apply to the conversion of units within either the customary or the metric system:

- Multiply when converting larger units to smaller ones.
- Divide when converting smaller units to larger ones.

If a problem asks you to convert between the customary and metric systems, you will be given the necessary formulas to use.

Units of Time

Units of time are inexact because they have evolved over centuries and are based on the movement of the sun and the moon:

- The second is the basic unit.
- 60 seconds make 1 minute.
- 60 minutes make 1 hour.
- 24 hours make 1 day.
- 7 days make 1 week.
- 4-plus weeks make a month, which varies in length from 28 to 31 days.
- 52 weeks make just under a year (364 days).
- 365 days make a year.
- 12 months make a year.
- 10 years make a decade.
- 100 years make a century.

Fractions of a second are frequently used, especially in sports, science, and technology:

- Tenth of a second (10 make 1 second)
- Hundredth of a second (100 make 1 second)

- Millisecond (1000 make 1 second)
- Nanosecond (1,000,000 make 1 second)

The last two fractions of a second are metric measures (*nano* means 0.000001, or one millionth).

Example A. The average life expectancy of an American is about 80 years. How many seconds is this?

First change years to days. Since a day is a smaller unit of time than a year, multiply: $365 \times 80 = 29,200$ days. Next, since an hour is smaller than a day, multiply: $24 \times 29,200 = 700,800$ hours. Since a minute is smaller than an hour, multiply: $60 \times 700,800 = 42,048,000$ minutes. Finally, since a second is smaller than a minute, multiply by 60 again: $60 \times 42,048,000 = 2,522,880,000$ seconds. This is the average life expectancy of an American in seconds.

Example B. How many centuries are there in 500 months?

First, change 500 months to years. Since a year is a larger measure of time than a month, divide: $500 \div 12 = 41.\overline{6}$ (recall, $.\overline{6} = .666\cdots$). Since a century is larger than a year, divide again: $41.\overline{6} \div 100 = 0.41\overline{6}$ centuries. Five hundred months equals $0.41\overline{6}$ centuries.

Units of Length

The table below summarizes the names and relationships between units of length.

Customary	Metric
foot is the basic unit	meter is the basic unit
3 feet make 1 yard	10 meters make 1 *deca*meter
5280 feet make 1 mile	100 meters make 1 *hecto*meter
12 inches make a foot	1000 meters make 1 *kilo*meter
	0.1 meters make 1 *deci*meter
	0.01 meters make 1 *centi*meter
	0.001 meters make 1 *milli*meter

Example C. Doreen needs 90 feet of fencing to enclose her vegetable garden. She goes to the store and finds that fencing comes in 2-yard sections. How many sections of fencing will she need?

Change the 90 feet into yards by dividing by 3. She needs 30 yards. Each section of fencing is 2 yards, so divide 30 by 2 to get 15 sections.

Example D. Julia trained for her track meet by running 500 meters, 350 meters, 600 meters, and 550 meters on four consecutive days. How many kilometers did she run on these four days altogether?

Add the four distances to get the total distance in meters: $500 + 350 + 600 + 550 = 2000$. The total distance she ran was 2000 meters. Since a meter is smaller than a kilometer, divide by 2000 by 1000 to get 2 kilometers.

Example E. A baseball player and a golfer wanted to compare the distances they hit a ball. The baseball player could hit a baseball 400 feet, while a golfer could hit a golf ball 280 yards. Which one hit the ball farther and by how much (in feet)?

Since the answer is to be in feet, convert the yards the golfer hit the ball to feet. Since a yard is longer than a foot, multiply 280 by 3: $3 \times 280 = 840$ feet, compared to 400 feet for the baseball player. Subtract 400 from 840: the golfer hit the golf ball 440 feet farther than the baseball player hit the baseball.

Units of Liquid Volume

The table below summarizes the names and relationships between units of liquid volume.

Customary	Metric
cup is the basic unit	liter is the basic unit
2 cups make 1 pint	10 liters make 1 *deca*liter
2 pints make 1 quart	100 liters make 1 *hecto*liter
4 quarts (8 pints) make 1 gallon	1000 liters make one *kilo*liter
8 liquid ounces make 1 cup	0.1 liters make 1 *deci*liter
(a liquid ounce is a measure of volume, not weight)	0.01 liters make 1 *centi*liter
	0.001 liters make 1 *milli*liter

Example F. How many liquid ounces of milk make a half gallon?

Work from a half gallon back to liquid ounces. It takes 8 liquid ounces to make 1 cup and 2 cups to make a pint. Therefore, it takes $8 \times 2 = 16$ liquid ounces to make a pint. Since it takes 2 pints to make a quart, it takes $2 \times 16 = 32$ liquid ounces to make a quart. Finally, since it takes 4 quarts to make a gallon, it takes only 2 quarts to make a half gallon. Therefore, it takes $2 \times 32 = 64$ liquid ounces to make a half gallon.

Units of Weight

The table below summarizes the names and relationships between units of weight.

Customary	Metric
ounce is the basic unit	gram is the basic unit
16 ounces make 1 pound	10 grams make 1 *deca*gram
2000 pounds make one ton	100 grams make 1 *hecto*gram
	1000 grams make 1 *kilo*gram
	0.1 grams make 1 *deci*gram
	0.01 grams make 1 *centi*gram
	0.001 grams make 1 *milli*gram

Example G. One dose of a certain medicine is 5 milligrams. How many doses does a 1-gram bottle of this medicine contain?

First change to a common unit. Since a milligram is smaller than a gram, use milligrams because it involves multiplication instead of division. There are 1000 milligrams in the bottle. Since each dose is 5 milligrams, there are $1000 \div 5 = 200$ doses in the bottle.

Example H. An elevator has an inspection certificate stating that the elevator has a 2500-pound capacity. Assuming an average weight of 200 pounds, what should be the maximum number of people allowed on this elevator?

Divide $2500 \div 200 = 12.5$. To be safe, no more than 12 people should be allowed on this elevator.

Units of Temperature

The table below summarizes the units of temperature.

Customary	Metric
degrees Fahrenheit (F)	degrees Celsius (C)
water freezes at 32° F	water freezes at 0° C
water boils at 212° F	water boils at 100° C

Because Americans travel to other parts of the world, it is useful to be able to move between temperature in Fahrenheit and Celsius measures. Here are the formulas, where C and F stand for the temperature measured in Celsius and Fahrenheit:

- $C = \dfrac{5}{9}(F - 32°)$

- $F = \dfrac{9}{5}C + 32°$

Example I. Alicia is planning to shop one day while on vacation in Australia. She calls the hotel front desk, and she is told the forecast calls for a high temperature of 15° C. What is this temperature in degrees Fahrenheit?

Since we need to change from degrees Celsius to degrees Fahrenheit, use the formula $F = \dfrac{9}{5}C + 32°$. Substitute 15° for C and multiply: $\dfrac{9}{5} \times 15° = 27°$. Then add: $27° + 32° = 59°$. Alicia should probably wear a sweater!

Measurement Practice

1. Tom has 523 minutes remaining on his disposable cell phone. How many hours and minutes is this?
   a. 5 hours, 23 minutes
   b. 7 hours, 15 minutes
   c. 8 hours, 43 minutes
   d. 9 hours, 3 minutes

2. Charlotte picks $\frac{1}{3}$ acre of blueberries on her farm from 9:30 to 12:00. If she takes an hour for lunch and has a 1-acre farm, at what time would she finish?
   a. 5:30 pm
   b. 6:00 pm
   c. 6:30 pm
   d. 7:00 pm

3. When Chris woke up yesterday morning, the temperature was 12° F below zero. By the time he got to work, it was 22° F. How many degrees F did the temperature rise?
   a. 10°
   b. 18°
   c. 24°
   d. 34°

4. A cruise ship is 1545 feet long. If a football field is 100 yards long, how many football fields long is the cruise ship?
   a. 4.85
   b. 5.15
   c. 5.75
   d. 15.45

5. A patient must receive 15 milliliters of glucose an hour. How many liters of glucose will the patient receive in 12 hours?
   a. 180
   b. 18
   c. 1.8
   d. .18

6. A chemist must add 5.48 kilograms of a substance to a mixture. How many grams of the substance is this?
   a. 0.0548
   b. 54.8
   c. 548
   d. 5480

7. The temperature in New York is 86° F. How does this compare with 30° C? Use the formula $C = \dfrac{5}{9}(F - 32°)$.

    a. They are the same.

    b. 86° F is hotter.

    c. 30° C is hotter.

    d. They can't be compared.

8. Sharon needs 2.25 gallons of paint to paint her living room. How many pints of paint is this?

    a. 5

    b. 9

    c. 18

    d. 21

9. Michelle buys a 50-ounce container of laundry detergent. What is this weight in pounds?

    a. $2\dfrac{1}{2}$

    b. 3

    c. $3\dfrac{1}{8}$

    d. 4

10. Last week Bill worked for 36 hours, and this week he worked for 52 hours. He gets paid $100 for each 8-hour day or part of a day with no overtime. What was Bill's pay for these 2 weeks?

    a. $900

    b. $1000

    c. $1100

    d. $1200

LESSON 11 Geometry

Geometry is the study of shapes. **Plane geometry** is about shapes on planes (flat surfaces or two dimensions), such as triangles, rectangles, hexagons, and circles. **Solid geometry** is about shapes in space (three dimensions), such as boxes, balls, pyramids, and cones.

You see geometry all around you. The rails of train tracks are parallel lines. The letter T consists of perpendicular lines. The yield sign is a triangle. The stop sign is an octagon. The headquarters of the U.S. Department of Defense is a pentagon. Common three-dimensional shapes are cereal boxes, water glasses, and ice cream cones. The great pyramids of Egypt are the best-known examples of that shape.

The review of geometry begins with definitions and facts about lines and angles. We then discuss triangles, quadrilaterals, other polygons, circles, and polygons.

Lines and Angles

The **point** named *A* is a location in space, represented by a dot. The **line** named $\overleftrightarrow{AB}$ goes through points *A* and *B* in both directions forever (indicated by the two-headed arrow). The **segment** named $\overline{AB}$ is a line with **endpoints** *A* and *B* (no arrowheads). Finally, $\overrightarrow{AB}$ names the **ray** that starts at endpoint *A* and continues forever through *B* (a single arrowhead over *B*).

The *length* of segment $\overline{AB}$ is called *AB*. There is no line above the letters. To find the length of a segment, put its endpoints on a number line and subtract the location of the left endpoint from the location of the right endpoint. For example, suppose $\overline{AB}$ had the left endpoint of a segment at 3 and the right endpoint at 7. Then *AB* would be $7-3=4$. Segments that have the *same length* are called **congruent**. In a figure, tick marks are used to indicate that two segments are congruent. Since lines and rays have infinite length, congruency does not apply to these.

The **midpoint** of a segment is the point *halfway* between the endpoints. The midpoint of the segment with endpoints at 3 and 7 is 5. A line, a segment, and a ray are shown in the figure below.

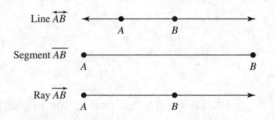

Parallel lines, segments, or rays lie in a plane and never intersect (cross each other), like railroad tracks. The arrows in the figure indicate that the two lines are parallel. The symbol ‖ means "is parallel to." In the figure below, $\overleftrightarrow{AB} \parallel \overleftrightarrow{CD}$.

Perpendicular lines, rays, or segments form a right angle (90°), like a plus sign (+). The symbol ⊥ means "is perpendicular to." In the figure below, $\overleftrightarrow{AB} \perp \overleftrightarrow{CD}$.

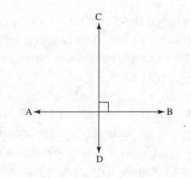

An **angle** consists of two rays with the same endpoint. The common endpoint is called the **vertex** of the angle, and the rays themselves are called the **sides** of the angle. The **degree measure** of an angle (symbolized by °) indicates the amount of *rotation* from one side to the other (how "wide open" the angle is). The degree measure of ∡*A* is called ∠*A*. There is no arc through the ∠ symbol when naming its measure. **A protractor**, shown below, is used to determine the degree measure of an angle. Angles are said to be **congruent** if they have the *same degree measure*.

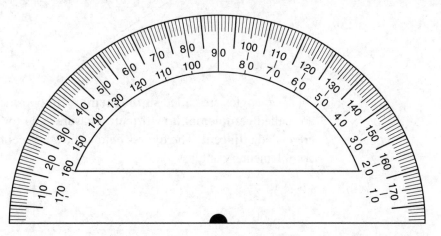

An angle is typically named by its vertex: ∡*A* is shown below. If there are more than two rays with a common endpoint *A*, you need three letters to name an angle. The three rays shown below form the three angles ∡*BAC*, ∡*CAD*, and ∡*BAD*. The vertex for all three is *A*, the middle letter of the name.

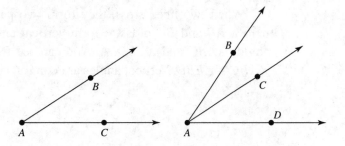

An angle with measure 90° is called a **right** angle.

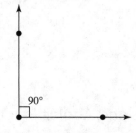

An angle with measure 180° is called a **straight** angle.

An angle with measure less than 90° is called **acute**, and an angle with measure greater than 90° is called **obtuse**.

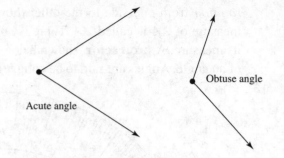

Acute angle

Obtuse angle

Two angles are called **supplementary** if their measures add to 180°, and they are called **complementary** if their measures add to 90°. Angles that share a side are called **adjacent**. The figures below show adjacent supplementary and adjacent complementary angles.

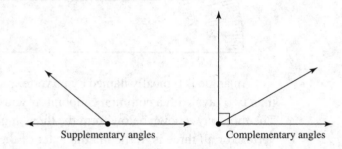

Supplementary angles   Complementary angles

When two lines cross, they form two pairs of **vertical** angles. In the figure below, $\overrightarrow{AB}$ and $\overrightarrow{BC}$ cross to form vertical angles $\angle ABE$ and $\angle CBD$ and vertical angles $\angle ABC$ and $\angle EBD$. As you can see from this figure, $\angle ABE \cong \angle CBD$ and $\angle ABC \cong \angle EBD$. Vertical angles are congruent.

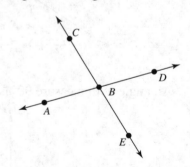

Lines and Angles Practice

1. A segment has its endpoints at −6 and 10 on a number line. What is its midpoint?
   a. −2
   b. 0
   c. 2
   d. 5

2. What is the complement of a 47° angle?
 a. 3°
 b. 43°
 c. 53°
 d. 133°

3. What is the supplement of a 55° angle?
 a. 25°
 b. 35°
 c. 45°
 d. 125°

4. An obtuse angle is one whose degree measure is
 a. less than 90°.
 b. equal to 90°.
 c. greater than 90°.
 d. greater than 100°.

5. In the figure, what is the measure of ∡*EBD*?
 a. 75°
 b. 105°
 c. 115°
 d. Cannot be determined

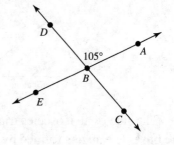

6. An angle whose measure is 100° is called
 a. a vertical angle.
 b. a right angle.
 c. an acute angle.
 d. an obtuse angle.

7. If two angles have degree measures of 85° and 95°, they are
 a. right angles.
 b. complementary angles.
 c. supplementary angles.
 d. acute angles.

Triangles

A **triangle** is a figure with three sides (segments that meet) and three angles. Triangles are named by their three vertices. The figure below displays $\triangle ABC$. The sides are labeled by the lowercase letter of the **opposite** angle. An **altitude** is a segment from one vertex that is *perpendicular* to the opposite side. A **median** is a segment from a vertex to the midpoint of the opposite side. Note that every triangle has three altitudes and three medians.

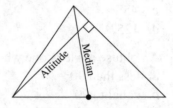

There are several special types of triangles. Three types of triangles are *classified by their sides*:

- A **scalene** triangle has *no* congruent sides.
- An **isosceles** triangle has *two* congruent sides.
- An **equilateral** triangle has *three* congruent sides.

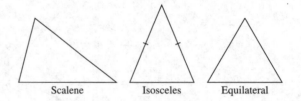

The side of an isosceles triangle that is not congruent to the other two is called the **base**. The angles formed by the base with each of the congruent sides are called **base** angles. The angle opposite the base is called the **vertex angle**. Angles that are *opposite* congruent sides are congruent angles. Therefore, the base angles of an isosceles triangle are congruent. This also leads to the conclusion that an equilateral triangle is also **equiangular**.

Three other types of triangles are *classified by their angles*:

- A **right** triangle has one 90° angle (also called a right angle).
- An **acute** triangle has three acute angles.
- An **obtuse** triangle has one obtuse angle.

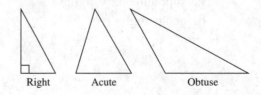

The *sides* of a right triangle that form the right angle are called **legs**. The side *opposite* the right angle is called the **hypotenuse**.

One of the most important facts in geometry is the **Pythagorean Theorem**. This theorem applies to right triangles and is illustrated in the figure below. In this figure, the legs of the right triangle have lengths a and b, and the length of the hypotenuse is c. The Pythagorean Theorem says $c^2 = a^2 + b^2$.

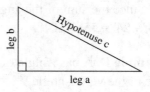

You can use this theorem to find the length of the third side of a right triangle given the lengths of the other two sides.

Example A. Suppose the legs of a right triangle have lengths 3 feet and 4 feet. What is the length of the hypotenuse?

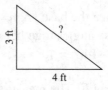

We need to find the value of c. According to the Pythagorean Theorem, $c^2 = 3^2 + 4^2 = 9 + 16 = 25$. Therefore, $c = \sqrt{25} = 5$. The hypotenuse is 5 feet long.

Example B. Suppose the length of one leg of a right triangle is 5 inches and the length of the hypotenuse is 13 inches. What is the length of the other leg?

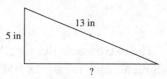

Let $a = 5$ be the length of the known leg. The length of the hypotenuse is $c = 13$. Using the Pythagorean Theorem, $5^2 + b^2 = 13^2$, or $125 + b^2 = 169$. Solve this equation for b^2 by subtracting 25 from both sides: $b^2 = 144$, so $b = \sqrt{144} = 12$.

The sum of the angle measures in *any* triangle is 180°. As a result of this fact, we know that the angles of a right triangle that are not the right angle *must be* acute (each less than 90°) and *complementary* (measures sum to 90°). Another result of this fact is that a triangle can have *at most one* obtuse angle (because two obtuse angles would have measures that sum to more than 180°). Finally, since the three angles of an equilateral triangle are congruent, the fact that the angle measures sum to 180° says each angle must measure 60° (180° ÷ 3).

Example C. Suppose two angles of a triangle have measures 24° and 55°. What is the measure of the third angle?

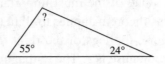

Since the sum of the angle measures is 180°, the measure of the third angle is $180° - 24° - 55° = 101°$.

Example D. A base angle of an isosceles triangle measures 70°. What is the measure of the vertex angle?

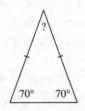

Since the base angles are congruent, the other base angle measures 70°, so the two base angles together measure 140°. Therefore, the measure of the vertex angle is $180° - 140° = 40°$.

Example E. The measure of the vertex angle of an isosceles triangle is 76°. What is the measure of a base angle?

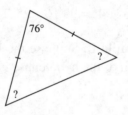

The two base angles together measure $180° - 76° = 104°$. Since base angles are congruent, each measures $104° \div 2 = 52°$.

Two triangles are **congruent** if the side lengths and angle measures of one triangle are equal to the side lengths and angle measures of the other. The same symbol ($\cong$) used for congruent segments and angles is used for triangles. If $\triangle ABC$ is congruent to $\triangle XYZ$, we write $\triangle ABC \cong \triangle XYZ$. The congruence statement says that vertex A matches with vertex X, vertex B matches with vertex Y, and vertex C matches with vertex Z. Therefore, when $\triangle ABC \cong \triangle XYZ$.

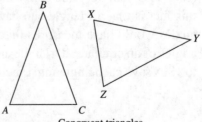

Congruent triangles

Two triangles are **similar** if the angles of one triangle are congruent to the angles of the other and the sides of the two triangles are proportional. Essentially, two triangles are similar if they have the same shape but not the same size. The symbol for similarity is ~ so that $\triangle ABC \sim \triangle XYZ$ means that $\angle A \cong \angle X$, $\angle B \cong \angle Y$, and $\angle C \cong \angle Z$ and $\dfrac{a}{x} = \dfrac{b}{y} = \dfrac{c}{z}$. A pair of similar triangles is shown in the figure.

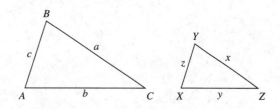

Example F. Suppose in the figure below that $\triangle ABC \sim \triangle XYZ$, $a = 12$, $b = 15$, and $x = 4$. Find y.

Since the side lengths of similar triangles are proportional, $\dfrac{12}{15} = \dfrac{4}{y}$. Cross multiply to get $12y = 60$. Divide both sides by 12 to get $y = 5$.

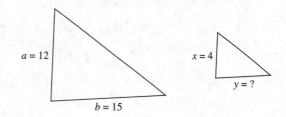

The **perimeter** of a figure is the distance around it. The area of a figure is the amount of space inside it. The length around a figure has the *same units* as the lengths of the pieces that make up the boundary of the figure. For example, if the lengths of the sides of a triangle are in feet, the perimeter is also in feet. The **area** of a figure is the amount of space inside it. For example, if the sides of a triangle are measured in feet, the area is measured in square feet (feet²).

Formulas for the perimeter and area of a triangle are shown in the figures below.

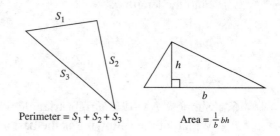

Perimeter $= S_1 + S_2 + S_3$ Area $= \frac{1}{b}\,bh$

Triangle Practice

Answer each question. Sketching a figure may help.

1. How should the triangle below be classified?

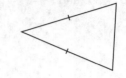

   a. Isosceles
   b. Right
   c. Scalene
   d. Equilateral

2. A scalene triangle has
   a. two congruent sides.
   b. two congruent angles.
   c. two right angles.
   d. no congruent sides.

3. Suppose $\triangle ABC$ is isosceles with vertex angle $\measuredangle C = 100°$. Find the measure of a base angle.
   a. 25°
   b. 30°
   c. 35°
   d. 40°

4. Suppose $\triangle XYZ$ is isosceles with base $\measuredangle X = 56°$. Find the measure of the vertex angle.
   a. 60°
   b. 64°
   c. 68°
   d. 72°

5. Suppose $\triangle ABC$ is a right triangle with the right angle at C, $a = 15$, and $b = 8$. Find the length c.
   a. 17
   b. 19
   c. 23
   d. 24

6. Suppose $\triangle ABC$ is a right triangle with the right angle at C, $a = 5$, and $c = 8$. Which of the following is the best approximation to the nearest hundredth for b?
   a. 5.91
   b. 6.24
   c. 6.87
   d. 7.00

7. Suppose $\triangle PQR \cong \triangle UVW$ and the measure of $\measuredangle Q = 73°$. What is the measure of $\measuredangle V$?
    a. 17°
    b. 27°
    c. 73°
    d. 107°

8. Suppose $\triangle DEF \sim \triangle LMN$, $e = 7$, $f = 9$, and $n = 18$. Find the length m.
    a. 14
    b. 15
    c. 16
    d. 17

9. A triangle has one side of length 10 inches, and the altitude to that side is 5 inches. What is the area of the triangle?
    a. 15 inches^2
    b. 25 inches^2
    c. 30 inches^2
    d. 50 inches^2

10. The three sides of a triangle have lengths 5.3 feet, 8.4 feet, and 6.7 feet. What is the perimeter of the triangle?
    a. 19.4 feet
    b. 20.4 feet
    c. 21.4 feet
    d. 22.4 feet

Quadrilaterals

A **quadrilateral** is a four-sided figure. A quadrilateral is named by its vertices, such as *ABCD* below. The angle measures of a quadrilateral sum to 360°. A **diagonal** is a segment whose endpoints are opposite vertices. The diagonals $\overline{AC}$ and $\overline{BD}$ are also shown in the figure.

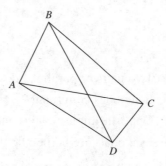

The most common quadrilaterals are rectangles, squares, and kites. Most people would recognize a parallelogram, rhombus, and trapezoid as well. It is important to know the properties of quadrilaterals so we can explain why a particular quadrilateral falls into a certain category. The names, properties, and shapes of quadrilaterals are summarized next. Familiarizing yourself with these properties is a good way to practice use of all the terminology.

Parallelogram

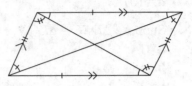

- Two pairs of parallel sides
- Opposite sides congruent
- Opposite angles congruent
- Diagonals bisect each other (cut each other in half)

Rectangle

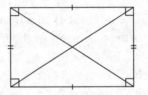

- Two pair of parallel sides
- Opposite sides congruent
- Four right angles
- Diagonals bisect each other
- Diagonals are congruent

Rhombus

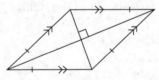

- Two pairs of parallel sides
- Four sides congruent
- Opposite angles congruent
- Diagonals are perpendicular

Square

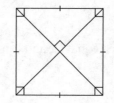

- Two pairs of parallel sides
- Four sides congruent
- Four right angles
- Diagonals congruent and perpendicular

Kite

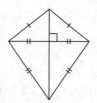

- Two pairs of *consecutive* congruent sides
- One pair of congruent opposite angles
- Diagonals are perpendicular
- One diagonal bisects the other

Trapezoid

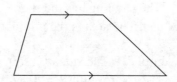

- Only one pair of parallel sides

We will only consider formulas for the perimeter and area of rectangles and squares. These formulas use lowercase letters to represent the lengths of the sides.

Rectangles

For the perimeter and area of a rectangle, we need to know only the lengths of the two sides—usually called the length l and width w, shown in the figure.

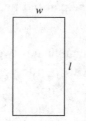

Perimeter equals twice the length plus twice the width.

$$P = 2l + 2w$$

Area equals length times width.

$$A = lw$$

Squares

Since all four sides are congruent, we only need one variable, s, to represent this length.

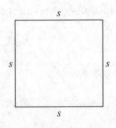

Perimeter equals four times the length of one side.

$$P = 4s$$

Area equals side times side, or side^2.

$$A = s^2$$

Example G. A painting is 3 feet high and 1.8 feet wide. What is its area?

The painting has the shape of a rectangle with a length of 3 feet and a width of 1.8 feet. The area is the product of these two numbers: 5.4 feet^2.

Example H. The side of a square is 5 meters long. What is its perimeter?

Use the formula $P = 4s$ with $s = 5$. The perimeter of the square is $4 \times 5 = 20$ m.

Quadrilateral Practice

Answer each question. It may help to sketch a figure for some problems.

1. A trapezoid has
   a. one pair of parallel sides.
   b. two pairs of parallel sides.
   c. one pair of opposite angles.
   d. congruent diagonals.

2. A rectangle has two pairs of parallel sides.
   a. Always true
   b. Sometimes true
   c. Never true

3. A rhombus has four congruent sides.
   a. Always true
   b. Sometimes true
   c. Never true

4. A parallelogram has
   a. two pairs of congruent sides.
   b. four right angles.
   c. congruent diagonals.
   d. None of the above

5. Which of the following statements is true?
   a. All rhombuses are squares.
   b. All squares are rhombuses.
   c. No squares are rhombuses.
   d. None of the above

6. A rectangle has sides of length 4.5 meters and 6.4 meters. What is its perimeter?
   a. 9.9 meters
   b. 10.9 meters
   c. 20.8 meters
   d. 21.8 meters

7. The side of a square is 7 mm. What is the area of the square?
   a. 14 mm^2
   b. 28 mm^2
   c. 36 mm^2
   d. 49 mm^2

8. What is the perimeter of a square whose side length is 2.4 inches?
   a. 4.8 inches
   b. 5.76 inches
   c. 8.6 inches
   d. 9.6 inches

9. The length of a rectangle is $5\frac{1}{2}$ centimeters, and its width is $3\frac{1}{4}$ centimeters. What is its area?
   a. $8\frac{3}{4}$ centimeters^2
   b. $15\frac{1}{8}$ centimeters^2
   c. $15\frac{3}{4}$ centimeters^2
   d. $17\frac{7}{8}$ centimeters^2

Other Polygons, Circles, and Solid Figures

Triangles and quadrilaterals are specific types of polygons. A **polygon** is a closed shape formed by segments touching end to end. Polygons are also convex, which means they *cannot* be shaped like a star. A **regular** polygon is one whose sides and angles are congruent to one another.

You should know the names of certain other types of polygons. A **pentagon** is a five-sided polygon. The headquarters of the U.S. armed forces is the building named the Pentagon because its five sides represent the five branches of the military. The shape of home plate is another pentagon, but not all the sides have the same length. A **hexagon** is a six-sided polygon. The heads of bolts are in the shape of a regular hexagon. Honeycombs of a beehive are also regular hexagons. Many homes have hexagonal tiling on their bathroom floors. These applications take advantage of the fact that the hexagon is an "efficient" shape. Finally, an **octagon** is an eight-sided polygon. A stop sign has this shape. A regular pentagon, a regular hexagon, and a regular octagon are illustrated below.

Pentagon   Hexagon   Octagon

The concepts of congruence and similarity apply to all polygons, not just triangles. Two *polygons* are **congruent** if the sides and angles of one are congruent to the sides and angles of the other. They are the *same* size and shape. Two *polygons* are **similar** if their angles are congruent and their sides are proportional. They have the *same* shape but *different* sizes. A pair of similar hexagons is shown below.

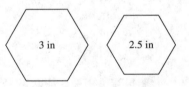

3 in   2.5 in

If asked for a definition of a circle, many of us would call it "a round thing." While this description is accurate, it needs to be more carefully defined to be studied mathematically. The *formal* definition of a **circle** is a set of points *equidistant* (same distance) from a given point. The given point is called the **center** of the circle, and the equal distance that the points on the circle are away from the center is called the **radius**. The distance around the circle is called its **circumference**. The circumference of a circle is like the perimeter of a polygon.

A **chord** is a segment that has its endpoints on a circle. The longest chord is the one through the center, called a **diameter**. The word "diameter" is also used to describe the *length* of a diameter. By definition, the diameter of a circle is *twice* as long as the radius.

Two lines have special relationships with circles. A line that touches a circle in one place is called a **tangent** (or tangent line). A line that touches a circle in two places is called a **secant** (or secant line).

A circle displaying these its radius, circumference, a chord, a diameter, and a tangent and secant is shown in the next figure.

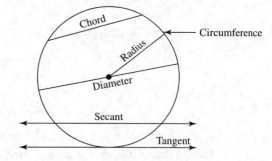

There are two important formulas you must know for circles. The circumference is π (pi) times the diameter: $C = \pi d$, where d stands for the diameter. Loosely speaking, the distance around a circle is a little more than three times the distance across ($\pi \approx 3.14$). Most calculators have a π button.

The other important formula is for the area of a circle: $A = \pi r^2$, where r stands for the radius. Since the diameter is twice the radius, the formula $C = \pi d$ is equivalent to $C = 2\pi r$. To summarize:

Circumference: $C = \pi d$ or $C = 2\pi r$

Area: $A = \pi r^2$

Example I. A porthole on a ship is the shape of a circle with a radius of 8 inches. What is the area of the porthole, rounded to the nearest tenth?

Use the formula $A = \pi r^2$: $\pi(8)^2 \approx 201.1$ inches^2.

Example J. An automobile tire has a radius of 16 inches. What is its circumference, rounded to the nearest tenth of an inch?

Use the formula $C = 2\pi r$: $C = 2\pi(16) = 100.5$ inches.

Solid figures are three-dimensional objects. Such an object has a volume, or the amount of space inside. The following summarizes five types of three-dimensional figures and formulas for finding their volumes. Look at objects around your household and see if you can name their shapes and find their volumes.

- **Rectangular prism** (shaped like a box)   Volume: $V = lwh$

- **Cube** (shaped like a die) $V = s^3$

- **Cylinder** (shaped like a can) $V = \pi r^2 h$

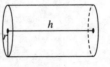

- **Cone** (shape like an ice cream cone) $V = \dfrac{1}{3}\pi r^2 h$

  The volume of a cone is one third the volume of a cylinder with the same radius and height.

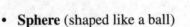

- **Sphere** (shaped like a ball) $V = \dfrac{4}{3}\pi r^3$

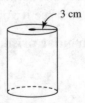

Example K. Find the volume of a cylinder with radius 3 centimeters and height 7 centimeters to the nearest cubic centimeter.

Use the formula $V = \pi r^2 h$: $V = (3.14)(3)^2(7) \approx 198$ centimeters³.

3 cm

Example L. Find the volume of a basketball, to the nearest cubic inch, if the radius is 4.7 inches.

Use the formula $V = \frac{4}{3}\pi r^3$: $V = \frac{4}{3}(3.14)(4.7)^3 \approx 435$ inches^3.

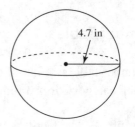

Practice on Other Polygons, Circles, and Solids

Answer the questions. Round answers to the nearest whole number. It may be helpful to sketch a diagram.

Suppose you know that the radius of a circle is 20 inches. Answer questions 1, 2, and 3.

1. What is the diameter of the circle?
2. What is the circumference of the circle?
3. What is the area of the circle?
4. What is a chord of a circle?
5. What is the name of the longest chord of a circle?
6. What is the name of a line that touches a circle at one point?
7. What is the name of a line that touches a circle at two points?
8. The edge of a Rubik's cube is 1 centimeter long. What is its volume?
9. A tissue box is 10 inches long, 4.5 inches wide, and 5 inches high. What is its volume?
10. A can of soup is 5 inches high and has a radius of 1.5 inches. To the nearest tenth of an inch, how much soup will this can hold?
11. Salt for snow removal is dumped in a pile the shape of a cone. The height of the pile is 3 meters, and it diameter is 12 meters. What is the volume of this pile?
12. The diameter of the earth is 12,742 kilometers. What is the earth's volume to the nearest billion cubic kilometers?

LESSON 12 Data Analysis

Data analysis means drawing conclusions from looking at number tables, charts, diagrams, or other visual methods of communicating information. You see these in newspapers and magazines and online all the time. There is no set way to interpret these figures. Careful reading of titles and labels is required to understand what is being presented. Several specific methods of visually presenting information are described in the sections below.

Number Tables

A number table is a list of categories and the number (or percent) of observations in each category. It is a fundamental way of displaying data.

Example A. The Centers for Disease Control lists the leading causes of death in the United States in 2014:

Cause	Number of Deaths
Heart disease	611,105
Cancer	584,881
Chronic lower respiratory diseases	149,205
Accidents (unintentional injuries)	130,557
Stroke	128,978
Alzheimer's disease	84,767
Diabetes	75,578
Influenza and pneumonia	56,979
Kidney disease	47,112
Suicide	41,149

How many times more likely is a person to die of an accident than diabetes? Look at the ratio $\frac{130,557}{75,578} = 1.7\cdots$. In 2014, a person was more than 1.7 times as likely to die of an accident as diabetes.

Bar Charts

Bar charts are a useful way of presenting counts of data categories. Bars are a uniform thickness, but their lengths represent the number observed in each category. A bar that represents 10 of something is twice as long as a bar that represents 5 of that thing. Bar charts usually have vertical lengths, although sometimes it is more effective to have the bar lengths going horizontally.

Example B. A survey was conducted in Anytown, USA, to determine the distribution of political party preference there. The bar chart below shows the number registered who preferred each party.

Democrat	4221
Republican	6015
Independent	3524
Other	1416

What percent of the voters were Independent?

Sum the numbers to find the total number of registered voters:

$$4221 + 6015 + 3524 + 1416 = 15,177$$

Then divide 3524 by 15,177 and multiply by 100: $\dfrac{3524}{15,177} \times 100 = 23.2\%$, rounded to the nearest tenth of a percent. About 23.2% of the registered voters were Independent.

Pie Charts

A pie chart is a circle divide into several "pieces of pie," technically called **sectors of a circle**. Each sector represents a percentage of a total by its relative area. The degree measure of a circle is 360°. If a category is 25% of a total, take 25% of 360°, which is 90°, and draw a 90° angle with its vertex at the center of the circle, as shown below.

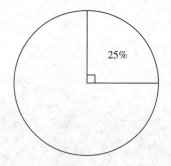

The area of the whole circle is a visual representation of the total, and the area of a sector is a visual representation of the size of that part of the total.

Example C. The pie chart below shows the number of federal prison inmates serving sentences for various types of offenses in 1998. Were more than half serving time for drug offenses?

Does the drug offense category take up more than half the circle? A quick glance shows that the answer is "Yes."

Line Graphs

A line graph is a useful way to show *changes* in the numbers or percentages *over time*. In a line graph, the data value for a particular time period, such as a month or a year, is identified with a point (dot), and the points are connected month by month or year by year to identify trends over time. More than one line graph can be displayed in a figure, such as the one below on educational attainment from 1940 through 2014. A quick look at this figure would readily lead to the conclusion that the educational attainment of people in the United States has risen since 1940.

Example D. By what percentage did the number of Americans age 25 and over who have less than a high school diploma decline between 1940 and 2014?

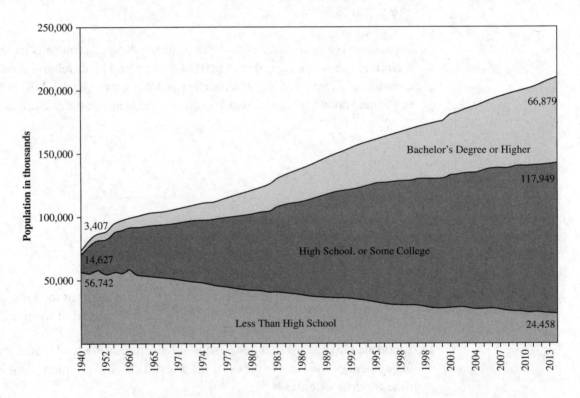

This number declined from 56,742 to 24,458, or by 32,284 people. This amounts to $\frac{32,284}{56,742} \times 100 = 56.9\%$, to the nearest tenth of a percent.

Example E. Justin walked to the store, spent 10 minutes there, and then walked home at a faster speed. Which graph shows this event? Choice B shows this. The flat portion of the graph shows the ten minutes at the store (no distance moved over time), and the steeper part of the graph going down shows the faster trip home.

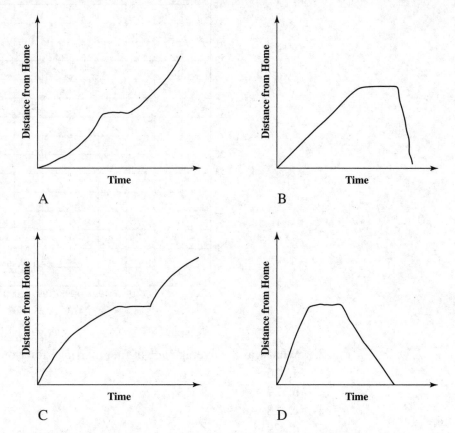

Data Analysis Practice

1. The pie chart shows the market share of four major cable TV companies. Which company has the greatest market share?

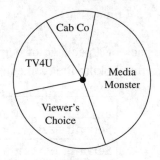

   a. Cab Co
   b. TV4U
   c. Media Monster
   d. Viewer's Choice

The graph below shows the average age of men and women at first marriage in Riverside for the years 1995–2002. Use this graph to answer Questions 2 and 3.

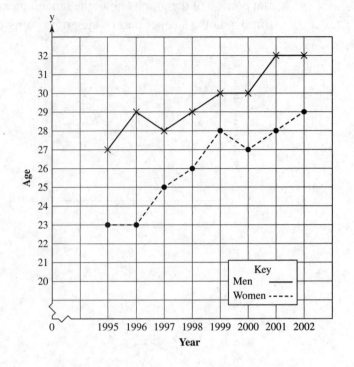

2. What was the average age at first marriage for women in 2000?

    a. 26

    b. 27

    c. 28

    d. 29

3. How many times did the difference in ages at first marriage increase from one year to the next?

    a. 1 time

    b. 2 times

    c. 3 times

    d. 4 times

The back of a package of oatmeal contains facts about nutrition as well as directions for cooking the oatmeal. Use this information to answer Questions 4–7.

Nutrition Facts	
Serving size	1/2 cup dry (40 g)
Servings per container	30

Amount per Serving	
Calories	150
Calories from fat	25

Percent Daily Value*		
Total fat	3 g	4%
Sodium	0 mg	0%
Total carbohydrate	27 g	9%

*Percent Daily Values are based on a 2000 calorie diet.

Cooking Directions		
Servings	2	4
Water (cups)	$1\frac{3}{4}$	$3\frac{1}{2}$
Oats (cups)	1	2
Salt (tsp)	$\frac{1}{4}$	$\frac{1}{2}$
Butter (tbsp)	$\frac{3}{4}$	$1\frac{1}{2}$

4. Doris plans to cook exactly 7 servings of oatmeal. According to the cooking directions, how many teaspoons of salt should she add to the uncooked oats?

   a. $\frac{7}{8}$

   b. $1\frac{1}{7}$

   c. $1\frac{3}{4}$

   d. $\frac{3}{4}$

5. A stick of butter contains 8 tablespoons of butter. What percent of a stick of butter is 3 tablespoons?
   a. 25%
   b. 30%
   c. 37.5%
   d. 45.5%

6. Ian measures 7 cups of water to cook oatmeal for breakfast. According to the cooking directions, how much dry oatmeal should be added to the water?
   a. 2 cups
   b. $2\frac{1}{2}$ cups
   c. 3 cups
   d. 4 cups

7. Pam is an athlete and is on a strict daily diet of 3000 calories. What percent of her daily calorie requirement is met by the calories from two servings of oatmeal?
   a. 5%
   b. 10%
   c. 15%
   d. 20%

The table below shows the number of residents of East Bridgewater and West Bridgewater who agree or disagree with a proposal to build a new bridge connecting the two towns. Use this table to answer Questions 8–10.

	East Bridgewater	West Bridgewater
Agree	175	250
Disagree	100	500

8. What fraction of East Bridgewater residents who participated in the survey agrees with the proposal?

   a. 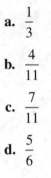 $\dfrac{1}{3}$

   b. $\dfrac{4}{11}$

   c. $\dfrac{7}{11}$

   d. $\dfrac{5}{6}$

9. Which pie chart shows how residents of West Bridgewater voted in the survey?

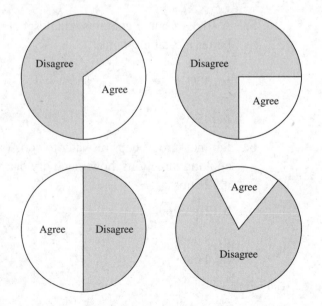

10. What percent of all those surveyed agree with the proposal?

    a. About 30%

    b. About 40%

    c. About 50%

    d. About 60%

LESSON 13   Statistics and Probability

A group of numbers is called a **data set**. These numbers may be the heights of students in a class, test scores, M&Ms in the bags at a convenience store, or cars that pass a certain intersection between 8:00 and 9:00 every morning. Averages are used to summarize these data sets with a single number, and they are an important element of the subject called **statistics**.

There are three ways of measuring "average" of several numbers. The most familiar is called the **mean**. This is found by adding up the numbers in the data set and dividing this total by how many numbers were added.

Example A. George had scores of 71, 83, 75, 90, and 78 on five math tests. What was his mean score?

Add 71, 83, 75, 90, and 78 to get a total of 397. Then divide by 5 to get a mean score of 79.4.

Another "average" is the **median**. Finding the median takes two or three steps, depending on whether there is an odd or even number of numbers. First, order the numbers from lowest to highest. If the number of numbers is *odd*, there is a middle number, and that is the median. If the number of numbers is even, there are two middle numbers, and the median is the mean of these two numbers.

Example B. The heights (in inches) of seven boys in an eighth-grade class were 63, 66, 58, 72, 61, 60, and 59. What is their median height?

First arrange the heights in order from smallest to largest: 58, 59, 60, 61, 63, 66, and 72. The middle number is 61, the fourth number. Three numbers are bigger, and three are smaller. The median is 61.

Example C. An eighth boy joins the class described in Example B. His height is 67 inches. What is the median height of the eight boys?

Including the new boy, the order of heights from smallest to largest is 58, 59, 60, 61, 63, 66, 67, and 72. Now there are two middle numbers, 61 and 63. The mean of these two numbers is $(61 + 63) \div 2 = 62$. The median height of the eight boys is 62.

The third type of average is called the **mode**. The mode of a data set is the number that occurs most frequently. If more than one number occurs most frequently, there is no mode. The mode is mostly used when the data set consists of counts in categories.

Example D. At a recent office party, there were 15 people with dark hair, 8 with blonde hair, and 4 with red hair. The mode of this three-category data set is dark hair.

The mean, median, and mode are three ways of summarizing a data set's average, or *center*. The spread of the numbers in a data set is another aspect of a data set that may be of interest. One very rough measure of spread is the **range**. This is the different between the largest and smallest number in the data set.

Example E. The range of the data set in Example B is 14 inches (58 – 72 inches). This is also the range of the data set in Example C.

A better measure of the spread of a data set is based on its **five-number summary**. Three of the five numbers are the median; the maximum, or max (largest number); and the minimum, or min (smallest number). The median of the numbers between the min and the median and the median of the numbers between the median and the max are the other two numbers in the five-number summary.

Example F. Suppose a data set consists of 13 numbers: 7, 8, 8, 9, 11, 12, 14, 14, 15, 15, 17, 18, and 20. The min is 7, the max is 20, and the median is 14 (the seventh number). $Q1$ is the median of the numbers 7, 8, 8, 9, 11, and 12. Therefore, $Q1 = 8.5$, the mean of the third and fourth numbers 8 and 9. $Q3$ is the median of 14, 15, 15, 17, 18, and 20. Therefore, $Q3 = 16$, the mean of the third and fourth numbers 15 and 17. Therefore, the five number summary is 7, 8.5, 14, 16, and 20.

The five-number summary divides the database into four parts, called **quartiles**. The number 10 in Example F is called the **first quartile**, and the number 17.5 is called the **third quartile**. The figure below shows the five-number summary for Example F. This figure is an example of a **box plot**.

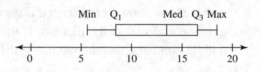

The numbers between the first and third quartiles make up the *middle half of all the numbers*. The difference between the first and third quartiles (third quartile minus first quartile) is called the **interquartile range**. The interquartile range for Example F is 7.5 (16 – 8.5). This, combined with the range, gives a pretty good idea of how the numbers in the data set are spread out.

Percentiles are similar to quartiles, except they divide a data set into 100 parts. Percentiles are used to place the position of an individual number in a large data set. A number in the 65th percentile, for instance, is larger than 65% of all the numbers in the data set. Note that the 99th is the largest possible percentile, as a number cannot be larger than 100% of all the numbers in a data set.

Probability is a way of measuring how likely an event is. If you roll a pair of dice many times, for example, you can measure how likely it is that any roll would result in seven spots facing up. Or, if you commute to work every day on the same route, you could measure how likely it is that you would make a green light at an intersection along the way.

The probability of an event is a number between 0 and 1. If a probability is 0, the event is impossible. If the probability is 1, the event is certain. If a probability is 1/2, there is a 50–50 chance that the event will occur. If a probability is less than 1/2, the chance that it will occur is less than 50–50. If the probability is more than 1/2, the chance that it will occur is more than 50–50.

Percentages can also be used to measure probabilities, simply by changing the proper fractions to percentages. There is a 0% chance of getting the impossible event, 100% chance of the certain event, and a 50% chance of an event that is as likely to occur as not.

Some probabilities are **theoretical**. For example, the probability of heads turning up when a fair coin is tossed is 1/2 because there are 2 possible *equally likely* outcomes, heads or tails, and only 1 (heads) is *favorable*. The probability of dealing an ace from a well-shuffled deck of cards is 4/52 because there are 52 cards in a deck, and only 4 are aces. Notice that the probability of dealing an ace is not 1/2 because dealing an ace and not dealing an ace are *not equally likely*.

Other probabilities are called **experimental**. These are probabilities that are based on observation. You might say that your probability of getting an A on a test is 1/4 if you have four tests and one received a grade of A. Or you could say the probability of making a green light at a particular intersection is 13/20 if you got a green light 13 times while commuting in the last 20 days.

Example G. At a certain college, 350 students take a bookkeeping course, 210 take a math course, and 82 take both. What is the probability that a student takes bookkeeping if the student also takes math?

Of the 210 students who take math, 82 also take bookkeeping. Therefore, the answer to the question is 82/210. This is about 0.39, or 39%.

There is one other important fact of probability. The probability that an event does *not* occur is 1 – the probability that it does occur. If the probability of an event is 0.3, then the probability that the event does not occur is 0.7.

Example H. Suppose the probability of winning a certain lottery is 1/1000. What is the probability of not winning this lottery?

Subtract 1/1000 from 1. The probability of not winning is 999/1000.

Statistics and Probability Practice

1. Suzanne scored 23, 19, 16, 18, 22, and 30 points in five basketball games. What was her mean number of points?
   a. 19
   b. 19.6
   c. 20.1
   d. 21.3

2. A cookie jar contains 6 chocolate chip cookies, 9 oatmeal raisin cookies, and 5 gingerbread cookies. Jason reaches into the cookie jar and takes a cookie without looking. What is the probability that he takes an oatmeal raisin cookie?

   a. 3/10
   b. 1/4
   c. 9/20
   d. 9/11

3. The costs of 10 electric ovens are $850, $900, $1400, $1200, $1050, $1000, $750, $1250, $1050, and $565. What is the median cost?

   a. $1000
   b. $1025
   c. $1050
   d. $1075

4. These are the annual number of deaths from tornadoes in the United States from 1990 through 2000: 53, 39, 39, 33, 69, 30, 25, 67, 130, 94, 40. What is the range?

   a. 13
   b. 28
   c. 100
   d. 105

Use this information for Questions 5 and 6. A survey of 100 households produced the following data on household income.

Income	Number of Households
$0–9999	5
$10,000–19,999	35
$20,000–29,999	30
$30,000–39,999	20
$40,000 or more	10

5. What is the probability that a household has an income of $20,000 or more?

   a. 1/5
   b. 3/10
   c. 3/5
   d. 4/5

6. What is the mode of income ranges?

   a. 20
   b. 35
   c. $10,000–19,999
   d. $20,000–29,999

7. Ted was keeping track of his gas mileage of his truck. He had 10 figures in miles per gallon written on a piece of paper. He discovered that he forgot to put the decimal point in the largest observation, writing 238 instead of 23.8. How would the mean have been affected by this error?
   a. Too small
   b. Too large
   c. Unaffected
   d. Can't know

8. Each of the letters in the word MISSISSIPPI is put on a piece of paper, folded, placed into a hat, and mixed thoroughly. One piece of paper is chosen without looking. What is the probability that the letter I is written on it?
   a. 4/11
   b. 2/5
   c. 1/3
   d. 1/4

9. A box has 5 quarters, 3 dimes, 8 nickels, and 17 pennies in it. You reach in the box without looking and pick a coin. What is the probability that the coin is a quarter?
   a. $\dfrac{5}{33}$
   b. 1/5
   c. 1/4
   d. 3/8

10. A family has 3 children. Assuming an equal chance of a child being male or female, what is the probability that exactly one is female?
    a. 1/8
    b. 1/4
    c. 3/8
    d. 1/2

LESSON 14 Patterns, Functions, and Algebra

Patterns

A **number sequence** is a list of numbers that follow a pattern of some sort. The counting numbers for a sequence: $1, 2, 3, \cdots$. Each number in the list is one more than the number preceding it. The even numbers also form a simple sequence: each number is double the corresponding number in the list of counting numbers. You may be asked to find the next number in a number sequence or the tenth number in a sequence where you are told the first three numbers. These can be challenging problems.

Example A. What is the next number in the sequence $1, 2, 4, 7, 11, \cdots$?

An inspection of the numbers in the list shows that each number is more than the one before it by 1, then 2, then 3, and so forth. Since 11 is 4 more than 7, the next number should be 5 more than 11. The next number should be 16.

Example B. What is the tenth number in the sequence $1, 4, 9, 16, \cdots$?

Each number is the square of the position occupied by the number. For example, 9 is in position 3, and it is equal to 3^2. Therefore, the tenth number should be $10^2 = 100$.

Example C. How many handshakes are there if 5 people are in a room?

In this problem, we have to develop the number sequence. With 2 people in the room, there is 1 handshake. When 3 are in a room, the third person can shake hands with each of the other 2, so there is the original handshake plus 2 more, or 3 handshakes. With 4 people, the 4th person can shake hands with 3 others, so there are the 3 handshakes with 3 people plus 3 new handshakes with the arrival of the 4th person. There are 6 handshakes altogether. With the arrival of the 5th person, there are the 6 handshakes among the 4, plus 4 more with the 5th person shaking hands with each of the other 4, so there are 10 altogether. In sum, there would be 10 handshakes if there were 5 people in a room. This problem is very similar to the problem in Example A.

Example D. What is the next number in the sequence: $1, 1, 2, 3, 5, 8, 13, \cdots$?

This example is the famous Fibonacci sequence. Each number is the sum of the two numbers preceding it: $2 = 1 + 1$, $3 = 2 + 1$, $5 = 3 + 2$, and so forth. Once you see this pattern, it's easy to calculate the next number as $21 = 8 + 13$.

Like a number sequence, the pictures in a sequence follow a pattern. The pattern is a visual one.

Example E. What is the next picture in the sequence?

Since the number of dots goes up 1 with each row, the next picture in the sequence should have 5 dots.

Patterns Practice

Name the next number in each sequence.

1. $2, 4, 6, \cdots$
2. $20, 17, 14, \cdots$
3. $-5, 10, -15, 20 \cdots$
4. $1, 3, 9, 27, \cdots$
5. $0, 3, 8, 15, 24, \cdots$
6. $4, 3, 1, -2, -6, \cdots$

Linear Functions and Graphs

A function is an equation that relates two variables, such as $y = 3x + 2$. Choose a number for x, say $x = 4$, and calculate $y = 3(4) + 2 = 14$. It is useful to think of a function as an input–output machine: the input is x, and the output is $3x + 2$. Since an output *depends* on what value is chosen as the input, y is called the **dependent variable**, and x is called the **independent variable**.

A **table of values** of a function displays selected x values with the corresponding y values. For the function $y = 3x + 2$, a table of values might look like this:

x	$y = 3x + 2$
0	2
1	5
2	8
3	11
4	14

Notice that the y values have a pattern. When x goes up by 1, y goes up by 3. This would be true regardless of which numbers were selected for x. To continue the amusement park application, each time the number of rides x goes up 1, the cost goes up 3.

A **graph** is a *picture* of a function. A graph is drawn on a grid consisting of two perpendicular number lines that intersect at $x = 0$ and $y = 0$, shown in the figure below. A shorthand way of naming a location (**point**) on a grid is to put x and y values in parentheses, with x first. The point $(0,0)$ is called the origin. The table of values corresponds to the points $(0,2), (1,5), (2,8), (3,11), (4,14)$. To graph these points, you put a *dot* where each (x, y) value is. The 5 points from the table of values and the line that goes through them are graphed on the grid below.

The pattern mentioned earlier is also evident from the graph. The dots appear to lie in line. In fact, if the table of values consisted of all pairs of real numbers (an infinite number) that make the equation $y = 3x + 2$ true, the graph would actually consist of an infinite number of points that lie on a line—the line itself! For this reason, the function $y = 3x + 2$ is called a **linear** function.

The function $y = 3x + 2$ could represent the cost of entering an amusement park and going on x rides. It costs \$2 to enter an amusement park and \$3 for each ride.

The value 3 in the function $y = 3x + 2$ is a **rate of change**. In the amusement park example, the rate of change is the cost of one more ride. On the graph of $y = 3x + 2$, the rate of change 3 is called the **slope** of the graph. The slope is the rate of change and measures how *steep* the line is. The number 2 in $y = 3x + 2$ is called the **y intercept** of the graph. This would be the cost of entering the amusement park even if no rides are taken.

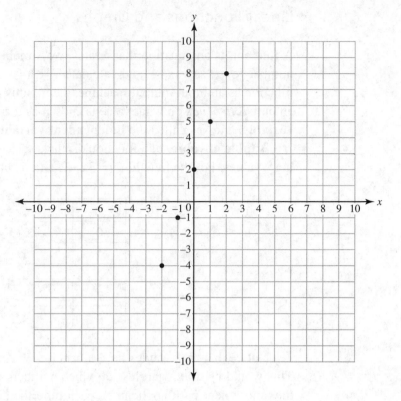

Example F. Tom just took a sales job. He will make a base salary of $2000 monthly plus a commission of $50 for each unit of the product he sells that month. Write the linear function that represents this situation. What will he earn if he sells 100 units of the product this month?

The linear function is $y = 50x + 2000$. Substitute 100 for x in this equation: $50(100) + 2000 = 7000$. Tom will earn $7000 this month if he sells 100 units.

Example G. Morgan has already prepared $\frac{1}{2}$ pound of pizza dough and will continue preparing 1 pound of pizza dough per hour. Write a linear equation that shows the amount of dough y as a function of the number of hours more x she works. Use your equation to show how much pizza dough she has after 5 hours of work.

The linear equation is $y = x + \frac{1}{2}$. After 5 hours of work, she will have $5\frac{1}{2}$ pounds of pizza dough. You should also be able to read a graph to answer a question such as this.

Example H. The graph below shows the charge for repairing a car as a function of the length of time it takes to repair. If the cost was $380, how much time did it take to repair the car?

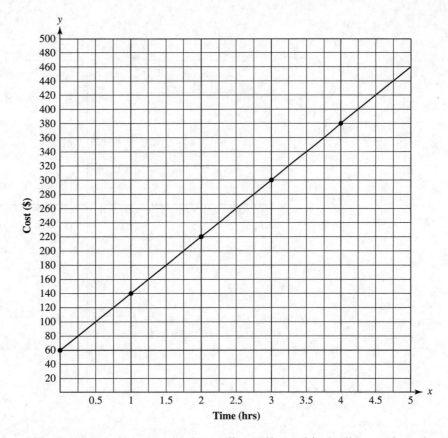

Go to 380 on the y-axis; move horizontally until you hit the line; and go down to the x-axis. It took 4 hours to repair the car.

Linear Functions and Graphs Practice

Find y, given x.

1. $y = 4x - 1$; $x = 3$
2. $y = -5x + 2$; $x = -1$
3. $y = x + 7$; $x = 3$

Build a table with at least three x–y pairs and sketch each graph on the grid below.

4. $y = 2x - 3$
5. $y = -1 - 4x$

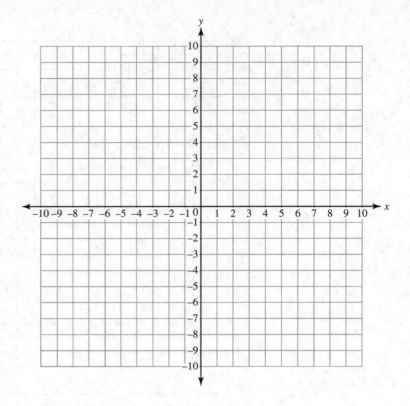

Solving Equations

An equation is a sentence that says one quantity equals another. If there is a variable in an equation, you can **solve** the equation by determining a number that makes the equation true when it is substituted for the variable. Sometimes an equation can be solved easily by inspection.

Example I. Solve $5 + x = 8$.

The solution is $x = 3$ because $5 + 3 = 8$.

Example J. Solve $6x = 24$.

What number, multiplied by 6, makes 24? The solution is $x = 4$ because 6 times 4 equals 24.

Example K. Solve $\dfrac{x}{3} = 4$.

What number, divided by 3, equals 4? The solution is $x = 12$ because 12 divided by 3 equals 4.

More often than not, the solution to an equation is not as obvious as this, so we need a method that will work for more difficult equations. The following examples show the method for "easy" equations. The central idea is to keep the equation *balanced* while *isolating* the variable.

Example L. Solve $5 + x = 8$.

The variable can be isolated by subtracting 5. To maintain the balance, 5 must be subtracted from both sides of the equation:

$$5 + x - 5 = 8 - 5$$
$$x = 3$$

$5 + x = 8$ and $x = 3$ are called **equivalent equations** because they have the same solution. When you keep an equation balanced by doing the same thing to both sides, you get an equivalent equation. Once you have $x = 3$, the solution is obviously 3, so 3 is also the solution to the original equation.

Example M. Solve $6x = 24$.

The variable can be isolated by dividing by 6. To maintain the balance, both sides must be divided by 6:

$$\frac{6x}{6} = \frac{24}{6}$$
$$x = 4$$

Example N. Solve $\frac{x}{3} = 4$.

The variable can be isolated by multiplying by 3. To maintain the balance, both sides must be multiplied by 3:

$$3\left(\frac{x}{3}\right) = (3)(4)$$
$$x = 12$$

These are all examples of **one-step equations**. To solve a **two-step equation**, you still want to isolate the variable and maintain the balance.

Example O. Solve $3x - 7 = 2$. To isolate the variable, first add 7 to both sides. Then divide both sides by 3:

$$3x - 7 = 2$$
$$3x - 7 + 7 = 2 + 7$$
$$3x = 9$$
$$\frac{3x}{3} = \frac{9}{3}$$
$$x = 3$$

Example P. Solve $4x - 3 = 5x + 1$.

First subtract $4x$ from both sides:

$$4x - 3 - 4x = 5x + 1 - 4x$$
$$-3 = x + 1$$

Then subtract 1 from both sides:

$$-3-1 = x+1-1$$
$$-4 = x$$

The fact that x is on the right side of the equation doesn't matter; $x = -4$ is the solution.

Example Q. Solve $x+3 = \dfrac{x}{2} - 5$.

When there is a fraction in an equation $\left(\dfrac{x}{2}\right)$, it is usually easiest to multiply by the least common denominator. In this case, there is only one denominator, 2. First multiply both sides of the equation by 2 and use the distributive properties for addition and subtraction:

$$2(x+3) = 2\left(\dfrac{x}{2} - 5\right)$$
$$2x+6 = x-10$$

Then subtract 6 from both sides and subtract x from both sides:

$$2x+6-6 = x-10-6$$
$$2x = x-16$$
$$2x-x = x-16-x$$
$$x = -16$$

Whenever x's are on both sides of an equation, it's possible that there is no solution.

Example R. Solve $3x = 3x+6$.

Subtract $3x$ from both sides of the equation:

$$3x-3x = 3x+6-3x$$
$$0 = 6$$

No value of x would make $0 = 6$, so there is no solution.

Practice Solving Equations

Solve each equation for x.

1. $4x-3 = 5$
2. $-2x+6 = 4$
3. $3x+5 = 4$
4. $5x+2 = 3x+6$
5. $3-2x = 3+x$
6. $4x-3 = x+6$

This lesson is about "story problems" that may involve setting up an equation and solving it. A four-step method to accomplish this is described below:

1. **Define a variable**. In most cases, begin by letting x stand for the quantity you are asked to find.

2. **Write an equation using the information given**. One approach is to choose a number for x and determine how that number would be used in a calculation based on the given information. This step will be clearer in the examples.

3. **Solve the equation**. Use the method outlined in Lesson 6.

4. **Check your solution**. Use the answer in the original problem and determine that it works.

The examples that follow are organized into the four steps outlined above.

Example A. One number is 3 more than another. The sum of the numbers is 24. What are the numbers?

1. Let x be the smaller number.

2. The other number is $x + 3$. Suppose x were 5. Then the other number would be 8. You have to add 5 and 3 more than 5 (8). In this problem, when you add the two numbers, you get 25: $x + (x + 3) = 25$.

3. Solve the equation.

$$x + (x + 3) = 25$$
$$2x + 3 = 25$$
$$2x + 3 - 3 = 25 - 3$$
$$2x = 22 \qquad \text{The two numbers are 11 and 14.}$$
$$\frac{2x}{2} = \frac{22}{2}$$
$$x = 11$$
$$x + 3 = 14$$

4. Check: $11 + 14 = 25$.

Example B. Alex answered all the questions on his math test but got 10 wrong. He earned 4 points for each correct answer, and his score was 76. How many questions were on the test?

1. Let x be the number of questions on the test.

2. Suppose there were 50 questions on the test. If he got 10 wrong, then he got 40 $(50 - 10)$ correct. At 4 points each correct answer, his score would have been $4(40) = 160$. We had to subtract 10 from the number of problems on the test (x) and multiply the result by 4 to get the score of 76. The equation is $4(x - 10) = 76$.

3. Solve the equation.

$$4(x-10) = 76$$
$$4x - 40 = 76$$
$$4x - 40 + 40 = 76 + 40$$
$$4x = 116$$
$$\frac{4x}{4} = \frac{116}{4}$$
$$x = 29$$

There were 29 questions on the test.

4. Check: If there were 29 questions on the test and Alex got 10 wrong, he got 19 right. At 4 points each, his score was $4 \times 19 = 76$.

Example C. Brian read the first 114 pages of a book. This is 3 pages more than a third of the book. What is the total number of pages in the book?

1. Let x stand for the total number of pages in the book.

2. If the book had 300 pages, 3 pages more than a third of the book would be $\frac{1}{3}(300) + 3 = 103$. The equation is $\frac{1}{3}x + 3 = 114$.

3. Solve the equation.

$$\frac{1}{3}x + 3 = 114$$
$$\frac{1}{3}x + 3 - 3 = 114 - 3$$
$$\frac{1}{3}x = 111$$
$$3\left(\frac{1}{3}x\right) = 3(111)$$
$$x = 333$$

There are 333 pages in the book.

4. Check: If the book has 333 pages, a third of the book is 111 pages, and 3 more than that is 114 pages.

Other types of problems don't really require solving a equation. They just need to be reasoned through. Experience is the best teacher for these types of problems. One tip: since all of the questions on the Applied Mathematics section of the test are multiple choice, **backsolving** is an option. This means trying each answer until you find one that meets the conditions of the problem.

Problem Solving and Reasoning Practice

1. Alicia and Cassie start a tutoring business. They rent office space for $500 per month and charge their students $35 per hour. If they have 20 students per hour each week, what is their monthly profit? (Assume 4 weeks per month.)
   a. $2000
   b. $2300
   c. $2600
   d. $2900

2. Two cell phone companies are competing for your business. Company A charges a fixed rate of $55 per month and $.12 per minute of use. Company B charges a fixed rate of $45 and $.15 per minute of use. How many minutes (to the nearest minute) must a cell phone be used each month if the two companies to charge the same amount?
   a. 300 minutes
   b. 325 minutes
   c. 333 minutes
   d. 349 minutes

3. The length of a rectangle is 6 feet more than its width, and the perimeter of the rectangle is 40 feet. What is the length of the rectangle?
   a. 7 feet
   b. 7.5 feet
   c. 8 feet
   d. 8.5 feet

4. Tony has $327.50 in his savings account. If he saves $12.50 per week, how long will it take him to have $515 in his savings account?
   a. 12 weeks
   b. 15 weeks
   c. 17 weeks
   d. 20 weeks

5. Grace is selling lemonade for 25 cents a cup. If she had sold 12 more cups on Tuesday, she would have made $10. How many cups of lemonade did she sell on Tuesday?
   a. 40
   b. 36
   c. 28
   d. 24

6. Raymond and Oscar are having a 200-meter race. Oscar can run at a speed of 5 meters per second, while Ray's speed is 4 meters per second. How many meters' head start should Oscar give Ray to make the race fair?
   a. 10 meters
   b. 20 meters
   c. 30 meters
   d. 40 meters

7. Tammy is 5 years younger than Doris. In 4 years, Doris will be twice as old as Tammy. How old is Tammy now?
   a. 1 year old
   b. 2 years old
   c. 3 years old
   d. 4 years old

8. Linda is planning to give her money to two friends. She will give her friend Marcia $10 more than she gives her friend Karen. The ratio of the two amounts she gives away is 5 to 3. How much money does she give away altogether?
   a. $13
   b. $23
   c. $40
   d. $45

9. Mary Ellen has 6 more apples than she has oranges. She has 15 apples and oranges altogether. How many apples does she have?
   a. 5
   b. 7
   c. 11
   d. 13

10. Matt took a test consisting of 20 problems. Each correct answer earns 5 points, but each incorrect answer loses 1 point. Matt answered all the questions, and his score was 76. How many questions did he answer correctly?
    a. 12
    b. 14
    c. 16
    D. 18

Answer Keys to Practice Problems

Lesson 1 Decimals

Place Value

1. 738	**5.** 90,002,070	**9.** 240
2. 5.37	**6.** 3.14	**10.** 0.0008
3. 10,529	**7.** 0.00745	
4. 82.04	**8.** 460,000	

Scientific Notation

1. 5.345862×10^6	**4.** 3.9×10^{-9}	**7.** 0.00000905
2. 6.34×10^{-7}	**5.** 4,440,000	**8.** 0.00000063
3. 5.613×10^{10}	**6.** 5,328,000,000	

Decimal Arithmetic

1. 10.97	**4.** 3.2	**7.** 222.5	**10.** 7.36
2. 3.76	**5.** 17.03	**8.** 0.5	**11.** 73.92
3. 4.14	**6.** 7.57	**9.** 175.76	**12.** 0.3

Rounding to a Place Value

1. 9.7	**3.** 57,300	**5.** 2.345	**7.** 350	**9.** 5.02
2. 84	**4.** 0.02	**6.** 85.7	**8.** 0.001	**10.** 4100

Lesson 2 Fractions

Reducing Fractions

1. $\dfrac{1}{2}$	3. $\dfrac{4}{3}$	5. $\dfrac{5}{3}$	7. $\dfrac{2}{3}$	9. 3
2. $\dfrac{3}{8}$	4. $\dfrac{1}{3}$	6. $\dfrac{5}{12}$	8. $\dfrac{3}{4}$	10. $\dfrac{2}{3}$

Multiplying Fractions

1. $\dfrac{12}{35}$ 3. $\dfrac{56}{21}$ 5. $\dfrac{12}{5}$ 7. $\dfrac{4}{7}$ 9. $\dfrac{7}{3}$

2. $\dfrac{3}{32}$ 4. $\dfrac{4}{7}$ 6. $\dfrac{15}{32}$ 8. $\dfrac{5}{4}$ 10. 1

Dividing Fractions

1. $\dfrac{9}{10}$ 3. $\dfrac{5}{4}$ 5. $\dfrac{1}{2}$ 7. $\dfrac{15}{8}$ 9. $\dfrac{5}{16}$

2. $\dfrac{2}{3}$ 4. 16   6. 14   8. 2   10. $\dfrac{9}{20}$

Adding and Subtracting Fractions

1. $\dfrac{10}{7}$ 3. $\dfrac{13}{12}$ 5. $\dfrac{23}{30}$ 7. $10\dfrac{2}{3}$ 9. $2\dfrac{14}{15}$

2. $\dfrac{2}{11}$ 4. $\dfrac{1}{12}$ 6. $\dfrac{7}{12}$ 8. $1\dfrac{7}{24}$ 10. $\dfrac{1}{10}$

Ratio and Proportion

1. a   3. c   5. d   7. d   9. d
2. b   4. c   6. b   8. c   10. c

Lesson 3 Percent

1. 5   3. 35   5. 25   7. 40%   9. 250
2. 20%   4. 20%   6. 6.92   8. 3.6   10. 24

Lesson 4 Integers

Adding Integers

1. 3   3. 22   5. −18   7. 17   9. −4
2. 5   4. −8   6. −13   8. −19   10. 5

Subtracting Integers

1. 15   3. 3   5. −14   7. 17   9. 7
2. −13   4. 6   6. 7   8. 2   10. −5

Multiplying and Dividing Integers

1. −24   **3.** 9   **5.** −96+   **7.** −4   **9.** 5

2. −35   **4.** 90   **6.** 3   **8.** 10   **10.** −14

Mixed Integer Arithmetic

1. 25   **3.** −17   **5.** −3   **7.** −7   **9.** 5

2. −18   **4.** −6   **6.** 5   **8.** 60   **10.** −3

Lesson 5 Order of Operations

1. 22   **3.** −1   **5.** 8   **7.** −1   **9.** −29

2. 6   **4.** 3   **6.** 3   **8.** −7   **10.** −2

Lesson 6 Algebraic Operations

Properties of Exponents

1. x^{10} **4.** x^{12} **7.** y^6 **9.** $\dfrac{1}{36}$ **11.** $\dfrac{1}{u^2}$

2. x^8 **5.** x **8.** $\dfrac{1}{4r^2}$ **10.** 1   **12.** 1

3. $8z^3$ **6.** x^8

Simplifying Algebraic Expressions

1. $13x$ **6.** $-3x$ **11.** $-a$ **16.** $4x^2$ **21.** a^4b^4

2. $12xy$ **7.** $4x^2$ **12.** $5q$ **17.** $-20pq$

3. 2   **8.** $-6u^3$ **13.** a^8 **18.** $x-y^2$

4. $\dfrac{2p}{q}$ **9.** $8p+12p^2$ **14.** $11x^2$ **19.** $y+3x$

5. $6x+5y$ **10.** 3   **15.** $\dfrac{1}{w^2}$ **20.** $6x$

Lesson 7 Number and Number Operations

1. whole number, integer, rational number, real number
2. counting number, whole number, integer, rational number, real number
3. integer, rational number, real number
4. rational number, real number
5. irrational number, real number
6. rational number, real number
7. rational number, real number

8. integer, rational number, real number
9. rational number, real number
10. rational number, real number
11. $2.09, 2.1, \dfrac{5}{2}$
12. $2, \dfrac{9}{4}, \dfrac{8}{3}$
13. $\dfrac{7}{16}, 0.5, \dfrac{9}{16}$
14. $-\dfrac{2}{3}, -0.6, 0.001$
15. $-.341, -0.34, -0.339$
16. $-9, \sqrt{59}, 8$
17. $-\sqrt{2}, -1, 0$
18. $\sqrt{80}, 9.01, 9.1$

Lesson 8 Computation in Context

1. c	**3.** d	**5.** c	**7.** c	**9.** d
2. c	**4.** a	**6.** c	**8.** a	**10.** c

Lesson 9 Estimation

1. b	**3.** a	**5.** a	**7.** d
2. d	**4.** b	**6.** b	

Lesson 10 Measurement

1. c	**3.** d	**5.** d	**7.** a	**9.** c
2. b	**4.** b	**6.** d	**8.** c	**10.** c

Lesson 11 Geometry

Lines and Angles

1. c	**3.** d	**5.** d	**7.** c
2. b	**4.** c	**6.** d	

Triangles

1. a	**3.** d	**5.** a	**7.** c	**9.** b
2. d	**4.** c	**6.** b	**8.** a	**10.** b

Quadrilaterals

1. a	**3.** a	**5.** b	**7.** d	**9.** d
2. a	**4.** a	**6.** d	**8.** d	

Polygons, Circles, and Solids

1. 40 inches
2. 126 inches
3. 1257 inches^2
4. A chord is a segment with its endpoints on the circle.
5. diameter
6. tangent
7. secant
8. 1 centimeter^3
9. 225 inches^3
10. 35 inches^3
11. 113 meters^3
12. 868 billion kilometers^3

Lesson 12 Data Analysis

1. c	**3.** c	**5.** c	**7.** b	**9.** a
2. b	**4.** a	**6.** d	**8.** c	**10.** b

Lesson 13 Statistics and Probability

1. d	**3.** b	**5.** c	**7.** b	**9.** a
2. c	**4.** d	**6.** c	**8.** a	**10.** c

Lesson 14 Patterns, Functions, and Algebra

Patterns

1. 8	**3.** −25	**5.** 35
2. 11	**4.** 81	**6.** −11

Linear Functions and Graphs

1. 11
2. 7
3. 10

4. Answers may vary. One answer:

x	0	1	2
y	−3	−1	1

5. Answers may vary. One answer:

x	−1	0	1
y	3	−1	−5

Solving Equations

1. $x = 2$ **3.** $x = -\dfrac{1}{3}$ **5.** $x = 0$

2. $x = 1$ **4.** $x = 2$ **6.** $x = 3$

Lesson 15 Problem Solving and Reasoning

1. b   **3.** a   **5.** a   **7.** a   **9.** c

2. c   **4.** b   **6.** d   **8.** c   **10.** c

LESSON 1: Surprises

When Mike Rinaldi first interviewed for a job at Ace Computer Chip Company, he wondered why the Human Resources Manager, Sue Mendez, asked him about school subjects. You may recall that Mike liked and excelled in math and computer courses. He did not like his English courses, especially writing. He thought that he was finished with English composition when he started working at Ace Computer. He was wrong.

The first surprise occurred when he enrolled at Brightwater Community College.

Words to Know

Matriculating	Enrolling at a college
Inflammatory	Able to arouse strong emotion
Employee evaluation	A written or oral statement of the employee's work

New Information

Sue had given Mike information about the college. He recalled that Ace Computer had an alliance with Brightwater. Mike was still surprised that he was required to take the TABE, which included a test of his English language skills. He even asked Sue if he could skip the TABE. After all, he was just going to be working on the computer. Sue answered, "Mike, as I told you, our agreement with Brightwater allows you to take any course that Ace does not offer in its training program. Ace does not require employees to take the TABE, but Brightwater requires all *matriculating* students to take the TABE for placement in courses."

Mike was almost afraid to ask the next logical question. "What kind of writing will I have to do for the company?" He was surprised to learn that he would have to write weekly summaries and monthly reports of his work. He would be expected to write even more if he wanted to advance in the company. His report-writing skills would be assessed in his *employee evaluations*. He had no idea how to write these reports. Sue, suspecting that this was a surprise to Mike, told him that she or Alicia Buchanan, her assistant, would work with him on his first few reports.

Mike saw Michelle frequently at Brightwater. They talked about her progress in pursuing her goal to become a registered nurse. She, too, was concerned about the writing that she would be doing at the job she hoped to get some day. At the moment she was concentrating on updating her résumé. She needed to find a new part-time job that would accommodate her school schedule. Eventually, Michelle and Mike found themselves—and each other—in a business/career writing course. At the second meeting, the entire class took a language pretest not unlike the one you are about to experience. But first, the students took a few minutes to think about writing in their lives. You should start by filling out the form that follows.

Reflection: Writing in My Daily Life

I estimate that I write _____ hours a week, including reminder notes or lists for myself and notes or letters to communicate with others.

I estimate that I write _____ hours a week for work-related tasks.

I enjoy writing _____.

I want to improve my ability to write _____ for my personal satisfaction.

I want to improve my ability to write _____ for job or career advancement.

Composition

I am able to organize my thoughts and express myself clearly when I need to write

Instructions: ___Yes ___No ___Need practice ___I don't know

Business letters: ___Yes ___No ___Need practice ___I don't know

Reports: ___Yes ___No ___Need practice ___I don't know

I understand the meaning of "Standard English" and can recognize it when I read it.   ___Yes ___No ___Need practice ___I don't know

Editing

I am able to correct   ___Yes ___No ___Need practice ___I don't know my own writing.

	Yes	No	Need practice	I don't know
I know how to check my own writing for:				
Plan, purpose, and tone	——	——	——	——
Correct use of words	——	——	——	——
Complete sentences	——	——	——	——
Organized paragraphs	——	——	——	——
Spelling	——	——	——	——
Punctuation	——	——	——	——
Capitalization	——	——	——	——

Spelling

I am able to identify the correct spelling of a word when I am given more than one choice.　——Yes ——No ——Need practice ——I don't know

I can identify the correct spelling of a word by the way it "looks."　——Yes ——No

I can identify the correct spelling of a word by knowing the rules.　——Yes ——No ——Need to review the rules

I know how to use Spell Check.　——Yes ——No ——Need practice

Language Skills Assessment

Read the following email reminder. Use it to answer Questions 1–3.

Good morning, Brown Auto Maintenance team:

The holiday season is upon us! I want to remind everyone about our annual holiday party on Saturday December 16. Join us for drinks hors d'oeuvres and entertainment starting at 7 p.m. at Crystal Bay Resort.

Please respond to this email by December 10 indicating whether or not you will attend. You may bring one guest. Dress to impress: we will take company photos!

Please email me at sforrest@brownauto.com if you have any questions. See you on the 16th!

Best regards,
Steve

---

1 A comma should be inserted following which words?

   A   I want to remind

   B   You many bring one

   C   Please respond to this email

   D   annual holiday party on Saturday

2 A comma should appear after which word

   A   annual

   B   drinks

   C   bring

   D   company

3 A comma should be inserted following which word?

   A   holiday

   B   season

   C   may

   D   None of the above

Read these paragraphs from a company manual. Each is a segment taken from a longer discussion. For Questions 4–13, look at the numbered underlined parts and choose the word or phrase that best fills those spaces.

Company Manual
Preparing for Meetings

(4) <u>Meetings is</u> an essential part of every business environment. We want every meeting you attend to be productive and (5) <u>taking place</u> in a positive environment. One of the best ways you can ensure a productive meeting is to prepare an agenda. All attendees should know, in advance, the purpose and direction of the meeting.

4

   A Some meetings is

   B Meetings is scheduled

   C Every busyness environment sched-ule meetings

   D Meetings are

5

   A to take place

   B to taking place

   C in place

   D None of the above

Managing Conflict

How do we manage conflict among staff at Davenport Health Care (6) <u>Center.</u> First, we take the emphasis off people and concentrate on gathering ideas. We discourage remarks (7) <u>such as "Bill,</u> why did you ever decide to close the recreation room between 7 P.M. and 9 P.M.? You know very well that that is (8) <u>our residents'</u> favorite time to use the facility. How could you do that?"

6

   A Center?

   B Center!

   C Center.

   D Center;

7

   A such, as "Bill

   B such as, "Bill

   C such as Bill

   D Correct as is

8

   A our resident's

   B time residents'

   C our residents

   D Correct as is

What does it mean to take the emphasis off people and (9) <u>then concentrating</u> on gathering ideas? To begin, it means that the leader of the group diffuses personal statements by redirecting attention to gathering facts. For example, in the situation detailed above, what could the leader or a participant say (10) <u>and that would</u> get to the facts yet not be *inflammatory?* Think about how this would (11) <u>work; Let's</u> look at our daily schedule. When can we free the recreation room for residents' use?

9

   A concentrate instead

   B concentration on

   C and starting concentrate on

   D concentrate with

10

   A that would

   B and do you think that would

   C and that wouldn't

   D and that would likely

11

    A   work, "Let's

    B   work, Let's"

    C   work? "Let's

    D   work: "Let's

For Questions 12 and 13, read the following two paragraphs from a progress report. In each case, choose the sentence that best fills the blank and completes the thought process in the paragraph.

12 _____. As the committee predicted, we will have the new procedure in place by January 1. Our first task was to choose several new suppliers. Now, three months before our start date, we have lined up all the suppliers we need.

    A   Our plan to revamp the stock ordering system is progressing according to schedule.

    B   We have just begun to plan our approach to choosing new suppliers.

    C   Yesterday, I met with the committee for the first time.

    D   There are no suppliers who want to do business with us.

13 The companies we chose have excellent records for on-time, on-budget deliveries. In addition, they will guarantee to deliver stock to us two to three days faster than our former supplier did. _____.

    A   We can't be certain these new companies will deliver on schedule.

    B   Since speed of delivery is not important to us, we chose companies based on different criteria.

    C   Better service to us will result in faster service to our customers

    D   Fortunately for our company, service to our customers is no longer important.

Read the following sentences. For Questions 14–19, choose the sentence that is written correctly _and_ has the correct capitalization and punctuation.

14

    A   The employees, and the owner, and some of the management.

    B   One of those employees is giving a talk on benefits she offers very important information.

    C   They'll all meet at dinnertime to talk about the seminars.

    D   Knowing that the main speaker is the vice president of the United States.

15

    A   Will and me gave our shopping list to someone else that was not complete.

    B   After walking for a very long time, Will and me gave up.

    C   Me and Elezondo was fixing the tire lying in the dirt.

    D   Looking intently at the laptop on display, Will and I had the same question.

16

   A   Ann asked the manager about the team's performance Reviews and she had very little to say.

   B   I told the operator that John's phone was not working.

   C   Let your Customers know that they're looking for feedback.

   D   New manuals should not be given to Teams until they have been checked into the company library.

17

   A   On the northeast corner of Simpson Avenue, you will see a new office building.

   B   She wrote a book called, "Adventures of a house Cat."

   C   He said, "don't forget to meet me in the cafeteria at 12 sharp!"

   D   She replied, "If I can't be there on time, i'll call you?"

18

   A   The Officer thanked them for their loyalty, dedication and because they never left their stations during the blackout.

   B   This computer is fast, user-friendly, and on sale until March 1.

   C   Let's put more emphasis on education, training, and Travel Experiences.

   D   Why don't you choose your courses, sign up for them, and when you'll meet us for dinner.

19

   A   Pick up the following; 2 dozen pencils, 6 legal pads, and a toner cartridge for my printer.

   B   Mr. Sadwin; from Illinois, is a member of the house of representatives.

   C   I dislike one of my office mates; however, I don't allow that to affect how well I do my job.

   D   I never did expect my boss to be my best friend; just to be fair.

For Questions 20–22, choose the answer that best completes the sentence.

20   An estimate of the costs for new bathrooms, office furniture, and window treatments _____ beyond the scope of this report.

   A   are

   B   is

   C   are going

   D   are spiraling

21   We think this fabric is _____ than the one we originally chose.

   A   more appropriate

   B   most appropriate

   C   more appropriater

   D   many appropriater

22 Many of our best ideas _____ left out of the final version of the report.

    A was

    B is

    C has been

    D were

In Questions 23 and 24, read the underlined sentences. Then choose the answer that best combines those sentences into one.

23 <u>I could not find the email update on the Johnson order.</u>
<u>Rob was supposed to forward me the update on Friday.</u>

    A I could not find the email update on the Johnson order because Rob was supposed to forward it to me on Friday.

    B I could not find the email update on the Johnson order and Rob said he forwarded it to me on Friday.

    C I could not find the email update on the Johnson order that Rob was supposed to forward me on Friday.

    D I could not find the email update on the Johnson order because I forwarded the update to Rob on Friday.

24 <u>Suddenly I remembered what had happened.</u>
<u>Rob took care of the update because I was out sick.</u>

    A Suddenly I remembered Rob took care of the update because I was out sick.

    B Suddenly I remembered Rob was out sick so no one took care of the update.

    C Suddenly I remembered I never asked anyone to follow up on the matter.

    D Suddenly I remembered what had happened. Rob sent me the update because I was out sick.

For Question 25 choose the word or words that best complete the sentence.

25 Whoever calls the _____ has the advantage of an early appointment.

    A sooner

    B more sooner

    C most soonest

    D soonest

To the Student: As you check your answers, record the results in this chart. Use the three columns next to the Answer Key to mark your answers as *Correct, Incorrect,* or *Skipped.* Use the other columns to record additional information you want to remember about the individual questions. Total the number of your responses in each column at the bottom of the chart. Then read the recommendations that follow.

Language Skills Assessment: Answers and Skills Analysis

Item Answers	Correct T	Incorrect X	Skipped O	I have a question about this item.	I need instruction.	Refer to these lessons.	Reading Skill Categories*
1 B						1	32
2 B						5	26
3 A						5	26
4 D						2	4
5 A						6	13
6 A						5	25
7 B						5	29
8 D						5	30
9 A						6	13
10 A						6	13
11 D						5	29
12 A						6	15
13 C						6	16
14 C						2	12
15 D						2	1
16 B						2	2
17 A						5	20
18 B						5	26
19 C						5	27
20 B						2	4
21 A						4	6
22 D						5	29
23 D						6	12
24 A						6	12
25 D						4	6
TOTALS	Correct	Incorrect	Skipped	Questions	Instruction	Lessons	Skills

*Key to Language Skill Categories
1 Usage
2 Antecedent Agreement

(Continued)

3 Tense
4 Subject/Verb Agreement
5 Easily Confused Verbs
6 Adjective
7 Adverb
8 Choose Between Adjective/Adverb
9 Use Negatives
10 Sentence Formation
11 Sentence Recognition
12 Sentence Combining
13 Sentence Clarity
14 Paragraph Development
15 Topic Sentence
16 Supporting Sentences
17 Sequence
18 Unrelated Sentence
19 Connective/Transition
20 Capitalization
21 Proper Noun
22 Name
23 Title of Work
24 Punctuation
25 End Mark
26 Comma
27 Semicolon
28 Writing Conventions
29 Quotation Marks
30 Apostrophe
31 City/State
32 Letter Part

Note: These broad categories of language skills are broken down into subcategories. Question numbers are aligned with the subcategories as well as the lesson to which you can return to review the concept(s).

Language Skills Analysis

USAGE

PRONOUN

Subjective   15   (See Lesson 2)

Objective

Possessive

NAME		
Geographic Name		
TITLE OF WORK		
PUNCTUATION		(See Lesson 5)
END MARK		
Question Mark	6	
COMMA		
Series		
Appositive	2	
Introductory Element	3	
Parenthetical Expression		
SEMICOLON	19	
WRITING CONVENTIONS		(See Lesson 5)
QUOTATION MARKS	11, 22	
Comma with Quotation	7	
End Marks with Quotation		
APOSTROPHE		
Possessive	8	
CITY/STATE		
LETTER PART		
Date	1	
Address		
Salutation		
Closing		

To identify the areas in which you need to improve your language skills, do three things:

1. Total your number of correct answers out of the 25 possible answers. You should have 90 to 95 percent correct (or 23 correct answers).

2. Total the number of correct answers in each subset of skills. For example, in the subcategory *Comma,* there are three correct answers. To score a passing grade, you should have 95 percent correct (or at least 2 correct answers).

3. Wherever your score is below 95 percent, go back to that lesson (the lesson number is indicated in parentheses) and review the skill.

Mike and Michelle met for coffee to compare notes about their first writing assignment. The assignment had just been returned, and neither of them looked too happy. They both realized that they had a lot of work to do to bring their work up to a higher standard.

Mike was puzzled by some of the errors and the instructor's markings. "What's wrong with this part?" Mike asked. He pointed to the following sentences from his assignment, a personal statement on a résumé:

"I really enjoy learning new business software. Me and my friends keep up with all the new developments."

Michelle thought she knew what was wrong with the second sentence. Do you? Read on for answers to your questions.

Words to Know

Perceived	Noticed
Image	Picture
Résumé	A summary of work and education

The Bottom Line

Whenever we speak or write, we put ourselves on display. We all want to be perceived in a positive way. Frequent errors in writing and speaking, however, project a negative image. Can we allow a résumé to be sent to a prospective employer with errors in usage or spelling? At work, should we send emails with errors in punctuation or grammar? Of course not! We need to find out what we can do to improve our writing. In this section you will read about some of the most common errors made by writers and speakers of English. Then we will give you some advice on how to correct these errors.

Your English teachers all tried to convince you that it was important to understand English grammar. You may have hated the subject when you were in school. You probably feel the same way now. The bad news is that you will still need to learn, or at least review, some basics of English grammar. The good news is that you probably know much more than you think you do. We'll help you refresh your knowledge and put it to work.

The first thing you need to do is look at your language pretest results. Find your areas of obvious weakness. The chart on page 189 will help you identify your strengths and weaknesses. Although we suggest that you review all of the areas covered in this section, remember to pay special attention to the items that you found difficult.

Let's begin by observing that you *do* know a great deal about English; after all, you construct English sentences from the moment you get up in the morning until you go to sleep at night (and probably in your dreams as well). And therein lies the secret: You started learning how to construct sentences from the time you were born. We begin by reviewing the parts of speech and how they are used.

We have a *name* for each of the words in the sentence below; for example, *noun, pronoun, verb, adjective, article,* and so on.

1. Article Adjective Noun Verb Article Noun Preposition Article Noun

   The talented ballplayer hit the ball over the wall.

2. Each of these words has a *job* to do in the sentences we construct. For example, nouns function as *performers* or *receivers* (known in grammatical terms as the *subject* or the *object*), verbs are *action* or *being* words, pronouns are words that *take the place of other words,* adjectives *describe other words,* and so forth.

 FYI

One very important kind of adjective is called an *article.* We have three articles in English: *the, an,* and *a.* Articles are *definite* or *indefinite.* The definite article *the* makes the noun more specific, or definite ('the ball in my hand," that is, the one ball that I am holding). The indefinite articles *a* and *an* make the noun more general or imprecise ("a ball on the field," that is, one of many balls on the field). *An* is used before nouns or adjectives preceding the noun that begin with a vowel.

Let's identify the jobs or functions of the parts of the sentence.

Describes Subject Action Describes Object IntroPrep Describes Object
                                              Phrase

The talented ballplayer hit the ball over the wall

You may have forgotten—or perhaps you never really learned—the names, definitions, and uses of grammatical terms. That's OK. We can help you become very competent users of English, written and spoken, with a limited emphasis on grammatical terms and rules. The grammatical terms and rules that you *do* learn will help you write and speak correctly.

Starting with Sentences

You are probably aware that you use different types of sentences when you write or speak. The following are all sentences and complete thoughts.

- The statement: You wrote that letter.
- The question: Did you write that letter?
- The exclamation: You wrote that letter!
- The command: Write that letter.

What do these sentences have in common? That is the subject of this lesson: *performers* (also known as *subjects*) and *actions* (also known as *verbs*) and how they work in sentences.

In the sentences above, which word tells you the *action* that is taking place? Everyone would probably agree that the action word is *write/wrote.* Who performs/ performed the action? In the first three sentences, the *performer* is quite obvious: The word *you* is the performer. What about the fourth sentence? Because it is a command, it starts with the action word, *Write,* but where is the performer (subject)? The simple answer is that we understand that the performer is there, implied—the same *you* as in the other three sentences. Read the following three commands.

Arrive on time tomorrow!

Hand in your papers.

Don't forget to turn off the lights before you leave.

When someone tells you to do something or perform actions like these do you have any doubt about the performer of the command? Certainly not: it's *you.*

Subjects and Verbs: Singular and Plural

What else do you have to know about performers and actions? Essentially, you have to know that one affects the other, especially in time and number. What does this mean? It means, first of all, that actions agree with performers in number: singular or plural.

Mike drives to the college library.

What action do you see in this sentence? Of course, it is *drives.* Who performs the action? Mike does; he is the performer. What changes take place in the following sentence?

Mike and Michelle drive to the college library.

What is the action word? You are right again: it is *drive.* Who are the performers? Mike and Michelle are the two performers. That is why the action word takes a slightly different form: *drive* instead of *drives.*

This may not seem logical to you because an *s* at the end of a word in English often signals more than one, or plural. For example, look at these words that might function as performers:

Employee

Computer

Car

Textbook

How do you change these words to their plural forms? Add an *s* to each:

Employees

Computers

Cars

Textbooks

But what does an *s* at the end of an action word mean? It means just the opposite. You add an *s* to an action word so it agrees with the singular performer. You remove the *s* so it agrees with the plural performer. We usually do this correctly and without even thinking. Sometimes we are fooled by an extra word or two in the sentence. For example:

An important characteristic of computers make them easy to use.

What is wrong with this sentence? Use the same technique you used above, to decide whether or not the verb agrees with the subject in number. The sentence talks about the subject, *characteristic.* The subject is singular. What is the action word or verb? It is *make.* Put those two words together without extra words between them. How would you write them?

An important characteristic make them easy to use.

or

An important characteristic makes them easy to use.

You probably know that the second sentence is the correct one just by the way it sounds. You also know that it is correct because you have just learned that an *s* at the end of the verb usually indicates that it is singular. *Characteristic* is singular and *makes* is singular; they agree in number.

Practice 1

Read each sentence. Decide whether the subject and verb agree in number. Correct any errors. Only one sentence is correct. *Hint:* Don't be fooled by extra words between the subject and the verb.

1 The flower, in addition to other greens, sit in water.

_____

2 This book, with hundreds of pages, needs your attention.

_____

3 A bank account in any of those branches pay a higher dividend.

_____

4 The magazine, *Consumer Guides,* sell all over the world.

_____

5 The customers on Terry's list needs a new car or truck.

_____

In each sentence above, the subject or performer, is expressed in one word: flower, book, account, magazine, and customers. At times, you want to write about more than one person or thing (a compound subject) in a sentence. That makes the subject plural, and the action word/verb follows suit. For example:

Clarissa and Mario open the office every day.

The action word/verb in the sentence is *open.* If the subject were *Clarissa,* how would the action word (verb) change? Remember what you read above. You add an *s* to the action word (verb) if the subject is singular.

Clarissa open*s* the office every day.

Now try these sentences. Circle the correct action word (verb).

Practice 2

1 Ceil (try/tries) to be on time.

2 Raoul and his brother never (misses/miss) an episode of Extreme Sports.

3 Marie and John (plan/plans) the company's picnic each summer.

4 Tomas (rewrites/rewrite) his résumé every six months.

5 Paper and paint (provides/provide) lots of fun.

More Challenges

What other subject–verb agreement challenges do you need to know about? A few word combinations cause many common writing and speaking errors.

- The subject contains an *either/or* combination. Think of the subject as *either* one *or* the other, which makes the subject singular. Choose a singular verb.

  Either Marie *or* John plans the company's picnic each summer.

  BUT

- The subject is compound and contains an either/or combination. The verb is singular or plural depending on the number of the second subject word.

  Either my brother or his children plan the reunion.

Brother and *children* are the two subject words. *Children* is the second subject word and it is plural; therefore, the plural verb form, *plan,* is correct.

- The subject of the sentence is *any.* Any is singular and used when the choice involves three or more.

  Any of your classmates meets the requirements for the biology course.

  Any one of your players is good enough to play on a pro team.

  You will learn more about subject–verb errors in later lessons. For now, let's face the challenges in the following practice exercise.

Practice 3

Choose the correct verb in each sentence. If you are in doubt, look back to the explanations above.

1 Either this course or that one (fill/fills) the requirement.

2 Any one of those outfits (look/looks) suitable for a job interview.

3 Hattie and her daughter (eat/eats) lunch together every Saturday.

4 Either this book or the videos (make/makes) a wonderful gift.

5 Children and a dog (make/makes) me smile.

Practice 4—Review

Correct each sentence. Look for errors in subject–verb agreement in number and use of pronouns as subjects. Look out for word combinations we discussed above that might confuse you.

1 Me and Amy share recipes all the time.

_____

2 Amy and me share CDs, too.

_____

3 Amy and I walks in the park every day.

_____

4 Amy's dog need to walk in the park twice a day.

_____

5 Either Amy or a family member walk the dog.

_____

Practice 5

Identify and rewrite statements that are not complete thoughts. Some of the statements are complete thoughts and won't require rewriting.

1 Concerning my request for a raise.

_____

2 I'll defer my request until next year.

_____

3 Return the cart to the store!

_____

4 A full explanation at the end.

_____

5 In community colleges where certificate programs are available.

_____

Practice 6

Read the following paragraph taken from a memo. Nick Bucci wrote the memo on January 4, 2016. Correct any errors you find.

> About the recycling program. We needs to discuss what our community is doing now. What do the community recycle? We should compare what we do to the national model we read about. Us and members of the town council should sit down to talk and plan. When do you think we can get together?

Something Else About Verbs

Verbs also indicate time, or what grammarians call *tense*. We can use any of the sentences from the exercises in this lesson to demonstrate the time or tense of verbs.

1 Present: Marie plans the company picnic each year.
Past: Marie planned the company picnic each year.
Future: Marie will plan the company picnic each year.
Past with helping word, has, have, or had: Marie has planned the company picnic each year.

2 Present: Mike walks to the library.
Past: Mike walked to the library.
Future: Mike will walk to the library.
Past with helping word, has, have, or had: Mike has walked to the library.

3 Present: Jack listens to the radio.
Past: Jack listened to the radio.
Future: Jack will listen to the radio.
Past with helping word, has, have, or had: Jack has listened to the radio.

So far, this is probably very easy for you; you change many verb forms—plan, planned, will plan—without even thinking about it. We say that these verbs change time in an organized, *regular* way. Think of yourself as doing any one of these actions. Place a pronoun in front of the verb to start. The first one, *I plan*, is done for you. Continue from there.

Present	Past	Future	Past + helping word, *has, have, had*
I plan	planned	will plan	has, have, had planned
walk	walked	will walk	has, have, had, walked
listen	listened	will listen	has, have, had walked
count	counted	will count	has, have, had counted
use	used	will use	has, have, had used

You probably use these verb forms often. You never think about the changes you make; you do it naturally. If you look at these verbs very carefully, however, a pattern emerges.

Present	Past	Future	Past + helping word, *has, have, had*
They walk	They walk + ed	They walk + will	They walked (past form) + helping word (have walked)
count	count + ed	count + will	counted (past form) + helping word (has counted)

What changes occur in these action words in the past tense and with helping words? The answer, of course, is that you add *-ed* to form the past tense. You add a forward-looking word, such as *will,* to the present tense, to form the future tense. You add a helping word to the past tense form to express the past tense that continues into the present. *(They have walked to work for three years.)* And you do all this without even thinking about it!

Why do we even bring this up if we handle this automatically and correctly? The answer is that we don't always use the correct forms. English takes some strange turns. And that is why you need to be aware of the common verb use errors. We'll explore the topic further in the section entitled "There's More?"

Practice 7

Complete this chart. The first verb, *call,* is done for you.

Present	Past	Future	Past + helping word, *has, have, had*
call	called	will call	have called
change			
check			
include			
use			
clean			

Practice 8

Complete the sentences using the verbs listed. The sentences will give you clues to the tense of the verb. Change the verb endings when necessary.

load   guide   trip   enter   arrive

1 Yesterday I _____ over that wire.

2 According to the chart, you will _____ the dishwasher every night this week.

3 As I _____ the room, I can see my favorite chair.

4 My newspaper has _____ on time every Sunday.

5 Your map _____ me to the campsite.

There's More?

It would be comforting to think that you now know everything you need to know about action words/verbs. Unfortunately, that is not the case. You recall that you worked with verbs that changed tense in a regular pattern—adding *-ed* to form the past, and so forth. Now you need to learn about *irregular* action words/verbs. These are verbs whose spellings change to a greater degree to indicate tense. They are called *irregular* verbs—for a reason.

Many errors in writing and speaking occur because of these irregular verb changes. Study the list that follows to see if you use the correct forms. As you study the list, what one characteristic do you see that remains the same with every verb? *Hint:* Look at the future tense.

Present	Past	Future	Past + helping word, *has, have, had*
begin	began	will begin	have begun
bend	bent	will bend	have bent
bet	bet	will bet	have bet
bite	bit	will bite	have bitten
bring	brought	will bring	have brought
burst	burst	will burst	have burst
buy	bought	will buy	have bought
choose	chose	will choose	have chosen
cost	cost	will cost	have cost
dig	dug	will dig	have dug
dive	dived or dove	will dive	have dived
drink	drank	will drink	have drunk
drive	drove	will drive	have driven
fling	flung	will fling	have flung
fly	flew	will fly	have flown
forbid	forbade	will forbid	have forbidden
forget	forgot	will forget	have forgotten
freeze	froze	will freeze	have frozen
get	got	will get	have gotten
grind	ground	will grind	have ground
hang	hung	will hang	have hung
have	had	will have	have had
know	knew	will know	have known
lay (place)	laid	will lay	have laid
lend	lent	will lend	have lent
lie (recline)	lay	will lie	have lain
mistake	mistook	will mistake	have mistaken
ride	rode	will ride	have ridden
ring	rang	will ring	have rung
run	ran	will run	have run

Present	Past	Future	Past + helping word, *has, have, had*
see	saw	will see	have seen
seek	sought	will seek	have sought
send	sent	will send	have sent
shake	shook	will shake	have shaken
shine	shone	will shine	have shone
shrink	shrank	will shrink	have shrunk
sing	sang	will sing	have sung
sink	sank	will sink	have sunk
slide	slid	will slide	have slid
speak	spoke	will speak	have spoken
spin	spun	will spin	have spun
spring	sprang	will spring	have sprung
steal	stole	will steal	have stolen
sting	stung	will sting	have stung
strike	struck	will strike	have struck
swear	swore	will swear	have sworn
swim	swam	will swim	have swum
swing	swung	will swing	have swung
take	took	will take	have taken
tear	tore	will tear	have torn
think	thought	will think	have thought
throw	threw	will throw	have thrown
wake	woke	will wake	have waken
weep	wept	will weep	have wept
wind	wound	will wind	have wound
wring	wrung	will wring	have wrung

Practice 9

Choose the correct form of the verb in each sentence. Look back at the list whenever you are in doubt about the correct form to use.

1 I (did/done) my homework very carefully.

2 Mac has (sing/sung) in the choir for years.

3 Lydia and Tomas have (teared/torn) up their credit cards.

4 Last summer, I (swimed/swam) a half mile every day.

5 I went back home because I had (forgot/forgotten) my license.

6 Our dog (shaked/shook) his wet fur furiously.

7 According to the recipe, I should have (grinded/ground) the meat.

8 Betsy and David (drived/drove) over an hour a day to work.

9 The student (laid/lain) his paper on the teacher's desk.

10 Jim's family (flew/flown) to Disney World for vacation.

Practice 10—Review

Practice everything you have learned in Lesson 2. Correct the error in each sentence.

1 Me and my dog start every day with a long walk.

2 Either you or me will have to lend Barney lunch money.

3 Ted, Dan, and Jose (play/plays) on the company's softball team.

4 This office plus people from the other building (share/shares) a parking lot.

5 Any of your choices (work/works).

Practice 11

Read the following paragraph. All of the sentences, except two, contain errors. Rewrite them to correct the mistakes.

> I have learnt that the English language has a history of changing. What's wrong usage today may be accepted years from now. Just takes a long time. Me and my friends struggle to learn the rules. For example, Mike and me always say, "We swimmed the mile race last summer." That might be right some day. Don't know if we can wait that long!

_____

_____

_____

_____

Answer Key

Practice 1
1. flower–sits
2. book–needs (Correct as it is.)
3. account–pays
4. magazine–sells
5. customers–need

Practice 2
1. tries
2. miss
3. plan
4. rewrites
5. provide

Practice 3
1. fills
2. looks

3. eat
4. make
5. make

Practice 4
1. Amy and I
2. Amy and I
3. walk
4. needs
5. walks

Practice 5
1. I am writing this memo concerning my request for a raise.
2. Correct
3. Correct
4. I have provided a full explanation at the end.
5. Adults attend community colleges where certificate programs are available.

Practice 6
From: Nick Bucci

Date: January 4, 2003

Subject: The Recycling Program (Avoid the incomplete sentence in the paragraph. Use this as the subject line of the memo.)

We need to discuss what our community is doing now. What does the community recycle? We should compare what we do to the national model we read about. We should sit down with members of the town council to talk and plan. When do you think you and I can get together?

Practice 7

call	called	will call	have called
change	changed	will change	have changed
check	checked	will check	have checked
include	included	will include	have included
use	used	will use	have used
clean	cleaned	will clean	have cleaned

Practice 8
1. tripped
2. load
3. enter
4. arrived
5. guided

Practice 9

1. did
2. sung
3. torn
4. swam
5. forgotten
6. shook
7. ground
8. drove
9. laid
10. flew

Practice 10—Review

1. My dog and I start every day with a walk.
2. Either you or I will have to lend Barney lunch money.
3. play
4. shares
5. works

Practice 11

1. I have learned that the English language has a history of changing.
2. Change (*or* It) just takes a long time.
3. My friends and I struggle to learn the rules.
4. For example, Mike and I always say, "We swam the mile race last summer."
5. I don't know if we can wait that long!

LESSON 3: The Good News and the Bad News

Mike had been going to his computer class for several weeks. Not only did he thoroughly enjoy all the new information he was learning, but he was also happy to meet people with whom he had a lot in common.

Leaving computer class one day, a new friend, Tim McNeil, talked to Mike.

"I love this class! I enjoy it because I understand it. English is completely different for me now. I been speaking English my whole life and I ain't got a decent grade on my work yet!"

Mike answered, "I know what you mean, Tim. My friends and I are having the same problem, but I think that if we stick with it, we'll get the idea."

The good news is that Mike has learned to say, "My friends and I . . . ," but Tim still has some work to do in agreement of subjects and verbs. Did you find Tim's errors? Read on for an explanation.

Words to Know

DVD	A compact disc that stores a large amount of information
Construction	The way in which something has been built

Contraction	A shortened form of a word or words
Infamous	Having a bad reputation

Another Kind of Verb

Up to now, we have discussed only one kind of verb: *action* words such as *write, return, plan, arrive, make, look,* and so forth. The subjects of the sentences did something. For example:

The batter hit the ball over the wall.

The action in this sentence is very clear: *hit.* Who did it? The *subject,* or *batter,* did it.

Now we will explore another type of verb that does not tell what the subject was doing. This verb tells what the subject was *being.* Some people call these *being verbs,* while others refer to them as *non-action* or *linking verbs.* For example:

The other team *was* angry.

You can see that there is no action in the sentence, but there is a description of how the team members *felt*—how they *were.* The verb, *was,* links *team* to the describing word, *angry.* (We go into more detail about words that describe in Lesson 4.)

The being verb, *was,* is a good place to start the discussion because we use it so much. It is, in fact, one of the forms of the very common linking verb *to be.* A number of other linking verbs are listed later in this lesson. For now, we will start by listing all the forms of *be,* using the same chart that you worked with in Lesson 2. The chart combines tense (present, past, and so forth) with number (we use singular or plural pronouns as subjects). Again, it is a convenient way to show how the number of the subject changes the spelling of the linking verb. With pronouns as subjects, the authors can show subject–verb agreement in number. In your writing or speaking, you use whatever subject is appropriate.

Linking Verbs

Present	Past	Future	Past with helping words *have, has, had*
I am	was	will be	have been
You are	were	will be	have been
He, she, it, is	was	will be	has been
We are	were	will be	have been
They are	were	will be	have been

Consider yourself very fortunate if you have heard and spoken English since birth. Most of what you have seen above simply comes naturally to you. Imagine what it must be like to learn English as a second language—so many irregularities and changes to memorize!

But don't become too comfortable. Common errors occur when people use non-action or linking verbs. How many times have you heard this doubleheader?

Me and Jim was on our way to work.

The first error, of course, is the infamous pronoun error. You can easily correct it by *mentioning Jim first* and *choosing a subject pronoun for yourself, I.* Now decide whether the subject—*Jim and I*—is a singular or plural subject. Yes, it is plural (there are two people in the subject), and it requires a plural non-action verb. Look back at the chart. If you substituted a pronoun for *Jim and I,* which one would it be? Of course, *we* would be the correct pronoun.

We were on our way to work.

We is a plural subject and *were* is the plural linking verb.

Practice 1

Choose a linking verb in each sentence. If you need help, look at the chart above.

1 Angelo (is/are) the biggest eater in our crowd.

2 We (was/were) not even close to his athletic ability.

3 Only one of us (were/was) a big enough eater to compete. (*Hint:* Don't be fooled by words between the subject and linking verb.)

4 Bill and Ann (is/are) always late.

5 This new computer program (is/are) much easier to install than the last one was.

When you read the instruction above, you learned that non-action verbs are also called *linking* verbs. You will see how appropriate this name is when you consider what follows linking verbs. For example:

Don is handsome.

Les is president.

I was really angry at her.

They were sick for a week.

Tomorrow is Thanksgiving.

What is linked in each sentence? In each one, the subject is linked to one of two things: a describing word (handsome, angry, sick) or a word that means the same as the subject (president, Thanksgiving). Because of the linking verb, you can turn any of these sentences around and still make sense of the meaning.

Now take a look at a longer list of linking verbs.

Linking Verbs

are	am	appear	become
is	feel	seem	smell
was	were	grow	taste
be	sound	remain	

Practice 2

Fill each blank with a linking word from the list above. There may be more than one correct choice for some sentences.

1 My children _____ tired of that TV show.

2 Do you _____ as groggy as I do today?

3 I'll _____ president of the PTA for this year at least.

4 The first apples of Fall _____ tart and crispy.

5 Marge _____ sick.

Practice 3

Underline the linking verb in each sentence above. What does the linking verb link? Draw an arrow from the subject to the describing word or the word that means the same as the subject. The first one is done for you.

My children <u>are</u> tired of that TV show.

1

2

3

4

5

Practice 4

Read the sentences and decide if they are correct. Change any words that are used incorrectly.

1 These pies tastes so good.

2 We was here on time; where was you?

3 A DVD sound so much better than a video cassette.

4 Ron, Fred, and Barney feels left out.

5 Either a guitarist or a pianist are needed.

6 Ellen and Lacy is co-chairs of the event.

7 The dog is a terrier.

8 The scouts growed weary from climbing the mountain.

9 The Santos and their dog is home after their vacation.

10 The appliances appears broken.

Linking Verbs and Pronouns

Pronoun usage is a problem for many people. Many of these problems have to do with linking verbs. Is the correct form "It is I"? Or is it "It is me"? Should you say, "It's between you and he"? Or is this correct: "It's between you and him"? Is there an easy way to make these decisions? Actually, there is. Just by dividing pronouns into three groups, you will avoid not all, but many, pronoun problems.

In Lesson 2, you learned that words have names (noun, verb, and so forth) and they have jobs (subject, action or linking word, and so forth). You can explain pronouns in the same way. You know that pronouns (that is their name) take the place of nouns (that is their job). In addition, pronouns can be placed in three groups according to what they do.

Pronouns That Act	Pronouns That Are Acted Upon	Pronouns That Own or Follow the Linking Verb (Receive Action)
I	me	my, mine
you	you	your, yours
he, she, it	him, her	his, her, hers, its
we	us	our. ours
they	them	their, theirs
who	whom	whose

Look at these sentences. Some contain linking verbs and others contain action verbs.

The new council president is *she*.   (*She* follows the linking verb and equals the *council president.*)

Our greatest resource is *he*.   (*he* follows the linking verb and equals *resource*)

These two sentences are correct, but they are too formal for everyday speech or writing. Instead, you might say, She is the new president. He is our greatest resource.

I gave the appointment to *him*.   (*I* acts; *him* receives the action)

The lunch bag is *yours*.   (*yours* shows ownership)

Betty and *I* gave *you* an extra   (*I* acts; *you* receives the action)
day off this week.

 FYI

As you work with the sentences below, remember this: The pronoun that follows a linking verb either (1) describes the subject or (2) equals the subject.

Describes the subject: The new office is *ours. Ours* is an ownership pronoun. *Ours* describes office.

Equals the subject: The fastest runner is *she. She* equals the subject. The best test of the subject and the pronoun being equal is this: You can turn the sentence around and achieve the same meaning.

She is the fastest runner.
She is the new council president
He is our greatest resource.

The authors know that most people do not answer the phone by saying, "Yes, this is he/she." In many cases, that would be too formal and unnatural. You need to make a choice based on the situation. At those times when being casual is not appropriate, you need to know the correct pronoun form.

Practice 5

Choose the correct pronoun in each sentence.

1 It was (they, them) who stole the money!

2 The winner is (him, he).

3 Tina and (I, me) called you.

4 The Smiths are (them, they).

5 The winner is (who, whom)?

Practice 6—Review

Use all that you have learned to choose the correct pronoun in each sentence.

1 The child had a new dog; the child loved (her, she) immediately.

2 Shirley and (me, I) leave for lunch at exactly 1 P.M.

3 A new lunch hour was set for Shirley and (me, I).

4 Mike and (him, he) plan to share an apartment.

5 It is (she, her) who committed the crime!

Another Group of Pronouns

Just when you thought you were familiar with all pronoun categories, here is another group. *Indefinite* pronouns are used often, but they are different in an important way. They don't replace a specific noun. That is why they are called *indefinite*. For example:

Each has the right to choose one person.

Someone chose Lynn.

Just as subjects and verbs have to agree in number, so do pronouns and verbs:

Each has a new uniform. (*Each* is singular, *has* is singular)

Both have new uniforms. (*Both* is plural, *have* is plural)

The following list will help you match indefinite pronouns with the correct verbs.

Indefinite Pronouns

Singular	Plural	Singular or Plural
any	many	some
anybody	few	all
each	plenty	most
everything	more	none
nothing	several	
either, neither	both	
much		
one		
someone		
more		
plenty		
less		

Practice 7

Choose a verb to agree with the indefinite pronoun in each sentence. The pronoun is italicized.

1 *Both* of the recipes (is, are) delicious.

2 *Anybody* (are, is) welcome to come.

3 *Few* (was, were) able to attend.

4 *One* of us (has, have) to take responsibility.

5 *Several* of us (is, are) leaving at the same time.

6 *None* of us (is, are) responsible for the damage. (Meaning none of us as individuals.)

7 *None* (was, were) sad about the results. (Meaning none of a group of people.)

Another Pronoun Problem

Another problem occurs when a pronoun comes later in the sentence but refers to something before it. The word the pronoun refers to is called the *antecedent.* You learned that subjects and verbs must agree in number. The same rule applies to a pronoun and its *antecedent.* For example:

A new employee will pick up their own uniform.

What is the subject of the sentence and is it singular or plural? *Employee* is the subject, and it is singular. *Their* is a plural pronoun that refers to *employee,* the *antecedent.* But that can't be correct, can it? Either both words must be plural or both must be singular.

A new *employee* will pick up *his* or *her* own uniform.

or

All new *employees* will pick up *their* own uniforms.

Sometimes plural words come between the subject and the referring pronoun:

Each one of the women hired *their* own babysitter.

What is the subject? Each is the singular subject. No matter how many plural words (women) follow the subject, the next pronoun must be singular:

Each one of the women hired *her* own babysitter.

In addition to the singular/plural decision, you have one more decision to make: Is the pronoun reference clear? For example:

The employee told the repairman that his computer was down.

Whose computer is down? Does it belong to the employee? Or does it belong to the repairman? Rewrite the sentence:

The employee told the repairman that his, the employee's, computer was down.

Here's another example:

Larry and Juan moved the equipment to the new office, but he could not stay past 6 P.M.

Who could not stay? Larry? Juan? Rewrite the sentence:

Larry and Juan moved the equipment to the new office, but Juan could not stay past 6 P.M.

Practice 8

Choose the correct pronoun in each sentence. If necessary, rewrite the sentence for clarity. One sentence is correct.

1 Don't give new employees materials until they have been date stamped.

2 Laura told the receptionist her phone was not working. [*Hint:* Whose phone was not working?]

3 Each of our sons wants a car for themselves.

4 Many of their friends get their cars before they are eighteen years old!

5 Anybody in this group who thinks they are done are sadly mistaken.

Special Forms of Linking Verbs

We often take shortcuts when we write or speak. We can take a shortcut using linking words. A linking word can be combined with another word to construct a new word, a *contraction*. In each case, one letter is left out of the combination.

Contraction	Example	Letter Left Out
I'm = I am	I'm here to help.	a
He's = He is	He's always right!	i
She's = She is	She's my best friend.	i
It's = It is	It's your turn.	i
You're = You are	You're wrong as usual.	a
We're = We are	We're a great team.	a
They're = They are	They're following us.	a

Note: Without the apostrophe, *its* is used to indicate possession. For example: The cat took the kitten to *its* new home.

Once again, if you have been speaking and writing English all of your life, the information above is not a great challenge. However, the same problem—agreement in number—does remain a challenge. Sometimes we use a contraction when we should not. For example:

There's many problems with your plan. = There is many problems with your plan.

What is wrong with this sentence? *Problems* is the subject, and it is plural. A plural subject agrees with a plural linking verb. Change *is* to *are*. The correct construction should be:

There are many problems with your plan.

Here is another example:

Here's the magazines you asked for. = Here is the magazines you asked for.

What is wrong with this sentence? *Magazines* is the subject and it is plural. Once again, you need to use a plural linking verb. Change *is* to *are*. The correct construction should be

Here are the magazines you asked for.

A New Wrinkle

What happens when the contraction is negative? Add *not* to the following:

is + not = isn't

are + not = aren't

will + not = won't

were + not = weren't

was + not = wasn't

Very Wrinkly

Never use the contraction *ain't*. Think about what it takes the place of and use the correct form instead.

I ain't (am not) finished yet.	I'm not finished yet.
You ain't (are not) finished yet.	You aren't finished yet.
She ain't (is not) finished yet.	She isn't finished yet.
They ain't (are not) finished yet.	They aren't finished yet.
We ain't (are not) finished yet.	We aren't finished yet.

Even though you will find *ain't* in some dictionaries, it is not correct usage, ever.

Practice 9

Find the errors in the following sentences. One is correct as written.

1 My problems isn't the worst in the world!

2 Wasn't you and Miguel expected at 8 A.M.?

3 Ain't I ever going to get any credit?

4 I can't sign up at the community college until September.

5 There's plenty of apples on that tree.

Read the paragraphs. Decide if any underlined word is incorrect. The underlined words are listed below each paragraph. Correct any errors.

1 Employees, if <u>they're</u> smart, <u>prepares</u> for every performance evaluation. Preparations should <u>begin</u> immediately following the last evaluation session. Rewrite any notes that you took so that <u>they're</u> very clear to you. Look at the goals that you and the manager <u>decided</u> were appropriate for the next six months. <u>Plan</u> how you will implement the goals.

    A they're
    B prepares
    C they're
    D decided
    E Plan

2 <u>Are</u> you interested in taking online courses? <u>There's</u> pluses and minuses to online learning. Being able to keep your own schedule as you learn <u>is</u> a very big consideration for some people. The computer <u>doesn't</u> know if you are learning at 5 P.M. or A.M. <u>Neither</u> does your instructor.

    A Are
    B There's
    C is
    D doesn't
    E Neither

3 On the other hand, <u>are</u> you independent and reliable enough to assume the responsibilities? There <u>ain't</u> going to be an instructor to face in person, therefore no face-to-face reminders about assignments. Although <u>you'll</u> have an online instructor, you <u>won't</u> have someone at your side to help you with homework and research.

    A are
    B ain't
    C you'll
    D won't

Another Kind of Agreement

Verbs also express time or tense.

I walk the dog each morning.

I walked the dog this morning.

I will walk the dog tomorrow morning.

I have walked the dog every morning this week.

The action verb, *walk,* is in the present; *walked* in the past; *will walk* is about the future, *have walked* is about the past and continues into the present.

Now let's look at the linking verb in time.

Present: I am angry.   I appear pale.

Past: I was angry.   I appeared pale.

Future: I will be angry.   I will appear pale.

Past with helping word: I have been angry. I have been pale.

The Challenge

In a sentence or a paragraph, the writer needs to keep the time of the verbs consistent. For example:

(1) The scene *is* set. (2)The atmosphere *is* hushed. (3) The curtain *rises* and the audience *applauds.*

Every verb in this paragraph—whether action or linking—is in the same tense.

1 is

2 is

3 rises, applauds

Obviously, the writer decided, in the first sentence, that all the verbs would be in the *present* tense. You need to check your writing, as well as your speech, for inconsistencies in tense. Start with the following practice:

Practice 11

Read the paragraphs. Look particularly for inconsistent verb tense. Choose the answer that shows the incorrect verb tense. Correct the error.

1 (A) We decided to leave for the airport three hours before our flight time. (B) Believe it or not, we didn't have any extra time. (C) It takes us a long time to park. (D) The airport parking lot was so crowded. (E) We ran to the departure gate.

   A decided

   B didn't

   C takes

   D was

   E ran

2 (A) We were the last to board the plane. (B) None of us had window seats. (C) This was a no-frills flight, which meant that no food was served. (D) In the last minute rush, we also forget to buy some food for lunch. (E) What a mistake that was!

    A were

    B had

    C was, was

    D forget

    E was

3 (A) We settled in for a three-hour trip. (B) Unfortunately, we spent the first two hours waiting to take off. (C) Have you ever spent five hours on a plane with someone else's three-year-old? (D) By the time we took off, the child had visited every passenger. (E) Finally, the flight attendant talks to the parents and they control the child.

    A settled

    B spent

    C spent

    D had visited

    E talks, control

Answer Key

Practice 1

1. is
2. were
3. was
4. are
5. is

Practice 2

1. are, were, grew, became, appeared
2. feel
3. remain, be
4. tasted, were, are
5. was, is, became, felt, remained, seemed

Practice 3

1. My children <u>are</u> tired of that TV show.

2. Do you <u>feel</u> as groggy as I do today?

3. I'll <u>remain</u> president of the PTA for this year at least.

4. The apples <u>tasted</u> tart and crisp.

5. Marge <u>became</u> sick.

Practice 4

1. taste
2. were, were
3. sounds
4. feel
5. is
6. are
7. Correct as written
8. grew
9. are
10. appear

Practice 5

1. they
2. he
3. I
4. they
5. who?

Practice 6

1. her
2. I
3. me
4. he
5. she

Practice 7

1. are
2. is
3. were
4. has
5. are
6. is
7. were

Practice 8

1. Don't give new employees materials until the materials have been date stamped.
2. Laura told the receptionist that Laura's phone was not working.
3. Each of our sons wants a car for himself.

4. Correct

5. Anybody in this group who thinks that he or she is done is sadly mistaken.

Practice 9

1. aren't

2. Weren't

3. Aren't

4. Correct as written

5. There are

Practice 10

PARAGRAPH 1

1. B; prepare

PARAGRAPH 2

2. B; There are

PARAGRAPH 3

3. B; isn't

Practice 11

PARAGRAPH 1

1. C; took

PARAGRAPH 2

2. D; forgot

PARAGRAPH 3

3. talked, controlled

LESSON 4: SPEAK UP!

Mike met Ken on campus, after Ken's math class.

Mike asked, "How was class today?" Ken replied, "Same." "Coffee?" Mike asked. "Sure," Ken answered.

This conversation between Mike and Ken consists of mostly non-sentences: "Same." "Coffee?" "Sure." In casual conversation, incomplete thoughts are acceptable. You will see incomplete thoughts in written language as well as in conversation. What is noteworthy, however, is the lack of color in such sentences. Adding color to your speech and writing is the subject of this lesson.

Words to Know

Adjective	A word that describes a noun or pronoun
Adverb	A word that describes a verb, an adjective, or another adverb
Preposition	The first word in a group of words that describes another word, usually a noun, in the sentence

| Reluctant | Feeling no enthusiasm for something |
| Dilemma | A situation in which you must choose one of two unsatisfactory solutions |

A More Colorful Approach

This bears repeating: A complete sentence must have a subject and a verb, and that makes it a complete thought. Does that make it an interesting thought? Not necessarily. You need to introduce more colorful additions to the basic thought. This is true whether the sentence is organized around an action verb or a linking verb. Look at a sentence with an action verb.

The child leads.

Subject = child   Action verb = leads

We don't usually write or speak such simple thoughts. We want to describe both the subject and the verb. We accomplish that by adding adjectives and adverbs to sentences.

The assertive, older child leads very effectively.

Assertive and older describe child. Effectively describes leads. Very describes effectively.

With these words, adjectives (*assertive* and *older*) and adverbs (*effectively* and *very*), the reader has more information. The question becomes, "If all of the words describe, why do they have different names?" The answer is simple. You recall that words have both *names* and *jobs*. In this case, the adjective's (that is its name) job is to describe or give more information about nouns, or names of people, places, or things. Here are a few examples:

Adjective	Noun
older	child
small	town
big	meal
tall	gentleman
large	crowd

As you learned in Lesson 3, adjectives also work with linking verbs. A linking verb links the subject of the sentence with a describing word (adjective). Retool the sentence above:

The assertive, older child is effective at work.

Child is still the noun/subject of the sentence. However, the verb is now a linking verb (*is*) instead of an action verb (*leads*). What two words does the linking verb bring together? The answer, of course, is *child* and *effective*. *Effective* describes *child*.

Here is another example:

My job is challenging.

Noun	Linking verb	Adjective
job (noun)	is (linking)	challenging (adjective describes job)

STUDY TIP
You have been studying adjectives that follow the linking verb. What about other adjectives in the sentence? For example, in the sentence above, what about the word *my? My* certainly describes job, telling whose job it is. *Job* is a noun; therefore, the describing word, *my,* is an adjective. If *my* looks as if it should be called a pronoun, you are right. Some pronouns act as if they are adjectives: The kind of job they do in the particular sentence affects what they are called! Remember, words have names and they have jobs, too.

Here's another example:

Your job seems impossible.

job (noun) seems (linking verb) impossible (adjective describes job)

After reading the study tip above, what job do you think the word *your* does in this sentence? If you said it describes, you were correct. What word does it describe? The correct answer is *job.* Again, you see a pronoun acting as an adjective.

Practice 1

Now try these sentences on your own. Underline the linking verb and find the subject. Draw an arrow from the adjective to the noun or pronoun it describes.

1 We grew tired of a very long argument.

2 That pie tastes so good.

3 You are swamped with work.

On the Other Hand . . .

The job of adverbs is to describe a verb, an adjective, or another adverb. For example:

The assertive, older child leads very effectively.

Effectively describes *leads.*

Very describes *effectively.*

Here's another example:

I gave the present reluctantly.

Reluctantly describes *gave.*

Practice 2

Now try these sentences on your own. Draw an arrow from the adverb to the verb it describes. In Sentence 3, there is also an adverb that describes another adverb.

1 The student in the next room played music loudly.

2 Our cousins arrived unexpectedly.

3 I'll ask very politely.

Practice 3

Read the five sentences in the "On the Other Hand" and Practice 2 sections above. List the adverbs that describe verbs

1

2

3

4

5

Note: What conclusion can you draw about the way adverbs that describe verbs are most often spelled? Yes, they very often end in *-ly.* That spelling will be a clue for you when you are trying to decide if a word is an adverb.

The Challenge

The challenge is to use adjectives and adverbs correctly. There are several very common errors that you will want to avoid.

Well vs. Good

Well can be used as an adjective when you talk about health. For example:

I feel well now. (*Well* describes *I.*)

At all other times, *well* is an adverb and, as such, describes the action word:

My boyfriend drives racecars well. (*Well* describes *drives.*)

Important: Good never describes an action. What kind of word does it describe in the next four sentences?

My boyfriend is a good driver. (Not, "My boyfriend drives good." *Good* cannot describe the action *drives*.)

A good reader has an advantage on tests.

A good place to live is not always easy to find.

Use good paper to print that report.

We have *good driver, good reader, good place,* and *good paper.* The word *good* obviously describes people, places, and things. They are all nouns.

Practice 4

Choose the correct word to complete each sentence.

   1 One of my colleagues dresses (good/well).

   2 Our manager has not felt (good/well) for weeks.

   3 My brother-in-law is a (good/well) house painter.

   4 The choir sings (good/well).

   5 I rewrote my résumé, and it worked (good/well) for me.

Real vs. Really

Really describes another descriptive word. Did you notice the *-ly*? Yes, *really* is an adverb, and it describes or limits other descriptive words. For example:

Clara's computer is really outdated. (*Really* describes the adjective *outdated.*)

Aaron's excuse for being late was really lame. (*Really* describes the adjective *lame.*)

Real describes a person, place, or thing—a noun. For example:

This is a real dilemma. (*Real* describes the noun *dilemma.*)

The sofa is made of real leather. (*Real* describes the noun *leather*)

Practice 5

Choose the correct word in each sentence.

   1 The actress played a (real/really) lovable part.

   2 The hat was (real/really) too small to protect me from the sun.

   3 One problem is that our morning meetings start (real/really) early.

   4 One (real/really) problem is that our meetings are in the morning.

   5 Why don't you take a (real/really) break—an extra ten minutes.

Nice vs. Nicely

This is one of the most common errors in the use of descriptive words. Don't make this error!

The senator spoke nice at the town meeting.

Once again, you need to decide what job each word performs. *Nice* describes a person, place, or thing—a noun. *Nicely* describes an action—a verb. In the sentence above, what does *nice* try to describe? The answer, of course, is *spoke*. But *nice* cannot describe a verb; *nicely* does.

The senator spoke nicely at the town meeting.

If you wanted to describe the senator as nice, what would you say?

The nicely senator spoke at the town meeting.

or

The nice senator spoke at the town meeting.

Nice is an adjective and, as you know, adjectives describe nouns or persons, place, or things.

Practice 6

Choose the correct word in each sentence.

1 Because it was a (nice/nicely) day, we walked to work.

2 "(Nice/Nicely) done!" yelled the enthusiastic fan.

3 The manager spoke (nice/nicely) at the district meeting.

4 The (nice/nicely) manager spoke at the district meeting.

5 He's really a (nice/nicely) person.

Practice 7

Read the paragraph below. Choose the correct adjective or adverb in each sentence.

> Young people today have a (well/good) reason for learning to write a strong résumé. Research tells them that they will not have just one job in their lifetimes. It is (more/most) likely that they will have many jobs over time. For some, this is a (nice/nicely) opportunity to avoid boredom in their work lives. It is also a (real/really) good opportunity to become a lifelong learner. These young people—as well as older workers—must expect to change jobs. In addition, they will have to feel (good/well) about changing the kind of work they do. They have to be (real/really) ready, and trained for change.

An Important Change

There is another very important way that adjectives change to accommodate the meaning in a sentence. The change is called *comparison of descriptive words.* In the following examples, you can see why that term is appropriate.

The commuter train is *fast.*

The new German train is *faster.*

The French train is the *fastest* one of all.

Obviously, each sentence talks about the degree of speed. Sentence 1 simply states a fact—a certain train is fast. Sentence 2 sets up the comparison between the first train and the German train. The important fact here is that two things are compared and the English language adds an *-er* to indicate that of the *two,* one is faster. Sentence 3 shows a new level of comparison. Now it is clear that of the three trains being compared, the French train is the fastest. The word ending *-est* is used to show that comparison of three or more.

This simple comparison exercise is probably not much of a challenge for you. You use the following words, and many others, without a problem.

Adjective	Comparison of Two	Comparison of More Than Two
fast	faster	fastest
green	greener	greenest
blue	bluer	bluest
pretty	prettier	prettiest

Trouble Ahead

We tend to run into trouble in comparisons in two ways:

1 Sometimes adjectives change spelling in ways other than the addition of *-er* or *-est* to the base word. Some describing words are too long and become awkward when we place an extra syllable on the end. Consider this:

That is the *advancedest* course in our program.

The writer or speaker compared all of the courses in a program. The person decided that one of many courses was the most advanced. Because *advanced* is a three-syllable word and because it becomes a very awkward word, you must not add *-er* or *-est* to it. What do we do instead? Add *more* or *most* and keep the base word, *advanced.*

That course is the most advanced in our program. (The sentence indicates a comparison of three or more courses. The word *most* is used instead of adding *-est*.)

or

That course is more advanced than the one I took last semester. (The sentence indicates a comparison between two courses. The word *more* is used instead of adding *-er*.)

We sometimes, mistakenly, use *more* or *most* plus the *-er* or *-est* ending, and that is too much of a good thing:

That TV show is *more funnier* now than it was in the past.

The correct sentence should read:

That TV show is funnier now than it was in the past.

Here are some other words that need to use *more* and *most* in comparisons:

Adjective	Comparison of Two	Comparison of More Than Two
enormous	more enormous	most enormous
difficult	more difficult	most difficult
beautiful	more beautiful	most beautiful
quickly	more quickly	most quickly
valuable	more valuable	most valuable
wonderful	more wonderful	most wonderful

2 Some adjectives are spelled entirely differently when they are used to compare two or more things. Look at the following chart:

Adjective	Comparison of Two	Comparison of More Than Two
good	better	best
bad	worse	worst

What's wrong with the folllowing sentence?

That was the worse meal I've ever had.

I think we can assume that the writer has had more than two meals. How would you correct the sentence?

That was the worst meal I've ever had.

Try this:

That book is the better of the group.

This should read

That book is the best of the group.

Practice 8—Review

Find the error in each sentence. One sentence has no error. Write a correction in the space provided.

1 She has children who are enormouser than mine. _____

2 I run pretty quick for the bus. _____

3 Our garden looks good this year. _____

4 This is the worse training course I've had in my ten years with the company!

_____

5 You'll never find a more wonderfuler friend. _____

6 Tod's known as the most tenaciousest trainer in our group of runners.

_____

7 I feel good today. _____

8 Jan lives nearest to me than Carl does. _____

9 That episode was more funnier than any of the others. _____

10 She's real unhappy._____

Another Way to Describe

Occasionally, we need more than a single word to add meaning to a sentence. We add a phrase instead. For example:

The guitar screeched *on the high notes.*

The phrase *on the high notes* describes how the guitar screeched. The entire phrase acts as a descriptive word. If you had to decide whether the phrase was an adjective or adverb phrase, what would you say? You would first have to know what kind of word it describes. In this case, it is *screeched,* the verb. What kind of word describes a verb? If you said an adverb does, you are correct. You remember what you learned at the beginning of this lesson.

There is a practical reason for you to be able to recognize descriptive phrases. As you will see, they frequently come between or close to the subject or verb. For example:

A *summary* of all the chapters *is* in the last part of the book.

You needed to recognize that the word *chapters* is a part of the descriptive phrase. It is not the subject in the above sentence. The sentence below shows *chapters* as the subject. What happened to the verb? It became plural to agree with the plural subject.

The chapters are in the last part of the book.

STUDY TIP

Sometimes you need to identify the subject to decide if it is singular or plural. First, exclude the descriptive phrase. Then make your decision. Try this sentence:

The athletes at the stadium (park/parks) free.

What is the action verb? The answer is *park*. Who parks? The *athletes*. That is the subject. Is the subject singular or plural? The answer is plural. Which word should you choose? *Athletes park.* Try another sentence.

The recruits under the wire fence (was/were) stuck.

Remember, first remove the prepositional phrase, *under the wire fence*. What is left? *The recruits (was/were) stuck.* Now, choose the correct verb. *The recruits under the wire fence were stuck.*

A group of words that typically starts a descriptive phrase is called a *preposition*. Some common prepositions are listed below.

Prepositions

after	at	along	alongside	among	around
before	beside	between	by	except	for
from	in	into	of	off	on
over	to	through	under	up	with

Practice 9

Each sentence below includes a descriptive phrase. Each descriptive phrase starts with one of the prepositions listed above. Find the phrases and decide which word the phrase describes. Then find the subject and the verb. Place an *S* over the subject and a *V* over the verb.

1 The puppy fell into our swimming pool.

2 They are among our best friends.

3 Our children went through the woods to Grandmother's house.

4 All the houses between the brook and the forest (are/is) green, white, or gray.

5 The houses of Congress are divided in their thinking. (*Hint:* divided describes Congress. What does *in their thinking* describe?)

STUDY TIP

Do you remember the three kinds of pronouns? You recall that they act as subjects, are receivers of action, or show ownership. (If you need to, review Lesson 3, page 219.) Now you can follow this rule. Choose a pronoun from the second column and place it at the end of a prepositional phrase.

Save the books *for them.*
John sent an invitation *to her.*
An argument raged between *George and him.*

Practice 10

Choose the correct word in each sentence.

   1 The discussion was between you and (I, me).

   2 We'll make that decision among (us, we).

   3 Any final decision must go through (me, I).

   4 Will anyone arrive before (me, I)?

   5 The contest is between Jorge and (he, him).

Warning!

A descriptive or prepositional phrase should be placed next to the word it describes.

When prepositional phrases are misplaced, confusion results. For example:

The child yelled at her mother on the swing.

Who was on the swing, the child or her mother? You cannot say for sure after reading this sentence. Rewrite it like this:

The child on the swing yelled at her mother.

Or try this:

Tom ran down the newly polished hallway in slippery boots.

Who was wearing slippery boots, Tom or the hallway? Be more precise by placing the descriptive phrase closer to the word it describes. You can do this in more than one way:

In slippery boots, Tom ran down the newly polished hallway.

or

Tom, in slippery boots, ran down the newly polished hallway.

Practice 11

Find the incorrectly placed prepositional phrases in these sentences. Rewrite the sentences and place the phrases closer to the words they describe. If you have trouble recognizing the prepositions, look back to the list on page 228.

   1 The cow belongs to that farm with the black and white spots.

   2 The photographer relaxed after taking 100 outdoor pictures in his studio.

   3 I was finally able to hang on my wall my diploma.

   4 Show Lois outside the door the frisky dog.

   5 The drivers on the counter completed registration forms.

Answer Key

Practice 1

1. <u>grew</u> we (subject) tired

2. <u>tastes</u> pie (subject) good

3. <u>are</u> you (subject) swamped

Practice 2
1. played ⟵ loudly
2. arrived ⟵ unexpectedly
3. ask ⟵ very ⟶ politely

Practice 3
1. effectively
2. reluctantly
3. loudly
4. unexpectedly
5. politely very

Practice 4
1. well
2. well
3. good
4. well
5. well

Practice 5
1. really
2. really
3. really
4. real
5. real

Practice 6
1. nice
2. Nicely
3. nicely
4. nice
5. nice

Practice 7
1. good
2. more

   3. nice

   4. really

   5. good

   6. really

Practice 8

   1. more enormous

   2. quickly

   3. correct as is

   4. worst

   5. more wonderful

   6. most tenacious

   7. feel well

   8. nearer

   9. was funnier

 10. really

Practice 9

   1. puppy (subject) fell (verb) into our swimming pool (prepositional phrase describes *fell*)

   2. They (subject) are (verb) among our best friends (prepositional phrase describes *they*)

   3. Children (subject) went (verb) through the woods, to Grandmother's house (prepositional phrases describe the verb *go*)

   4. houses (subject) are (verb) between the brook and the forest (prepositional phrase describes *houses*

   5. houses (subject) are (verb) *of Congress* and *in their thinking* are prepositional phrases. *Of Congress* describes *houses. In their thinking* describes *divided.*

Practice 10

   1. me

   2. us

   3. me

   4. me

   5. him

Practice 11

   1. The cow with the black and white spots belongs to that farm.

   2. The photographer relaxed in his studio after taking 100 outdoor pictures.

   3. I was finally able to hang my diploma on the wall.

   4. Show Lois the frisky dog outside the door.

   5. The drivers completed registration forms on the counter.

At the Brightwater Community College student café, Mike and some friends were having their usual after-class get-together. Ken had a great deal to say (complain) about his English class. "I'm doing good—I mean well on my tests now. But I don't think I'll ever understand the teacher completely." Mike and Michelle couldn't wait to hear why. Ken always had such good stories.

Ken continued, "Today Ms. Santos gave back our third paper. I worked real—really—hard on that paper. She gave me a C! And she said to me, 'I don't think you like me, Mr. Brinkley.' I had absolutely no idea what she was talking about, so I stayed after class and asked what I had done. She said, 'If you cared about your reader, and I am your reader in this class, you would use punctuation more carefully. Your thinking skills are excellent, but sometimes I have to read a sentence two or three times in order to sort out your idea.'"

Ken asked, "What can I do about it?" She replied, "Come to see me during office hours and we'll go over your paper. I'll give you some extra materials to work through."

Here are some things Ken learned about punctuation and how it affects understanding. Ken was very surprised. Will you be?

Words to Know

Unenthusiastic	Not eager to do something
Interact	To have an effect on someone else
Diversity	Variety

Why Do We Need Punctuation?

Have you ever thought about the fact that we don't talk this way?

today comma Iapostrophem going to the mall right after work period my coworker comma Jennie comma has promised to take me to the best discount clothing store in the state exclamation point

Of course, we don't have to supply the punctuation and capitalization as we talk. Our voices provide all the necessary information. We pause for commas, and come to a stop for a period. Our tone rises for a question. We show appropriate emotion for an exclamation point. Obviously, on paper, we can't express endings, beginnings, excitement, and so forth. We need punctuation marks. That is what Ken had not taken into consideration when he eliminated commas, occasionally ran two sentences together, and misused or forgot quotation marks.

Much of punctuation use is logical. We avoid run-on sentences, for example, by using a period or a semicolon. What is wrong with the following sentence?

My friend is always hungry she'll want to eat before we go shopping.

My friend is always hungry, she'll want to eat before we go shopping.

These are classic run–on sentences. The sentences do exactly what their name implies; they run on from thought to thought with no punctuation or with the incorrect use of a comma (called a comma fault). Let's correct these sentences:

My friend is always hungry. She'll want to eat before we go shopping.

or

My friend is always hungry; she'll want to eat before we go shopping.

Either the period or semicolon is correct. You will learn more about choosing between a period and a semicolon later in this lesson. For now, keep in mind that sentences have to end. Always choose a period, a question mark, or an exclamation point: **.** or **?** or **!**

End Marks

The period (.), question mark (?), and exclamation point (!) are all end marks. They are the most commonly used punctuation marks. Without them and capital letters, our sentences would be chaos. For example:

> would you like to be able to learn something the minute you need to would you like to access information from a reliable source any time anywhere with new software people–friendly machines and knowledge of how people learn we will be able to create such a learning environment

The authors challenge you to read the above information quickly and tell us what you understood. You probably got some meaning on your first reading, but real comprehension came when you placed missing end marks and capital letters in the paragraph, as follows:

> Would you like to be able to learn something the minute you need to? Would you like to access information from a reliable source any time anywhere? With new software, people–friendly machines, and knowledge of how people learn, we will be able to create such a learning environment.

In this section, you will study end marks and capital letters simultaneously. One does, in fact, signal the other. The Study Tip below provides a list of capitalization rules. For the purposes of Practice 1, however, just remember that proper names of people and places are capitalized.

STUDY TIP

Here is a list of capitalization rules. Refer to this list whenever you are unsure about using a capital letter.

Capitalize the following:

- The first word in a sentence.
- The first word of a direct quotation.

- The word *I*.
- Names of important historical events, documents, and periods of history (World War II, Declaration of Independence, the Renaissance).
- The deity, place names, people's names, organization names, specific course names, languages.
- A title when it is a form of address: Lieutenant George Grant.
- The title of a book, play, magazine, or poem (just the first and important words in each, e.g., The Competent Writer: A Plan of Attack).
- Sections of the country, not directions. Example: I had lived in the East for many years.
- Days of the week, months, and holidays. Example: Thanksgiving is the fourth Thursday in November.

Practice 1

In the following paragraphs, place end marks and capital letters where they are needed. Do not worry about commas or any other punctuation marks.

1. if you ask me, our leader bruce m wheeler needs to learn more about leading a group successful group work depends to a great extent on the skills of the leader our leader absolutely does not believe in imposing any standards would you rather have no rules or a few sensible rules of procedure and conduct anything less must lead to anarchy

2. in june, we'll move to our new two-room office our moving list will include paper and pencil supplies yours should concentrate on furniture and lighting dan will concentrate on the computers and other hardware the office can be moved quickly if we all cooperate do you think we can be ready by may 31

3. yesterday i told my boss that i would be happy to work on the new project he was very glad to get my message he's had trouble selling the idea to our team management really wants full cooperation what do you do when four of the five team members are unenthusiastic pray

When Should I Use a Comma?

For many people, the comma is the most challenging form of punctuation. If, however, you keep the idea of logical use in mind, the process will be easier. Commas are meant to clarify meaning. Read the paragraph below. Where would you insert commas?

When you use the English language some rules are very clear. For example there is no dispute about the word ain't. You should not use it—ever. Neither do you say "I don't never want to see that textbook again." However when it comes to commas we don't seem to be as confident sure or secure in making decisions.

Now you will have the opportunity to study the important uses of commas and when you finish you will be very confident in your decisions.

Check your answers in the Answer Key. The following checklist will help you to understand the correct uses of commas and to correct any errors you may have missed in the sample paragraph.

Comma Use Checklist

1 Use a comma after a salutation in a friendly letter.

Dear Abby,

Use a comma after the closing in a business or friendly letter.

Sincerely,

Ruth

2 Separate items in a series with commas.

Feed the cat, walk the dog, and clean the bird's cage.

3 Use a comma to separate an introductory phrase from the complete thought.

When I am ready to leave for the airport, I go over my departure checklist one more time.

STUDY TIP

Take a careful look at this example. Writers sometimes make the error of thinking that the introductory words (When I am ready to leave for the airport) constitute a sentence. They do not. When you finish reading this, you want to ask, "What happens?" That is because it is an incomplete thought, a sentence fragment. Don't fall into the sentence fragment trap!

4 Insert commas to separate words that interrupt the flow of the sentence.

An electronic organizer, although I don't own one, is an essential tool for business trips.

STUDY TIP

Use this tip to test the need for commas. Words that interrupt the flow of the sentence can be eliminated. Eliminating the words will not affect the sentence's meaning.

An electronic organizer is an essential tool for business trips.

5 Commas set off the words *however, nevertheless,* and *therefore,* when they interrupt a complete thought.

Our meeting, however, cannot take place in the usual meeting room.

6 A comma separates two complete thoughts that are joined by a connecting word such as *but, for, or, and.*

We will look at all the available rooms, and we will choose the largest one.

7 Use commas to separate more than one descriptive word describing the same word.

A Series B, handheld, electronic organizer is the newest version.

8 Insert a comma to separate the name of a city from the name of a state or country.

Juan Moniz

196 Union Street

San Francisco, CA 00000

9 Insert a comma to separate a direct quotation from the rest of the sentence. For example:

"I'll never get to work on time in this traffic," he complained.

He shouted in his empty car, "I'll never get to work on time in this traffic!"

"Jason, I know I won't make it on time," Laura said to her assistant "so please start the meeting without me."

10 Insert a comma between the day and the year and between the year and the rest of the sentence.

Mike graduated on June 14, 2015, from Brightwater Community College.

Practice 2

Insert commas where they are needed. If you are not sure of your answers, check the list of rules above.

Citizens can make a difference in their community and in the world. Without doubt, the first step is to identify problems. Look at community needs strengths and resources. As a result of their investigation people can form and express opinions. Of course all involved in community action must be willing to work with others. In this way, citizens can impact their communities and the world around them.

Practice 3

Insert or remove commas wherever necessary.

How, do things get done in a community? When citizens have a common purpose they interact with others to get things done. In order to do that people must respect others. They, need first to understand the power of diversity.

Practice 4

For questions 1 through 5, decide if the underlined parts need correction. Write the correction or *correct as is* on the line provided.

1 How many times have you heard people complain about others' failure to communicat<u>e.</u>

_____

2 Believe it or <u>not people</u> benefit from poor <u>communication?</u>

_____

3 Poor communication allows people to hide their lack of <u>planning, others</u> can't see the whole picture. _____

4 <u>Or poor</u> <u>communication, makes</u> it easier to deny what plan was made.

_____

5 If you don't say things clearly, who can say you were wrong?

_____

Use Commas Logically

Do not insert commas where they are not needed. Avoid the following common overuses of commas.

1 Do not use a comma to separate two actions if the sentence has one subject/ performer.

Incorrect: <u>I bought</u> the car, and <u>went</u> to register it immediately.

Correct: <u>I bought</u> the car and <u>went</u> to register it immediately.

2 When a sentence starts with a complete thought, do not use a comma to separate it from the incomplete thought that follows.

Incorrect: You need to greet the guest, when he arrives.

Correct: You need to greet the guest when he arrives.

Reminder: You can see that the subject of commas frequently brings up the subject of sentence fragments. Keep this in mind as you do the review exercise.

Practice 5—Review

Find and correct errors in capitalization, end marks, and comma usage. For practice, look for three sentence fragments among these sentences.

1 I was ready to eat lunch, having finished the morning's work.

2 dear mom
please send money.
Love
Sam

3 I'll mow the lawn fertilize it and pull the weeds if you want me to

4 When I have finished and you are ready and the new equipment has arrived.

5 Because he was late six times this year John's pay was docked.

6 This long-standing committee will disband and a new team concept will be put in place.

7 If you think you can be available we'll meet on September 20, 2016.

8 "I cannot attend" she responded.

9 Before the event and after my promotion.

10 After outrunning the children and entering the cool house.

Stronger Than a Comma

A semicolon is stronger than a comma; it is actually more like a period. It expresses the close relationship between two complete thoughts. You will recall reading (page 233) that you can correctly put two thoughts together by using a semicolon. You read this example:

My friend is always hungry; she'll want to eat before we go shopping.

Remember that the two thoughts need to be closely related. Three rules apply.

1 Thoughts connected by a semicolon might otherwise be connected using a comma plus the words *so, for, but, and, or, nor.*

Use a period to end a declarative sentence, or use a question mark if it is a question.

or

Use a period to end a declarative sentence; use a question mark if it is a question.

2 What happens when you write two complete and related thoughts, one or both of which contain commas?

I was born on May 24, 1970, in Denver, Colorado; but my sister was born in Seattle.

According to Rule 1 above, two thoughts connected by *but* do not require a semicolon. In this sentence, however, there are three commas in the first thought. Using another one to separate the two thoughts might be very confusing. To avoid the confusion, use the stronger mark of punctuation, the semicolon.

3 When you use certain large connecting words to join two complete thoughts, use a semicolon. Use a semicolon, the connecting word, and a comma, in that order. The connecting words are *however, therefore, nevertheless,* and *inasmuch as.* For example:

I don't like my new schedule; however, I must stick with it for at least a year.

You haven't finished the report; therefore, I will not be able to present it.

We will continue our work; the report is due in three days, we have a great number of facts to discuss.

Practice 6—Review

Insert commas, end marks, and semicolons wherever they are needed. Look for run-on sentences and correct them.

1 Rod is taking a computer course an introduction to health care and a writing course

2 I'll be very busy at work all week please don't call me.

3 Shelley said that we should meet in the parking lot

4 Shelley said "Meet me in the parking lot."

5 I've already made plans therefore I won't be there.

6 Rain hail and snow followed us all the way to our destination.

7 When you visit us you will travel on Route 95 for an hour.

8 The child needed to have a blood test he howled at the sight of the needle

9 His mother did all that she could to comfort him however nothing seemed to work.

10 I want a sleek red fast sports car for my birthday do you think I'll get one

Quotation Marks

You have had some experience working with commas and quotation marks. You learned that quotation marks are used to set off the exact words someone says.

Direct quotation: The President of the United States said, "We need to learn to work together to solve problems."

Indirect quotation: The President of the United States said that we need to learn to work together to solve problems.

What one word changes the direct quotation to an indirect one? The answer, of course, is the word *that.* The word *that* turns the statement into a *report* of what the President said.

In order to use quotation marks correctly, you need to know a number of rules.

Quotation Mark Checklist

1   As you saw above, use quotation marks to indicate the exact words of a speaker. *Important:* Note the period inside the quotation marks at the end of the sentence. Also note the comma between the speaker and the words spoken.

The policeman said, "Stay right and move along."

2   Some quotations are called "broken," because the name of the speaker interrupts the sentence. In the first example, note the small letter on the first word of the second part of the quotation. In the second example, the second part of the quotation is actually a new sentence and requires a capital letter. Also look at the exclamation points. Just like the period, they are placed inside the quotation marks.

"Sure," shouted Audrey, "now that I'm finished, you want to help me!"

"Now that you're finished, you don't need my help," said Audrey. "Why didn't you call me earlier?"

3   Place a semicolon after the closing quotation marks.

I heard, "Pull over to the right"; so I did.

4   Never use two forms of punctuation at the end of a quotation. Use logic to decide where question marks and exclamation marks should be placed. If the entire sentence is a question, but the quotation is not, place the question mark after the closing quotation marks. If the entire sentence is an exclamation, but the quotation is not, place the exclamation point after the closing quotation mark.

Question mark: Did Ms. Santos say, "Your final exam is next Thursday"?

Exclamation point: I was so furious when you said, "I never told you that the reconditioned equipment would work again"!

5   Use quotation marks to enclose titles of poems, chapters, articles, or any part of a book or magazine. When the quoted title is followed by a comma, the comma should be placed inside the quotation marks.

"To Brooklyn Bridge," by Hart Crane, was written in 1930.

6 Use single quotation marks for a quotation within a quotation.

> The other day, Judy asked me, "Is it true that you said, 'I'm going on strike if I don't get more help at home' when you started spring cleaning?"

STUDY TIP

Here are some common mistakes made when using quotation marks. You will see that the addition of other punctuation marks often causes the problem. Errors include the misuse of commas, periods, question marks, and capital letters.

Problem 1: "Take the newspaper with you" his father suggested.

Solution: Insert a comma between the quoted words and the person who said them. Remember to place the comma inside the quotation marks.

"Take the newspaper with you," his father suggested.

Problem 2: "Take the newspaper with you," his father suggested. "In case you want something to read in the car."

Solution: When you write a broken quotation, do not capitalize the first word of second part of the quotation unless it starts a new sentence.

"Take the newspaper with you," his father suggested, "in case you want something to read in the car."

or

"Take the newspaper with you," his father suggested. "You may want something to read in the car."

Problem 3: His mother warned, "We're not stopping to eat, so remember to take food with you".

Solution: The period always goes inside the quotation marks at the end of a sentence.

His mother warned, "We're not stopping to eat, so remember to take food with you."

Problem 4: My son asked, "Is this all there is to eat"?

Solution: The quoted portion is a question; the entire sentence is not. Place the question mark inside the quotation marks.

My son asked, "Is this all there is to eat?"

Problem 5: Did your son say, "There's only enough food for me?"

Solution: The quoted portion is not a question; the entire sentence is a question. Place the question mark outside the quotation marks.

Did your son say, "There's only enough food for me"?

Practice 7—Review

Punctuate these sentences. Add capital letters where necessary.

1 The announcer said the manager must get the field in shape for the season

2 The announcer said that the manager must get the field in shape for the season

3 Two other people said that the manager must get the field in shape for the season

4 The announcer asked when will the manager get the field in shape for the season

5 Why didn't the announcer ask when will the manager get the field in shape for the season

6 Imagine if the announcer had said that the manager should get the field in shape for the season

7 The announcer shouted into the microphone the manager should get the field in shape for the season

Practice 8

Punctuate these sentences. Add capital letters where necessary.

1 "We asked them to come for dinner, she said

2 She said, We asked you to come for dinner, too"

3 The salesman said that we would receive our order within two weeks

4 I believe him do you

5 "If you are planning to drive the car back home" I said "Please be sure to check the tires first

6 After finishing the fourth chapter entitled "Getting Your Puppy Trained" I thought I could do a good job

7 After you drive the car out of the garage take out all the gardening tools she instructed

8 Did you say "Meet me in one hour"

9 "Did you hear that" Alice inquired

10 "Get off the stands. They're collapsing" the announcer shouted.

More Punctuation: Colon, Hyphen, Apostrophe, Dash, Parentheses, Brackets

Although we use them less frequently, we need to know how to use these forms of punctuation. Study the checklist below, and then try the practice exercise.

1 The Colon

Use a colon to introduce a list. For example:
Don't forget to bring up the following: the attendance report, the new employee kitchen, and raises.

Use a colon after the salutation in a business letter. For example:
Dear Mr. White:

Use a colon between numbers that show time. For example:
Please be home for dinner by 7:30.

2 The Hyphen

Use a hyphen to divide a word at the end of a line. Always divide words between syllables. For example:
Some people are natural-born athletes.

Use a hyphen to divide compound numbers from twenty-one to ninety-nine. For example:
forty-two, twenty-three, eighty-seven

Use a hyphen when you add some prefixes or when you add *self-* before another word. For example:
non-American   self-respect
ex-partner   self-reliant

3 The Apostrophe

Use an apostrophe to show that one or more letters have been left out of a word (a contraction). For example:
Mac isn't (is not) meeting us until 9 P.M.
I'll (I will) call you when we're (we are) ready to leave.
It's (It is) too hot in here.

Use an apostrophe to show possession. (a) Place the apostrophe before the *s* in singular words. (b) Place the apostrophe after the *s* in plural words. (c) Some words become plural by other spelling changes. For example:
the cat's meow (singular)
the cats' meow (plural)
the cow's pasture
the cows' pasture
the woman's office
the women's office
the baby's cries
the babies' cries
the child's school
the children's school

Names follow the same rules. For example:
Ms. Paulsen's coat   The Paulsens' property
Mr. Dawson's coat   The Dawsons' car
Ms. Jones's class   The Joneses' property

Use an apostrophe to show the plural of letters and numbers. For example:
Start the math game with the 1's in the top row.
Z's are the hardest letters to use in a word game.

STUDY TIP

Don't use an apostrophe in possessive pronouns: theirs, its, hers, whose. For example:

The house is theirs.
The animal carried its weight in supplies.
The blue one is hers.
Whose is this?

4 The Dash

Use dashes to mark an important interruption in the sentence. For example:
Your voice—as beautiful as it is—should not be heard above everyone else's.

Use a dash to sum up previous words. For example:
Promptness, enthusiasm, and knowledge—these are the things we're looking for in our new candidate.

5 Parentheses

Words in parentheses are not directly related to the main thought of the sentence. They are an *aside* or an *addition* not absolutely necessary to the thought. For example:
We definitely included that information (see Section 2.A).

Practice 9

Choose the correct word and punctuation in the parentheses.

1 (Its/It's) only 3 P.M.

2 Her thirteen-year-old is not as (self-reliant/self reliant) as she thinks she is.

3 That (restaurant's/restaurants) food is too expensive.

4 In your backpack, carry the (following;/following:) water, a pen knife, some crackers, cheese, and trail mix.

5 When I turned (thirty nine/thirty-nine), I stopped smoking.

6 Call me when (it's/its) time to go.

7 The mother cat carried (it's/its) kittens to safety.

8 Even though Evan knew the manager of the company, he started the letter, Dear Mr. (Murray,/Murray:).

9 The six town (councilors/councilors') decided to table the issue.

10 We planned our get-away(—in an antique car—/in an antique, car) following the reception.

Answer Key

Practice 1

1. If you ask me, our leader, Bruce M. Wheeler, needs to learn more about leading a group. Successful group work depends to a great extent on the skills of the leader. Our leader absolutely does not believe in imposing any standards. Would you rather have no rules or a few sensible rules of procedure and conduct? Anything less must lead to anarchy.

2. In June, we'll move to our new two-room office. Our moving list will include paper and pencil supplies. Yours should concentrate on furniture and lighting. Dan will concentrate on the computers and other hardware. The office can be moved quickly if we all cooperate. Do you think we can be ready by May 31?

3. Yesterday, I told my boss that I would be happy to work on the new project. He was very glad to get my message. He's had trouble selling the idea to our team. Management really wants full cooperation. What do you do when four of the five team members are unenthusiastic? Pray!

WHEN SHOULD I USE A COMMA?

When you use the English language, some rules are very clear. For example, there is no dispute about the word *ain't*. You should not use it—ever. Neither do you say, "I don't never want to see that textbook again." However, when it comes to commas, we don't seem to be as confident, sure, or secure in making decisions. Now you will have the opportunity to study the important uses of commas, and when you finish, you will be very confident in your decisions.

Practice 2

Citizens can make a difference in their community and in the world. Without doubt, the first step is to identify problems. Look at community needs, strengths, and resources. As a result of their investigation, people can form and express opinions. Of course, all involved in community action must be willing to work with others. In this way, citizens can impact their communities and the world around them.

Practice 3

How do things get done in a community? When citizens have a common purpose, they interact with others to get things done. In order to do that, people must respect others. They need, first, to understand the power of diversity.

Practice 4

1. communicate?
2. not, people communication.
3. planning. Others
4. Or, communication makes
5. Correct as is

Practice 5—Review

1. lunch having
2. Dear Mom,
   Please send money.
   Love,
   Sam
3. I'll mow the lawn, fertilize it, and pull the weeds if you want me to.
4. Fragment. Possible correction: When I have finished, and you are ready, and the new equipment has arrived, let's go home.
5. Because he was late six times this year,
6. will disband, and a new team
7. available, we'll meet September 20, 2016.
8. attend,"
9. Fragment. Possible correction: Before the event and after my promotion, we'll go out for dinner.
10. Fragment. Possible correction: After outrunning the children and entering the house, I showered.

Practice 6—Review

1. computer course, an introduction to health care, and a
2. week; please don't call me. OR week. Please
3. lot.
4. Shelley said, "Meet
5. plans; therefore, I
6. Rain, hail, and snow
7. visit us,
8. test. He
9. comfort him; however, nothing
10. sleek, red, fast sports car for my birthday. Do you think I'll get one?

Practice 7—Review

1. The announcer said, "The manager must get the field in shape for the season."
2. The announcer said that the manager must get the field in shape for the season.
3. Two other people said that the manager must get the field in shape for the season.
4. The announcer asked, "When will the manager get the field in shape for the season?"

5. Why didn't the announcer ask, "When will the manager get the field in shape for the season"?
6. Imagine if the announcer had said that the manager should get the field in shape for the season!
7. The announcer shouted into the microphone, "The manager should get the field in shape for the season!"

Practice 8
1. dinner," she said.
2. She said, "We
3. weeks.
4. I believe him; do you?
5. back home, " I said, "please . . . first."
6. chapter, entitled, "Getting Your Puppy Trained," I . . . a good job.
7. "After you . . . garage, take out . . . tools," she instructed.
8. Did you say, "Meet me in one hour"?
9. "Did you hear that?" Alice inquired.
10. collapsing!" the announcer shouted.

Practice 9
1. It's
2. self-reliant
3. restaurant's
4. following:
5. thirty-nine
6. it's
7. its
8. Murray:
9. councilors
10. —in an antique car—

LESSON 6: Constructing Sentences and Paragraphs

Ms. Santos continued to press her students for perfect English usage. She also insisted that they master another skill. They must use their best English in well-constructed sentences and paragraphs. Ken, Mike, and Michelle all agreed about one thing: The earlier discussion of punctuation, especially commas and semicolons, helped them. Now they were thinking much more about using punctuation effectively and correctly to combine ideas in sentences and in paragraphs.

Ms. Santos also wanted her students to think about the structure of paragraphs. After all, well-structured paragraphs would support their ideas and construct solid arguments. She explained that each sentence must lead to the next. They would soon know more about writing topic sentences and supporting details. You will learn more about this toward the end of this lesson.

Words to Know

Subordination	Making one part less important than another
Data	Information, such as facts and figures
Succinct	With no wasted words
Sporadic	Occurring occasionally
Commonwealth	A nation in which the people govern

One of the first discussions took place after Ms. Santos asked the class to punctuate the sentences in Practice 1. She also advised them that the sentences illustrated another problem.

First, can you find any incorrect punctuation in these sentences? Then, can you explain what is structurally wrong with these sentences? *Hint:* Decide if the words and thoughts are parallel. That is, is each part of the sentence expressed in the same grammatical form? Before you try Practice 1, read this example:

Check your bank statement   and contact the bank in a prompt way if you find errors.

In the first half of the sentence, the writer instructs you to report *honestly* (an adverb describes *write*). In the second half of the sentence, you are told to report the facts *in a succinct way.* How can you change that prepositional phrase (*in a succinct way*) to match the *-ly* adverb, *honestly?* The answer, of course, is to change the phrase to one word: *succinctly.* Now the sentence is parallel.

Check your bank statement *carefully* and contact the bank *promptly* if you find errors.

Practice 1

Correct any punctuation errors in these sentences. Rewrite the sentences so that they are parallel.

1 The long-time assistant was faithful; prompt, and with honesty.

2 Some doctors give patients very little nutritional advice; are saying little about exercise, and they're silent on lifestyle.

3 I like to sing in the shower and dancing in the kitchen.

4 The team worked on the project quickly; confidently, and efficient.

5 This weekend I will buy fabric for the new drapes, choose a paint color, and then I'll be emptying the cabinets.

6 Mike is not only a good computer analyst but a gifted mathematician also.

You probably realized that these sentences have more than punctuation problems. They are not parallel. Sentence 1, for example, contains two descriptive words, *faithful* and *prompt,* followed by a prepositional phrase, *with honesty.* As we have said, to be parallel, a sentence must repeat like structures. Change the prepositional phrase to a descriptive word. In addition, change the semicolon to a comma. (Look back to the comma-in-a-series rule.)

The long-time assistant was faithful, prompt, and honest.

Sentence 2 tries to inform us that doctors are deficient in advice on three topics. How can you express those three topics in a parallel way? Start by changing the semicolon to a comma in a series.

Some doctors give patients very little nutritional, exercise, or lifestyle advice.

Sentence 3 has no punctuation problem. However, the sentence does not have parallel structure. The actions, or verbs, are not the same: *to sing* and *dancing.* One or the other needs to change.

I like to *sing* in the shower and *dance* in the kitchen.

or

I like *singing* in the shower and *dancing* in the kitchen.

Sentence 4 uses a semicolon instead of a comma in a series. In addition, only two of the three descriptive words (adverbs) are parallel: *clearly* and *promptly.* How would you change *fair* to give it a parallel form? Think about what you learned regarding adverb endings.

The team worked on the project quickly, confidently, and efficiently.

Sentence 5 has two verbs that are parallel: *buy* and *choose.* The third verb, *emptying,* is in the *-ing* form. How can you change it to match the others? The answer, of course is, to remove the *-ing.* The correct form is *empty.*

This weekend I will *buy* fabric for the new drapes, *choose* a paint color, and *empty* the cabinets.

Sentence 6 says that Mike is two things: a *good computer analyst* and a *gifted mathematician.* What two phrases relate computer analyst to mathematician? You probably realize that the answer includes *not only* and *but also. Not only* comes directly before *computer analyst;* consequently, *but also* must be placed before *gifted mathematician.*

Mike is not only a good computer analyst but also a gifted mathematician.

You will read more about words that combine ideas later in this lesson.

Practice 2

Restructure these sentences. Correct errors to make each construction parallel.

1 Professor Egbert is fair and has intelligence.

_____

2 Yoga is both invigorating and makes me tired.

_____

3 Our mentoring program involves both managers and peers are involved too.

_____

4 I like to research the subject, write a first draft, and then I'm doing a final draft.

_____

5 I love gardening and to cook.

_____

Combining Ideas

Good writing is usually simple, correct, and natural sounding. However, you need to learn to connect thoughts in order to make sentences more interesting and more meaningful. The punctuation you have studied, plus connecting words, will help you create better sentences and paragraphs. Read this paragraph from a personal evaluation:

> I had not had the opportunity to help my coworkers address their concerns. It was a test of my ability as team leader to succeed in a totally different task. I had to maintain a balance of leadership and acceptance. It was my job to provide a creative environment.

There are no grammatical or spelling errors in this paragraph. Still, we can improve the sentences in this paragraph by combining the flow of ideas. First, every time you start a sentence with "_It was, It is,_ or _This is,_" stop and ask yourself how you might join the sentence with the one before. You will need a combining word and punctuation. For example, how would you combine sentences one and two and delete "It was"? How could you combine sentences three and four and, again, delete "It was"? Write your answers here.

_____

_____

_____

> You probably combined the sentences in this way:

> Before this, I had not had the opportunity to help my coworkers address their concerns, so it was a test of my ability as team leader to succeed in a totally different task. I had to maintain a balance of leadership and acceptance because it was my job to provide a creative environment.

or

Before this, I had not had the opportunity to help my coworkers address their concerns; consequently, it was a test of my ability as team leader to succeed in a totally different task.

or

Before this, I had not had an opportunity to help my coworkers address their concerns; therefore, it was a test of my ability as team leader to succeed in a totally different task.

STUDY TIP
The last words in a sentence "grab" your reader's attention.

Combining sentences sometimes requires you to make one part less important than the other. This is called *subordination*. First, you decide on your emphasis. For example, look at the last sentence in the sample paragraph above. The complete thought that comes after the comma receives the greater emphasis. True of sentences in general, the final words do receive the emphasis. What if the writer decided that *a balance of leadership and acceptance* required emphasis? Then the sentence could be turned around. The introductory words would then begin with a subordinating word: *Because.* And this is where the punctuation you studied becomes very important. When you use a subordinating word to start a sentence, you need to punctuate before the complete thought. Note the comma before the complete thought:

Because it was my job to provide a creative environment, I had to maintain a balance of leadership and acceptance.

Subordinating words are important to know about. Here is a list of them.

Subordinating Words

although   after   if   though

as   because   unless

when   since   where   whereas

Practice 3

Subordinate one part of the sentence to the other. Choose a subordinating word from the list above. Insert the appropriate punctuation.

1 You shred the unusable paper. I'll put the report together.

2 We bought a new computer. We figured out which system would work better for us.

3 You need to get the report to me by July 2. The data won't be on time to be considered.

4 We requested the supplies three weeks ago. They have not arrived yet.

5 You didn't take my advice. I pleaded with you.

You have also learned about using commas or semicolons to connect sentences. Below is a list of words used with commas and semicolons. In the first list, you will find words that combine sentences of equal importance. The second group of words also joins ideas of equal importance. However, these are used in pairs.

Words That Link Equal Ideas

and	also	nor
or	however	but
yet	moreover	for
so	further, furthermore	then
therefore	thus	accordingly
also	besides	consequently

Words That Link One Sentence Element to Another

either—or

neither—nor

both—and

not only—but also

whether—or

Practice 4

In these sentences, insert words that link equal ideas. Use the words in the list above. Remember that a semicolon follows longer connecting words.

1 I'll finish my work first. Then I'll leave.

2 I've put hours and hours into creating the new filing system. No one uses it.

3 You could take the bus. You could take the train.

4 Her boss wrote in the memo, "I like the work you've been doing. I'm going to recommend a promotion."

5 Our computers don't have enough memory. We will buy new computers for the support staff.

Practice 5

Fill the spaces in the sentences below with words from the list above.

1 _____ you _____ I have a reason to complain.

2 I've decided that I'll carry _____ my computer _____ my gym bag.

3 The scientist couldn't explain _____ the cause _____ the effect.

4 Your employment agreement promises _____ _____ a week of vacation _____ _____ seven sick days.

5 We have to decide _____ we have enough staff _____ if we need to interview more people.

Practice 6

Michelle attended a training seminar to prepare for a job interview. The following paragraph is an incorrect version of the training manual. Use all that you have learned about commas and semicolons to make this paragraph flow smoothly. Look above at the two lists of words that link ideas. Use any of these that are appropriate.

> You will graduate from the college in June. You will go on interviews. Prepare for the interview. It is something like a final exam. The interview is the exam. Do your homework. Study the company for the interview. Think about the questions you will be asked. Think about the answers you will give. Pass the exam. It means more than answering a few questions. Be courteous. Be poised. Look good.

_____

_____

_____

_____

_____

Practice 7

The training manual continues. Continue to link ideas by using words that bring thoughts together.

> Few people think about the waiting room. The interview does not begin when you meet the interviewer. It begins earlier. It is in the waiting room where the interview begins. You know not to be late. Arrive about 10 minutes early. Introduce yourself to the receptionist. Choose a place to sit. It should not be in a chair where you know that you will slouch. Display good posture. Don't chew gum. Don't talk on your cell phone. Don't read a book. Remember that you are already on view.

Building Paragraphs

When you write anything—a report, a letter, or memo, for example—you are building paragraphs. Most of the time, you begin with a topic sentence. You want your reader to know as quickly as possible what to expect. Read the following paragraph. Start by asking yourself, "What is this paragraph about?" Where is the answer to that question? That is the *topic sentence.*

Note: The paragraphs below and in Practice 9 are all about Presidential Medal of Freedom winners, from 1998 to 2001.

Maya Angelou, an award-winning black writer, went through many changes in her life. She even started life with a different name. She was born Marguerite Johnson in 1928. As a child, she shuttled back and forth between St. Louis, a tiny town in Arkansas, and San Francisco. After she was assaulted, she stopped speaking for four years. Only her brother Bailey heard her voice in those years.

You would probably agree that you knew the topic of the paragraph as soon as you read the first sentence. You expected the sentences that followed to list the changes. They are the supporting details. Make a list of the changes below.

_____

_____

_____

Find the topic sentence in the following paragraph. Underline it. What details support the topic? List them on the lines that follow.

The Presidential Medal of Freedom has been awarded for over 50 years. President John F. Kennedy wanted to honor civilians for service in peacetime. He wanted the award to be for great achievements in the arts and sciences. Many other fields have been recognized as well. President Lyndon B. Johnson awarded the first Medal of Freedom award after Kennedy's death. President Kennedy was awarded the medal posthumously.

_____

_____

_____

Sometimes writers want to summarize the main idea in the last sentence. They can do that by placing the topic sentence at the end of the paragraph. Look at the following paragraph. Which sentence contains the topic? Explain your answer on the lines below.

Maya Angelou went to high school in San Francisco until 1944. After she dropped out, she trained to become the first black cable car conductor in the city. Maya returned to high school and graduated in 1945. In the 1950s, she studied dance in New York and appeared as a singer in New York and San Francisco. Maya's education was sporadic and varied.

_____

_____

_____

Check your answer in the Answer Key.

Practice 8

Read these paragraphs. Find the topic sentence in each one and underline it. List at least two details that support the topic sentence.

A. Maya Angelou had a series of important jobs. She served as an assistant to the director of a school of music and drama in Ghana. She worked as an editor of *The Arab Observer.* She also worked as an editor for *The African Review.* In addition, Maya wrote "Black, Blues, Black" for educational television.

_____

_____

B. Maya Angelou's distinguished career continued. She became very well known in 1970 for her autobiography, *I Know Why the Caged Bird Sings.* She finished three more volumes of her autobiography by 1990. She continued to publish books and poetry until 2013, the year before her death.

_____

_____

Now you have a topic sentence. How do you organize the paragraph? Ideas are organized logically. As you have seen, paragraphs can be organized by dates. You can tell where each idea should appear. Look at the next paragraph. Decide where this sentence should be inserted: She even acted on television in 1987.

C. Other creative activities followed as Maya Angelou used all of her many talents. Angelou received an Emmy for her TV performance in *Roots.* On January 20, 1993, Angelou participated in President Bill Clinton's inauguration. She recited her poem, "On the Pulse of Morning."

_____

_____

Practice 9

Follow the directions for each of the following exercises. Compare your answers to those in the Answer Key. Your answers may be different, yet still correct.

Insert this sentence where it logically belongs in time: She was re-elected twice.

A. Wilma Mankiller: Campaigner for Civil Rights and Winner of the Presidential Medal of Freedom in 1998

    Born in 1945, Wilma Mankiller rose out of poverty and great hardship. Wilma was appointed principal chief of the Cherokee Nation of Oklahoma in 1985. In 1987, she became the first elected female leader of a major Indian tribe. Wilma was known for being an effective leader. She worked to reduce Cherokee infant mortality. She also improved the health and educational systems. Wilma was well known for promoting Cherokee business interests.

_____

_____

In the next paragraph, insert this sentence where it belongs: The name was given to the person charged with protecting the village.

B. Wilma Mankiller's family history goes back to 1907. Her great–grandfather was given land in Oklahoma. She lived on that land until her death in 2010. Mankiller is a family name and a military title. Wilma showed the same leadership. She became the first female in modern history to lead a major Native American tribe.

_____

_____

In the next paragraph, insert this sentence where it belongs: In 1974, she moved back to her homeland.

C. Wilma Mankiller's understanding of her people went back to her family's forced removal from Oklahoma. She was just a small girl when they were relocated to California. By 1969, though, her concerns for her people had grown immensely. She began teaching in preschool and in adult education programs. There, she worked to get grants for rural programs.

_____

_____

Move the Ideas Along

STUDY TIP

How else can you organize paragraphs? Instead of dates, you can use words to move the ideas along. These are called *transition* words. They move the reader from one idea to another. Here is a list of transition words. They fall into the categories named in the left column.

Category	Transition Words
Time:	now, later, after, before, last, first, while, then, first, second, finally, meanwhile, formerly
Addition:	moreover, in addition, besides, too, also, furthermore
Similarity:	just as, similarly, in the same way, likewise
Contrast:	yet, but, however, although, nevertheless, on the contrary, on the other hand, whereas, nonetheless
Illustration:	for example, for instance, to illustrate, specifically, in this way
Emphasis:	indeed, clearly, in fact, certainly
Conclusion:	therefore, consequently, in conclusion, in other words

Use these words from the time category in the following paragraph: *first, then, meanwhile, finally.*

Making brownies includes these steps. Shop for all the ingredients in the recipe. Have all of them handy before you begin. Preheat the oven to 350°. Mix the dry ingredients and add the wet ones. Pour the mixture into a greased, 11 × 13 pan and bake for 25 minutes.

Your paragraph may look like this. Other answers are possible.

Making brownies includes these steps. *First,* shop for all the ingredients in the recipe. Have all of them handy before you begin. *Then,* preheat the oven to 350°. *Meanwhile,* mix the dry ingredients and add the wet ones. *Finally,* pour the mixture into a greased, 11 × 13 pan and bake for 25 minutes.

Practice 10

Use two of these connecting words (contrast words) to build your paragraph: *however, on the other hand,* or *nevertheless.* Check your answer in the Answer Key.

A. Luis Muñoz Marin, also a Presidential Medal of Freedom winner, was born in 1898. Puerto Ricans consider the year important for another reason: The United States acquired Puerto Rico from Spain. It was Marin who showed Puerto Ricans how to use their freedom.

In paragraph B, you have two jobs. First, find the sentence that does not support the topic. Cross it out. Then use words that show addition of ideas. Choose one from this list: *in addition, besides, furthermore.* Insert the word in the paragraph.

B. As a senator, Luis Muñoz Marin was known for starting very important programs. He ran for the senate in Puerto Rico in the 1920s. While in the senate, he started Operation Bootstrap. This program encouraged Puerto Ricans to help themselves by improving health and education conditions. The program improved farming methods and created new industries.

In paragraph C, can you find two sentences that could easily be combined? Then, add the word *finally* to the beginning of a later sentence.

C. Marin was Puerto Rico's first elected governor. He was elected in 1949. He started Operation Commonwealth. The purpose of the program was to increase self-rule. In 1952, Puerto Rico became a commonwealth of the United States.

In the following paragraph, decide which sentence does not belong. Cross it out. Then, use these words to connect ideas: *for instance, in this way.*

D. Marin had one more phase to his plan. He put Operation Serenity into effect. Marin thought that Puerto Ricans could enjoy life more. Theater, dance, and literature could be a part of their lives. Marin encouraged development and enjoyment of the arts. In 1964, Marin decided not to run for a fifth term as governor.

Answer Key

Practice 1

1. The long-time assistant was faithful, prompt, and honest.
2. Some doctors give patients very little nutritional advice, say little about exercise, and are silent on lifestyle.
3. I like to sing in the shower and dance in the kitchen.
4. The team worked on the project quickly, confidently, and efficiently.
5. This weekend I will buy fabric, choose a paint color, and empty the cabinets.
6. Mike is not only a good computer analyst but also a gifted mathematician.

Practice 2

1. Professor Egbert is fair and intelligent.
2. Yoga is both invigorating and tiring.
3. Our mentoring program involves both managers and peers.
4. I like to research the subject, write a first draft, and then do a final draft.
5. I love gardening and cooking.
   or
   I love to garden and to cook.

Practice 3

Your sentences may look something like this:
1. After you shred the unusable paper, I'll put the report together.
2. When we figured out which system would work better for us, we bought a new computer.
3. Unless you get the report to me by July 2, the data won't be on time to be considered.
4. Though we requested the supplies three weeks ago, they have not arrived yet.
5. Although I pleaded with you, you didn't take my advice.

Practice 4

Your choice of connecting words may be different, yet correct. In sentence 4, for example, you might have chosen *therefore, thus,* or *accordingly.*
1. I'll finish my work first and then I'll leave. Study Tip: When two short sentences are combined with *and,* you don't need to use a comma between them.
2. I've put hours and hours into creating the new filing system, but no one uses it.
3. You could take the bus or you could take the train. (See the Study Tip above.)
4. Her boss wrote in the memo, "I like the work you've been doing; consequently, I'm going to recommend a promotion."
5. Our computers don't have enough memory; therefore, we will buy new computers for the support staff.

Practice 5

1. Neither you nor I
2. both my computer and my gym bag
3. either the cause or the effect
4. not only a week . . . but also seven
5. whether we have enough staff or if we need

Practice 6

When you prepare for interviews, think of them as final exams. Do your homework not only by studying about the company but also by thinking about answers to the questions you will be asked. Passing the exam means more than just answering a few questions; courtesy, poise, and appearance all count.

Practice 7

Your paragraph may look something like this.

Your interview begins before you meet the interviewer; it begins earlier, in the waiting room. Of course, you know not to be late, but did you know that you should arrive about 10 minutes early? First, introduce yourself to the receptionist. Then choose a chair in which you won't slouch and you will display good posture. Don't chew gum, talk on your cell phone, or read a book, because you are already on view.

Building Paragraphs

Paragraph 1
Her name was changed.
She shuttled between Arkansas and California.
She stopped speaking for four years.

Paragraph 2
Topic sentence: The Presidential Medal of Freedom has been awarded for over 50 years.

Details:

JFK wanted to honor civilians in peacetime for achievements in the arts and sciences.
Many other fields have been recognized as well.
President Lyndon B. Johnson gave the first medal after JFK's death.
President Kennedy was awarded the medal posthumously.

Paragraph 3
The main idea is summarized in the last sentence, "Maya's education was sporadic and varied." The other sentences support the main idea with details.

Practice 8

A. Topic sentence: Maya Angelou had a series of important jobs.
Supporting details:

    1 Assistant to the director of a school
    2 An editor of *The Arab Review*
    3 An editor of *The African Review*
    4 Wrote for educational television

B. Maya Angelou's distinguished career continued.

   1 had published *I Know Why the Caged Bird Sings*

   2 finished three more autobiographical volumes by 1990

   3 She continued to publish books and poetry until 2013, the year before her death.

C. Other creative activities followed as Ms. Angelou used all of her many talents.

   1 received an Emmy

   2 participated in Bill Clinton's inauguration

   3 recited her poem, "On the Pulse of Morning," at the inauguration

Practice 9

A. Insert "She was re-elected twice" after sentence three.

B. Insert after sentence four.

C. Insert as the next-to-last sentence.

Practice 10

A. Luis Muñoz Marin, also a Presidential Medal of Freedom winner, was born in Puerto Rico in 1898. However, Puerto Ricans consider the year important for another reason: The United States acquired Puerto Rico from Spain. But, it was Marin who showed Puerto Ricans how to use their freedom.

B. Delete this sentence: He ran for the senate in Puerto Rico in the 1920s.

As a senator, Luis Muñoz Marin is known for starting very important programs. While in the senate, he started Operation Bootstrap. This program encouraged Puerto Ricans to help themselves by improving health and education conditions. Furthermore (or in addition), the program improved farming methods and created new industries.

C. Combine the first two sentences.

In 1949, Marin became Puerto Rico's first elected governor. He started Operation Commonwealth. The purpose of the program was to increase self-rule. Finally, in 1952, Puerto Rico became a commonwealth of the United States.

D. Delete this sentence: In 1964, Marin decided not to run for a fifth term as governor.

Marin had one more phase to his plan. He put Operation Serenity into effect. Marin thought that Puerto Ricans could enjoy life more. For instance, theater, dance, and literature could be a part of their lives. In this way, Marin encouraged development and enjoyment of the arts.

Spelling Pretest

For numbers 1 through 20, choose the word that is spelled correctly and best completes the sentence.

1   A _____ wind blew the sailboat across the finish line.

   A   phenomenil

   B   phenominal

   C   phenomenal

   D   phenomenul

2   Was Tom _____ to you?

   A   referred

   B   refferred

   C   refered

   D   refurred

3   I am thinking of hiring Anna because of her reputation for great _____ .

   A   stubility

   B   stabilaty

   C   stebility

   D   stability

4   We did three new _____ for that product.

   A   comercials

   B   commertials

   C   commercials

   D   commertiels

5   Some people require very close _____ at work; others don't.

   A   managment

   B   management

   C   manugement

   D   manigement

6   Is this a _____ time for you?

   A   convenient

   B   convienent

   C   convinient

   D   conveinient

7   That is a _____ in the problem that we had not thought of.

   A   vareable

   B   variable

   C   varible

   D   vareable

8   The new bookcase is so large we will have to be sure it is _____ .

   A   stationery

   B   stationury

   C   stationerery

   D   stationary

9 We didn't go to bed until _____ .

A midnite

B midnihgt

C midnight

D midnieght

10 Your _____ whining will not get the job done any faster.

A incessant

B inseccent

C insessant

D incessunt

11 Can you imagine a _____ to *Titanic?*

A seqel

B sequal

C sequel

D sequil

12 We'll _____ at noon.

A conveen

B convene

C conveine

D conveene

13 Remember to show your _____ as you enter the conference.

A credentials

B credencials

C credentails

D credencails

14 That is one _____ step.

A unneccessary

B unneccesary

C unnessary

D unnecessary

15 This directive _____ all the others you have received.

A superceedes

B supersedes

C superseeds

D superceeds

16 That music has a _____ beat.

A rhithmic

B rhuthmic

C rhythmic

D rhithmyc

17 When this company decides to hire someone, Human Resources sends a letter of _____ .

A acceptunce

B acceptense

C acceptance

D acceptince

18 Our _____ is at least 30 hours per week.

A requirement

B requirment

C requiremunt

D requiremint

19 It is _____ to park in some places.

A illegil

B illegal

C ilegal

D illegall

20   Your children bear a remarkable _____ to you.

    A   resemblance

    B   resemblence

    C   resemblanse

    D   resemblince

Answer Key

1. C; phenomenal
2. A; referred
3. D; stability
4. C; commercials
5. B; management
6. A; convenient
7. B; variable
8. D; stationary
9. C; midnight
10. A; incessant
11. C; sequel
12. B; convene
13. A; credentials
14. D; unnecessary
15. B; supersedes
16. C; rhythmic
17. C; acceptance
18. A; requirement
19. B; illegal
20. A; resemblance

To the Student: As you check your answers, record the results in this chart. Use the three columns next to the Answer Key to mark your answers as *Correct*, *Incorrect*, or *Skipped*. Use the other columns to record additional information you want to remember about the individual questions. Total the number of your responses in each column at the bottom of the chart. Then read the recommendations that follow.

Spelling Skills Assessment: Answers and Skills Analysis						
Item Answers	Correct T	Incorrect X	Skipped O	I have this question.	I need instruction.	Spelling Skill Categories*
1 C						1
2 A						2
3 D						1
4 C						2
5 B						3
6 A						1
7 B						1
8 D						3
9 C						2
10 A						3
11 C						1
12 B						1
13 A						2
14 D						3
15 B						1
16 C						1
17 C						3
18 A						3
19 B						2
20 A						1
TOTALS	Correct	Incorrect	Skipped	Questions	Instruction	Skills

* Key to Spelling Skill Categories
1 Vowels
2 Consonants
3 Structural Units

Note: These categories of spelling skills are broken down into subcategories as well. On page 5, question numbers are aligned with the subcategories as well. Return to Section 5 to review the rules.

Spelling Skills Analysis

Vowel

Short	16
Long	6, 12, 15
Schwa	1, 3, 7, 11, 20

Consonant

Variant Spelling	4, 13
Silent Letter	9
Double Letter	2, 19

Structural Unit

Homonym	8
Similar Word Part	10, 14, 17
Root	5
Suffix	18

To identify the areas in which you need improvement in the Spelling Section, do three things:

Total your number of correct answers out of the possible 20 answers. To score a passing grade you should have 95 percent correct (or 19 correct answers).

Total the number of correct answers in each skill subcategory. For example, in the subset *Schwa*, there are five correct answers. To score a passing grade, you should have 95 percent correct (or 4 correct answers).

Keep a list of your spelling errors and follow the directions for improvement in the Study Tip on page 265.

How Do I Become a Better Speller?

STUDY TIP

Some people seem to be "natural" spellers. For others, correct spelling is not an easy skill to acquire. If spelling is a problem for you, try a more organized approach to learning. First, understand that you cannot learn to spell every word you need in a short time. Instead, take your time and do a small amount of studying at any one time. Try the following plan.

- Keep a small notebook handy to record words that you have spelled incorrectly or that are new to you.
- When you enter a word into the notebook, divide it into syllables. Make sure that you are spelling and pronouncing it correctly. Check with a dictionary or use the spelling/dictionary tool on your computer.
- Look at the word. Say it in syllables.
- Think about whether a common spelling rule applies.
- Close your eyes and picture the word.
- Write the word. Check it. Write it again if necessary.
- Review a word until you are sure you know how to spell it.

STUDY TIP

Do you remember the discussion of the different types of learners? You should think about how you prefer to learn when you study words. Do you prefer to move around as you study? Do it! Have your list handy and spell the words out loud as you walk.

If you learn better by listening, dictate the words into a recorder and then listen to the way the words are spelled. In any case, make writing one of the steps in the learning process. For some, the writing may not be the first step.

What You Have to Know

To improve your spelling, you need to know the following:

1 Vowels, a, e, i, o, u, and sometimes y
   A Vowel sounds can be <u>short</u>, as the *a* in *apple* or the *e* in *test*.
   B Vowel sounds can be <u>long</u>, as the *i* in *fine* or the *o* in *pole*.
   C The vowel *y* provides different sounds depending on the word in which it is used: *scary* (long *e*), *rhythmic* (short *i*).
   D Vowel sounds are sometimes dropped, or not clearly long or short. Listen to the *o* in *conclude* or the first *e* in *absence*. They are dropped vowel sounds. A dropped vowel sound is called a *schwa*. In the dictionary, the schwa is printed this way: ə.

2 Consonants, which are the rest of the alphabet
   A Single consonants such as *d* and *g* in *dog*
   B Combinations such as *sh* in *shut* and *ch* in *church*
   C Letters that have more than one sound, such as the *j* sound in *jaw* which becomes *dg* in *edge*

3 Combinations of consonants and vowels that sound the same but are spelled differently in different words: *par<u>tial</u>*, *cru<u>cial</u>*

4 Silent letters as in *ni<u>gh</u>t*

5 Homonyms, or words that sound the same but have different meanings, such as *stationary* (meaning *place*) and *stationery* (meaning *paper*)

6 Syllables, or how letters are put together in small units of sound. Any word that contains more than one syllable has an accent on one of those syllables.

Example: bi-Ó-gra-phy. This word is made up of four syllables. Say it out loud. Can you hear the *accented* or *stressed* syllable? Yes, the second syllable is stressed; therefore, it has an accent mark over it.

Practice 1

Say each of these words. Put an accent mark over the syllable you hear stressed.

1 Eng-lish

2 com-put-er

3 ab-sent

4 yes-ter-day

5 sig-na-ture

6 con-ta-gious

Rules

Don't try to learn too many rules at one time. Sometimes, however, a series of rules naturally go together. One such rule has to do with adding prefixes and suffixes to words. Prefixes are added to the beginning of a word; suffixes are added to the end.

Rule: In most cases, you can add a prefix to a word without changing the spelling of that word (add prefix *un-* to *necessary* and you have *unnecessary*).

Prefix	Meaning	Root Word	New Word
ir-	not	regular	irregular
un-	not	necessary	unnecessary
mal-	badly	nourished	malnourished

Practice 2

Use the negative prefixes below to make new words that are the opposites of the words listed.

ir-   il-   im-   un-

1 possible

2 legal

3 reverent

4 complicated

5 available

Rule: When you add a suffix that begins with a consonant, the spelling does not change (with few exceptions).

Word	Suffix	New Word
quick	-ly	quickly
careful	-ly	carefully
careless	-ness	carelessness
economic	-al	economical

Exceptions

true   -ly   truly
due   -ly   duly

Rule: When you add a suffix that begins with a vowel to a word that ends in *e*, drop the *e* before you add the suffix.

Word	Suffix	New Word
continue	-ous	continuous
fame	-ous	famous

Exceptions: Words that end in *ge* or *ce* must keep the final *e* in order to retain the soft sound of *g* or *c*.

Word	Suffix	New Word
notice	able	noticeable

Another exception is the word *dye*.

Dye + -ing = dyeing

Rule: Suffixes change the spelling of words that end in *y*.

Word	Suffix	New Word
happy	-ness	happiness
necessary	-ily	necessarily
hearty	-ily	heartily

Practice 3

Circle the word in each sentence that is spelled incorrectly.

1 The movie was not fameous for its good story.

2 Happyness means different things to different people.

3 She was noticably thinner after her illness.

4 I am truely sorry.

5 Carlessness is not an option.

Rule: When a one-syllable action word ends in a consonant preceded by a vowel, double the final consonant before you add the suffix.

run   runner

plan   planned

thin   thinner

Rule: When a two-syllable word ends in a consonant preceded by a vowel and is accented on the second syllable double the final consonant before you add the suffix.

refer   referred

occur   occurrence

Rule: In a two- or three-syllable word, if the accent changes from the final syllable to a preceding one when a suffix is added, do not double the final consonant.

prefer   preference

confer   conference

Practice 4

Circle the letter of the word spelled incorrectly in each line.

1 **A** unanimous **B** nominate **C** confer **D** suning

2 **A** occurred **B** painter **C** thinest **D** satisfactory

3 **A** developped **B** prefer **C** funny **D** wonderful

4 **A** preferrence **B** reference **C** refined **D** conferred

5 **A** except **B** occurred **C** baddly **D** stun

Practice 5

Read each sentence. Correct any word that is spelled incorrectly. If there is no error, leave the space blank.

1 It ocured to me to check the weather report before I left. _____

2 John was refered to me as a possible candidate for the job. _____

3 Your bad attitude has never deterred me. _____

4 I consider myself a runer, not just a fast walker. _____

5 Suning yourself day after day is not a healthy thing to do. _____

Rule: *i* before *e* except after *c*.

believe

receive

Exceptions: *e* before *i* in words that have a long *a* sound (neighbor).

neighbor

weigh

More Exceptions: weird, leisure, neither, seize

Practice 6

Choose the word in parentheses that is spelled correctly.

1 I will feel great (relief/releif) once I have finished my report.

2 Does your (neice/niece) come to stay with you every summer?

3 "(Sieze/Seize) the day" is a famous saying.

4 Once she (deceived/decieved) me, I couldn't be her friend.

5 We'll have more (liesure/leisure) time next month.

Rules: Here are nine rules for forming plurals of words.

1 Add an *s* at the end of most words.

rug	rugs
shoe	shoes

2 Add *es* to words ending in *o* preceded by a consonant.

hero	heroes
tomato	tomatoes

3 Add only an *s* to words ending in *o* preceded by a consonant that refer to music.

alto	altos
piano	pianos

4 Add *es* to words ending in *s, sh, ch,* and *x*.

boss	bosses
crush	crushes
church	churches
sex	sexes

5 Change *y* to *i* and add *es* to words that end in *y* preceded by a consonant.

fly   flies

story   stories

6 Words ending in *-ful* form their plurals by adding *s* to the end of the word.

mouthfuls

spoonfuls

7 A compound word forms its plural by adding *s* to the main word.

mother-in-law   mothers-in-law

babysitter   babysitters

8 Some words keep the same spelling for singular and plural forms. You must memorize these words.

sheep

deer

Chinese

trout

9 Some words form their plurals by irregular changes. You must memorize these words.

child	children
leaf	leaves
tooth	teeth
crisis	crises
thief	thieves
knife	knives
woman	women
louse	lice
alumnus	alumni
appendix	appendices

Practice 7

Circle the word that is spelled incorrectly in each line.

1 **A** holiday **B** bulletin **C** knifes **D** teeth

2 **A** father-in-laws **B** chairs **C** bows **D** towels

3 **A** lice **B** crises **C** childs **D** deer **E** bunches

4 **A** gestures **B** occurrences **C** bulletin **D** radioes

5 **A** trays **B** handsful **C** clients **D** women

Rule: *sede, ceed,* and *cede.* Only three words end in *ceed*

exceed   proceed   succeed

Only one word ends in *sede*:

supersede

All other words of this type are spelled with a *cede* ending.

Practice 8

Choose the correct word in each sentence.

1 This manual (superceeds/supersedes) the one from 2010.
2 (Procede/Proceed) to the corner and turn right.
3 At the meeting, Manuel (preseeded/preceded) me on the program.
4 Have you read about the states that wanted to (secede/seceed) from the union?
5 Your praise (exceeds/excedes) what I expected.

Spelling Review

Part I Find the word in each line that is spelled incorrectly. Write the word correctly. If all the words are correct, write *no error.*

1 **A** deferred **B** hoping **C** differences **D** tomatos _____
2 **A** preparing **B** walking **C** skiping **D** running _____
3 **A** ladies **B** geese **C** crises **D** teeth _____
4 **A** disappoint **B** imature **C** pianos **D** candies _____
5 **A** trucksful **B** illiterate **C** regularly **D** overrate _____
6 **A** content **B** definitly **C** unaccustomed **D** truly _____

Part II Find the word that is spelled incorrectly in each paragraph. Write the word correctly on the line provided.

1 In the absense of any bargains, we left the store. A friend had referred us to that store. Now we know that we have to do our own research. When we find a real bargain, we'll buy the sofa. _____

2 Without hesitancy, we told the salesperson, "That delivery time is not feasable. We don't even leave work until an hour later." She said, "We'll try our best to make it later." _____

3 Our changeing schedule is a problem. Many times, no matter how insistent we are about the delivery time, the item arrives before we get home. The delivery man can't leave the sofa at our front door! _____

4 We were complaining to a friend about our problem. He said, "I always insist on Saturday delivery. I tell them that if I am not there to recieve the item, they lose my business. It has always worked." _____

5 We've decided to start all over again. This time, we don't intend to loose the battle!

Part III Find the one word spelled incorrectly in each column.

Column A	Column B	Column C	Column D
really	themselves	unfold	visible
magazine	omission	pronunciation	omit
vision	studying	particular	whether
precede	weird	chief	usually
planing	efficiency	coming	defend
Wednesday	familiar	stubborness	wherever
preference	ignore	beggar	accomodate
reference	knowledge	height	challenge
salary	discipline	either	calendar
sufficient	noticable	women	ninety

Answer Key

Practice 1

1. Éng-lish
2. com-pút-er
3. áb-sent
4. yés-ter-day
5. síg-na-ture
6. con-tá-gious

Practice 2

1. impossible
2. illegal
3. irreverent
4. uncomplicated
5. unavailable

Practice 3

1. famous
2. happiness
3. noticeably
4. truly
5. carelessness

Practice 4

1. **D** sunning
2. **C** thinnest
3. **A** developed
4. **A** preference
5. **C** badly

Practice 5

1. occurred
2. referred
3. blank
4. runner
5. sunning

Practice 6

1. relief
2. niece
3. seize
4. deceived
5. leisure

Practice 7

1. **C** knives
2. **A** fathers-in-law
3. **C** children
4. **D** radios
5. **B** handfuls

Practice 8

1. supersedes
2. proceed
3. preceded
4. secede
5. exceeds

Spelling Review

PART I

1. **D** tomatoes
2. **C** skipping

3. No error

4. B immature

5. A truckfuls

6. B definitely

PART II

1. absence

2. feasible

3. changing

4. receive

5. lose

PART III

Column A	Column B	Column C	Column D
planning	noticeable	stubbornness	accommodate

Commonly Misspelled Words

Review the words that you have misspelled in the past. Try to master the spelling of ten words at a time. Use the techniques outlined in the beginning of this section.

STUDY TIP
Many Web sites offer lists of frequently misspelled words. You can also find spelling lists in many English language books. See Appendix B.

A		
abnormal	ageless	apparently
abolition	aggravate	appraisal
abscess	aggressive	appreciation
absence	aging	argument
accede	agitation	assent
accommodation	agreeable	assessment
accumulate	all right	assistance
acknowledgment	already	athletic
acquaintance	amateur	attendance
acquiesce	amplification	attendants
acquire	analogous	attorneys
actually	analysis	attribute
adaptation	analyze	auditor
adequate	answer	authentic
adjacent	anticipate	autumn
affix	anxious	auxiliary
affect	apparatus	

B

bachelor	biased	boycott
bacteria	bimonthly	brief
bankruptcy	biographer	bulletin
barely	bisect	bureau
basically	bombard	burglaries
believe	bondage	business
belligerent	bookkeeper	
benefited	boundary	

C

cafeteria	collateral	conscious
calendar	colonization	consensus
campaign	colossal	consistent
canceled	column	consultant
cancellation	commentator	continually
candor	communal	controller
census	computerized	corporal
certainty	concede	correspondence
challenger	conceive	courtesies
chameleon	concession	courtesy
changeable	conflagration	credentials
chief	congenial	criticism
chronological	congruent	cross-reference
classification	connoisseur	crucial
classified	connotation	currency
coincidence	conscience	custody
collaborate	conscientious	

D

debtor	delicious	discipline
deceive	dependent	disinterest
decision	derogatory	dispensable
deductible	descendant	dissatisfied
de-emphasize	desert	dissimilar
defective	desperately	distasteful
defendant	dessert (food)	documentary
deferred	develop	dossier
deficit	development	drastically
definite	dilemma	durable
deliberate	disappear	dyeing (to change color)

E

economical	enormous	excitable
economy	enthusiastic	exhaustible
effect	entrepreneur	exhibition
efficient	enumerate	exhibitor
elaborate	envious	exhilarate
embarrass	enzyme	existence
emergency	equipped	exonerate
emigrant	erroneous	exorbitant
eminent	error	external
emphasis	evasive	extraordinary
emphasize	exaggerate	extravagant
endorse	exceed	eyeing
endurance	excel	

F

facilitation	filament	fluorescent
facsimile	filmstrip	foliage
faculties	finalist	forcible
falsify	finally	foreign
familiarity	financial	foresee
fascinating	financier	forfeit
fastener	fissure	forty
fiendish	flecks	fourteen
fiery	flexible	function

G

gallery	glamour	grieve
galvanized	glucose	grievous
gauge	gnash	gruesome
generalization	government	guarantee
geographic	graft	guardian
geological	grammar	guidance
ghetto	grateful	guild
glamorous	gravitational	gymnast

H

handicapped	hemoglobin	hosiery
handkerchief	hemorrhage	hostage
harass	heterogeneous	hygiene
harassment	hindrance	hygienic
height	homage	hypocrisy
helium	hors d'oeuvre	

I

idiomatic	inference	intercede
ignorant	inflammatory	interim
illegitimate	influential	intermission
illustrator	infraction	interpretive
imminent	ingenuity	interruption
immovable	inhuman	intuition
impasse	innocuous	inverted
impenetrable	innuendo	involuntary
imprisonment	innumerable	irrelevant
inasmuch as	inoculate	irreparably
incidentally	input	irrigation
indict	insurance	irritable
indispensable	integrity	itemized
individual	intelligent	itinerary

J

jealous	jovial	jurisdiction
jeopardy	judgment	justice
journal	judiciary	

K

khaki	kindergarten	kinsman
kidney		

L

labeled	liable	linguist
laboratory	liaison	liquefy
ladies	libel	literally
latter	liberal	logical
league	liberate	loose
leased	license	lose
legion	lien	losing
legitimate	likeness	lovable
leisure	likewise	lucrative

M

maintain	medieval	millennium
maintenance	mediocre	miniature
maneuver	memento	minuscule
manual	merely	miscellaneous
marital	mileage	mischievous
mechanical	milieu	mislaid

M

misspell	muscle	movable
monkeys	mortgage	

O

oceanography	omitted	outdated
offense	optional	overview
omission	ordinary	overweight

P

pamphlet	pitiful	presumptuous
panicky	plagiarism	pretense
paradigm	planned	previous
parallel	playwright	principal
parasite	pneumonia	principle
pastime	politician	privilege
patience	portable	probably
patient	possession	procedure
peculiar	possibilities	proceed
people's	potato	profit
permissible	potatoes	programmed
perseverance	practically	promissory
persistent	preceding	pronunciation
persuade	preferable	pseudonym
phenomenal	preferably	psychiatric
phony	preference	publicly
physical	preparation	pursue
physician	prerogative	
picnicking	presume	

Q

quantities	questionnaire	queue
quartet		

R

raisin	regrettable	resources
rarefy	reinforce	responsibility
realize	relevant	restaurant
reasonable	rendezvous	rhapsody
receipt	repetitious	rhetorical
receive	rescind	rhyme
recognizable	resemblance	rhythm
recommend	resilience	rhythmic
reconcile	resistance	

S

sacrilegious	similar	subtlety
salable	sincerely	subtly
salaries	skeptic	succeed
salient	skillful	successor
satellite	souvenir	summarize
scenes	specialized	supersede
schedule	specifically	surprise
scissors	sponsor	surreptitious
seize	stationary (fixed)	surveillance
separate	stationery (paper)	symmetrical
siege	statistics	
sieve	strength	

T

tariff	tempt	threshold
taunt	theater	totaled
taxiing	theory	tragedy
technical	thesis	traveler
technique	thoroughly	
temperament	thought	

U

unanimous	unfortunately	unnecessary
unauthorized	uniform	unwieldy
unbearable	unify	usage
unconscious	unique	
undoubtedly	unmanageable	

V

vacancy	valuing	vinyl
vaccinate	vegetable	visible
vacillate	vengeance	volume
vacuum	verbal	voluntary
vague	villain	voucher

W

warrant	wholly	woeful
weather	width	woman's
Wednesday	wield	women's
weird	wiring	woolly
welfare	withhold	wrapped
whether	witnesses	wretched

Y

yacht	yield	yoke

Posttests

Reading

You may have heard about this famous story or even read it. The story is called "The Gift of the Magi" by O. Henry, an American who wrote in the late 1800s and early 1900s. Read a portion of the story and answer the questions.

One dollar and eighty-seven cents. That was all. And sixty cents of it was in pennies. Pennies saved one and two at a time by bulldozing the grocer and the vegetable man. One's cheeks burned with the silent charge of cost cutting that such close dealing implied. Three times Della counted it. One dollar and eighty-seven cents and the next day was Christmas.

There was clearly nothing to do but flop down on the shabby little couch and howl. So Della did it. Which sets off the idea that life is made up of sobs, sniffles, and smiles with sniffles in the majority.

While the mistress' tears gradually decrease, take a look at the home. A furnished flat, at $8 per week. It did not make description impossible, but it certainly had a beggary look.

In the hall below was a letter box with the name *Mr. James Dillingham Young.* But whenever Mr. Young came home and reached his flat, he was called Jim and greatly hugged by Mrs. Dillingham, or Della. Which is all very good.

Della finished her cry and tended to her cheeks with the powder rag. She stood by the window. She looked out dully at a gray cat walking a gray fence in a gray backyard. Tomorrow would be Christmas Day, and she had only $1.87 with which to buy Jim a present. She had been saving every penny she could for months, and with this result.

Twenty dollars a week doesn't go far. Expenses had been greater than she had calculated.

Now there were two possessions of the Youngs in which they took great pride. One was Jim's gold watch that had been his father's and his grandfather's. The other was Della's beautiful hair.

Suddenly she whirled from the window to see herself in the mirror. Rapidly she pulled down her long hair. It fell to its full length. Della went pale, and did it up again. A tear or two splashed on the new carpet.

On went her old brown jacket. On went her old brown hat. With a whirl of skirts, she went down the stairs to the street.

Where she stopped the sign read: Mme. Sofronie. Hair Goods of All Kinds. One flight up Della ran. She saw Mme. Sofronie and said, "Will you buy my hair?"

Adapted from *The Gift of the Magi,* by O. Henry.

1 O. Henry creates a dark atmosphere by

    A having Della whirl toward the mirror.

    B making the rent $18 a week.

    C using the colors brown and gray over and over again.

    D talking about Christmas presents over and over again.

2 You can conclude that Della and Jim live

    A well beyond their means.

    B on a very tight budget.

    C in one of the very best apartments in town.

    D apart for most of the time.

3 What do the words "such close dealing" mean in this context?

    A Living close together

    B Overspending regularly

    C Playing cards

    D Bargaining

4 How much rent does the couple pay?

    A $8 a month

    B $80 per week

    C $8 per week

    D $2800 per year

5 The author describes Jim's and Della's loving relationship. She sobs over her lack of money for a gift. The author's description

    A leads to why Della leaves Jim for another man.

    B builds toward Della's need to take extreme action.

    C explains why Della is unable to take any action.

    D reinforces why Della buys herself a new dress.

6 From reading Paragraphs 1 and 3, you can describe Della as

    A embarrassed about bargaining, but very caring about her husband.

    B very sorry she married Jim.

    C ready to look for a new apartment on Christmas day.

    D someone who can't get her work done in a reasonable amount of time.

7 After reading this part of the story, what do you think Della will do next?

    A She will sit and sob until Christmas.

    B She will hurry home to clean the apartment.

    C She will decide that buying a gift is unnecessary.

    D She will sell her hair and buy a gift for Jim.

Read the pages below from the FAFSA application and answer Questions 8–12.

Adapted for use in this exercise from OMB document # 18451.

FAFSA: Free Application for Federal Student Aid
FAFSA Page 2

Notes for questions 13–14 (page 3)

If you are an eligible noncitizen, write in your eight- or nine-digit Alien Registration Number. Generally, you are an eligible noncitizen if you are: (1) a U.S. permanent resident and you have an Alien Registration Receipt Card (I-551); (2) a conditional permanent resident (I-551C); or (3) an other eligible noncitizen with an Arrival-Departure Record (I-94) from the U.S. Immigration and Naturalization Service showing any one of the following designations: "Refugee," "Asylum Granted," "Indefinite Parole," "Humanitarian Parole," or "Cuban-Haitian Entrant." If you are in the U.S. on only an F1 or F2 student visa, or only a J1 or J2 exchange visitor visa, or a G series visa (pertaining to international organizations), you must fill in oval c. If you are neither a citizen nor eligible noncitizen, you are not eligible for federal student aid. However, you may be eligible for state or college aid.

Notes for questions 17–21 (page 3)

For undergraduates, full time generally means taking at least 12 credit hours in a term or 24 clock hours per week. 3/4 time generally means taking at least 9 credit hours in a term or 18 clock hours per week. Half time generally means taking at least 6 credit hours in a term or 12 clock hours per week. Provide this information about the college you plan to attend.

Notes for question 29 (page 3) — Enter the correct number in the box in question 29.

Enter **1** for 1st bachelor's degree
Enter **2** for 2nd bachelor's degree
Enter **3** for associate degree (occupational or technical program)
Enter **4** for associate degree (general education or transfer program)
Enter **5** for certificate or diploma for completing an occupational, technical, or educational program of less than two years

Enter **6** for certificate or diploma for completing an occupational, technical, or educational program of at least two years
Enter **7** for teaching credential program (nondegree program)
Enter **8** for graduate or professional degree
Enter **9** for other/undecided

Notes for question 30 (page 3) — Enter the correct number in the box in question 30.

Enter **0** for never attended college & 1st year undergraduate
Enter **1** for attended college before & 1st year undergraduate
Enter **2** for 2nd year undergraduate/sophomore
Enter **3** for 3rd year undergraduate/junior

Enter **4** for 4th year undergraduate/senior
Enter **5** for 5th year/other undergraduate
Enter **6** for 1st year graduate/professional
Enter **7** for continuing graduate/professional or beyond

2002-2003

The FAFSA ℠

Free Application for Federal Student Aid
For July 1, 2002 — June 30, 2003

OMB # 1845-0001

Step One: For questions 1-34, leave blank any questions that do not apply to you (the student).

1-3. Your full name (as it appears on your Social Security card)

1. LAST NAME

2. FIRST NAME

3. MIDDLE INITIAL

4-7. Your permanent mailing address

4. NUMBER AND STREET (INCLUDE APT. NUMBER)

5. CITY (AND COUNTRY IF NOT U.S.)

6. STATE

7. ZIP CODE

8. Your Social Security Number

9. Your date of birth

/ / 19

10. Your permanent telephone number

( ) –

11-12. Your driver's license number and state (if any)

11. LICENSE NUMBER

12. STATE

13. Are you a U.S. citizen? Pick one. See **page 2.**

a. Yes, I am a U.S. citizen. **Skip to question 15** .... ○ 1
b. No, but I am an eligible noncitizen. **Fill in question 14.** ...... ○ 2
c. No, I am not a citizen or eligible noncitizen. .... ○ 3

14. ALIEN REGISTRATION NUMBER

A

15. What is your marital status as of today?

I am single, divorced, or widowed ..... ○ 1
I am married/remarried .... ○ 2
I am separated .... ○ 3

16. Month and year you were married, separated, divorced, or widowed

MONTH YEAR

/

For each question (17 - 21), please mark whether you will be full time, 3/4 time, half time, less than half time, or not attending. **See page 2.**

17. Summer 2002	Full time/Not sure ○ 1	3/4 time ○ 2	Half time ○ 3	Less than half time ○ 4	Not attending ○ 5
18. Fall 2002	Full time/Not sure ○ 1	3/4 time ○ 2	Half time ○ 3	Less than half time ○ 4	Not attending ○ 5
19. Winter 2002-2003	Full time/Not sure ○ 1	3/4 time ○ 2	Half time ○ 3	Less than half time ○ 4	Not attending ○ 5
20. Spring 2003	Full time/Not sure ○ 1	3/4 time ○ 2	Half time ○ 3	Less than half time ○ 4	Not attending ○ 5
21. Summer 2003	Full time/Not sure ○ 1	3/4 time ○ 2	Half time ○ 3	Less than half time ○ 4	Not attending ○ 5

22. Highest school your father completed   Middle school/Jr. High ○ 1   High school ○ 2   College or beyond ○ 3   Other/unknown ○ 4

23. Highest school your mother completed   Middle school/Jr. High ○ 1   High school ○ 2   College or beyond ○ 3   Other/unknown ○ 4

24. What is your state of legal residence?

STATE

25. Did you become a legal resident of this state before January 1, 1997?

Yes ○ 1   No ○ 2

MONTH YEAR

/

26. If the answer to question 25 is "No," give month and year you became a legal resident.

27. Are you male? (Most male students must register with Selective Service to get federal aid.)

Yes ○ 1   No ○ 2

28. If you are male (age 18-25) and not registered, answer "Yes" and Selective Service will register you.

Yes ○ 1   No ○ 2

29. What degree or certificate will you be working on during 2002-2003? **See page 2** and enter the correct number in the box.

30. What will be your grade level when you begin the 2002-2003 school year? **See page 2** and enter the correct number in the box.

8 From what you have read in this application form, you can tell that an applicant

  A must know his or her Social Security number.

  B can get as much funding as he or she needs.

  C must be at least 29 years old to qualify for aid.

  D must be married to fill out the application.

9 Your permanent mailing address is

  A where your parent lives.

  B where you used to live.

  C where you live now.

  D where you are planning to move.

10 If you are a citizen, you can

  A answer Question 14.

  B skip Question 13.

  C skip to Question 15.

  D answer only questions about citizenship.

11 According to the information on page 2, one of the conditions for being an eligible non-citizen is

  A that you are a U.S. permanent resident and have an Alien Registration Receipt Card (I-551).

  B that you are a U.S. permanent resident and have an Alien Registration Receipt.

  C that you must have an F1 or F2 student visa only.

  D that you must have lived in the United States for 12 years.

12 You know that Mike Rinaldi has expressed a strong interest in working with computers. You can conclude that he may choose which of the following answers to Question 29?

  A 1, 2, or 7

  B 2, 4, or 7

  C 1, 2, or 4

  D 3, 5, or 6

Michelle decided to learn how to use her hometown library as well as the Bridgewater Community College library. She was very excited to learn that she could also do online research from home. Now all she had to do was learn how to do it! Her local library offered these instructions regarding online research from home. Read the instructions, and then answer Questions 13–17.

Online Research from Home

1. *Go to our home page at http://www.clan.lib.ri.us/nki/index.htm.*

2. *Click on "Online Research."*

3. *Click on the link for the subject you would like to research (e.g., click on "health" to look for health information). You may also choose "magazine and newspaper articles," "encyclopedia articles," "maps," or "photographs and images."*

4. *Click on the link for the online resource that you would like to use.*

5. *Type in your 14-digit North Kingstown Free Library Card number with no spaces between the numbers. (The card needs to be a North Kingstown card. If you have moved to North Kingstown and you have been using a CLAN card that you received from another library, you will need to get a new card by registering at the circulation desk.)*

6. *Start your research!*

7. *If you have any questions, call the Reference Desk at 294-3306.*

Be sure to check out our selected websites page at http://www.clan.lib.ri.us/nki/websites.htm.
Courtesy of North Kingstown Free Library, North Kingstown, RI 02852.

13 The main idea of this instruction sheet is to

    A help you do all your shopping online.

    B help you learn how to get your diploma.

    C help you learn how to copy answers from books.

    D help you learn how to do online research from home.

14 The first step you must take to start your search for information is

    A call the library immediately.

    B click on "maps."

    C go to the library's home page.

    D click on "Online Research."

15 If you plan to use the library or its online services, you can conclude that you will need to have

    A a CLAN card that was issued at this library.

    B a new home address.

    C a brand-new computer.

    D an appointment with a librarian.

16 If you were looking for a recent article in the *Boston Globe,*

    A you would click on the "magazine and newspaper articles" link.

    B you would first call the *Boston Globe.*

    C you would get a CLAN card from the *Boston Globe.*

    D you would click on the "health information" link.

17 Scan the instructions for the special selected websites page. What is the address for this page?

    A http://www.clan.lib.ri.us/nmi/index. htm

    B http://www.clan.lib.ri.us/nki/ websites.htm

    C http://www.clan.lib.ny.us/ny/ websites.htm

    D http://www.clan.lib.ma.us/bos/ wesites.htm

Michelle clicked on Online Research and went immediately to the page below. Read the information and answer Questions 18–21.

North Kingstown Free Library
Online Research

HELP! I don't know where to go.
Search for information in the following subjects and categories:

CLAN Catalog (Cooperating Libraries   Magazine & Newspaper Articles
   Automated Network)
Encyclopedia Articles   Literature & Authors
Biography (Past & Present)   Geography (Countries & States)
Health   History
Science & Math   Social Issues & Current Events
Maps (World & State)**   Photographs & Images

**For street maps and driving directions, sign up at the Reference Desk to use the Internet.

NKFL Home Page   Online Resources (in alphabetical order)   Reference Desk
Fiction Page   Young Readers' Page   Teen Page

   For help with online research, please ask at the Reference Desk or Young Readers' Desk.
   This computer does not have access to the Internet. To use a computer with Internet access, please sign in at the Reference Desk.

---

18 If Michelle does not know what step to take next, she should

  A leave immediately.

  B click on every underlined word on the screen.

  C call her friend Mike.

  D click on HELP.

19 One of the first things Michelle noticed is that even her young children could find books by clicking on

  A Maps.

  B Science & Math.

  C Young Readers' Page.

  D Social Issues & Current Events.

20 Before Michelle and Mike can access occupational information online at this library they need to

  A sign up at the Reference Desk.

  B click on Encyclopedia Articles.

  C click on Maps.

  D click on CLAN Catalog.

21 What does Michelle have to do to get back to this library's home page?

  A Click on any subject matter

  B Get help from the Reference Desk

  C Click on NKFL Home Page

  D Get help from her professor

Read the following information on learning. Then answer Questions 22–25.

Learning experts agree that some habits help you learn while others hinder your progress. For example, studies done with high school students revealed some interesting data. The studies showed that students did best in their most difficult classes at 11 A.M. Yet math homework was best done at 6:30 P.M. At that hour, students dealt best with calculations. When are you at your peak for math?

Experts also suggested that breaks in the study routine were important. A 5-minute break every 30 minutes worked well. That means, for example, getting up to stretch, walking around, or taking a drink of water. A different kind of break is important too. That is a break to review what you have studied. If you review what you have learned every 10 minutes, you will greatly increase future recall. Of course, reviewing at the end of a week also helps.

More good advice from the learning experts: Take care of your body and your mind. Exercising boosts the growth of new cells in the part of the brain called the hippocampus. That part of the brain is responsible for memory and learning. Some activities, however, work against the brain. For example, social drinking three or more times a week decreases cognitive, or knowledge gaining, skills.

Variety is the spice of life—and great for your brain function. Doing puzzles, for example, sharpens analytical skills. Puzzles also improve memory and learning. In addition, occasionally you should try looking at everyday things differently. Take a different route to work or school. You'll force your brain to use its mapping ability. To stimulate your brain, wear your watch upside down. You'll force yourself to see things differently.

22 In the first paragraph, *calculations* means

A instructions from the teacher.

B answers that are obviously wrong.

C exercises while you're studying.

D steps in working out the answer to a math problem.

23 The opposite of the word *variety* (used in the last paragraph) is

A mixture.

B assortment.

C diversity.

D sameness.

24 Including exercise in your schedule and variety in the way you do things

A affect your brain positively.

B make you too tired to study.

C prevent you from seeing your friends.

D guarantee success in your studies.

25 A major point made by some learning experts is that

A most habits hinder your learning.

B some habits help you learn while others hinder it.

C everyone has the same habits.

D the only good habit is to review often.

To the Student: As you check your answers, record the results in this chart. Use the three columns next to the Item Answers to mark your answers as *Correct, Incorrect,* or *Skipped.* Use the other columns to record additional information you want to remember about the individual questions. Total the number of your responses in each column at the bottom of the chart. Then read the recommendations that follow.

Reading Skills Assessment: Answers and Skills Analysis

Item Answers	Correct T	Incorrect X	Skipped O	I have a question about this item	I need instruction.	Refer to these lessons.	Reading Skill Categories*
1 C						6	5
2 B						5	4
3 D						5	5
4 C						6	4
5 B						6	5
6 A						6	4
7 D						6	5
8 A						2	3
9 C						4	1
10 C						2	3
11 A						2	3
12 D						5	4
13 D						2	3
14 C						2	3
15 A						5	4
16 A						3	5
17 B						2	3
18 D						3	5
19 C						2	3
20 A						2	3
21 C						3	5
22 D						4	2
23 D						4	2
24 A						6	3
25 B						2	3
TOTALS	Correct	Incorrect	Skipped	Questions	Instruction	Lessons	Skills

* Key to Reading Skill Categories

1 Interpret Graphic Information   2 Words in Context   3 Recall Information
4 Construct Meaning   5 Evaluate/Extend Meaning

Note: These broad categories of reading skills are broken down into subcategories. Question numbers are aligned with the subcategories as well as the lesson to which you can return for a review.

READING SKILLS ANALYSIS

Interpret Graphic Information

REFERENCE SOURCES

LIBRARY CATALOG CARD DISPLAY

Maps

Forms	9	(See Lesson 4)

WORDS IN CONTEXT

Same Meaning	22	(See Lesson 4)
Opposite Meaning	23	(See Lesson 4)

RECALL INFORMATION

Details	8, 11, 17, 19	(See Lesson 2)
Sequence	14, 10, 20	(See Lesson 2)
Stated Concepts	25	(See Lesson 2)

CONSTRUCT MEANING

Character Aspects	6	(See Lesson 6)
Main Ideas	13	(See Lesson 2)
Summary/Paraphrase		
Cause/Effect	24	(See Lesson 2)
Compare/Contrast		
Conclusion	2, 3, 12, 15	(See Lesson 5)
Supporting Evidence	4	(See Lesson 6)

EVALUATE/EXTEND MEANING

Fact/Opinion		
Predict Outcomes	7, 24	(See Lesson 6)
Apply Passage Element	16, 18, 21	(See Lesson 3)
Generalizations		
Effect/Intentions		
Author Purpose	5	(See Lesson 6)
Point of View		
Style Techniques	1	(See Lesson 6)
Genre		

To identify your areas for improvement in the Reading Section, do three things:

1. Total your number of correct answers out of the 25 possible answers. You should have 90 to 95 percent correct (or 23 to 24 correct answers).

2. Total the correct answers in each subcategory. For example, in the subcategory *Recall Information,* there are 8 correct answers. You should have 7 correct answers, or close to 90 percent correct.

3. Wherever your score is below 95 percent, go back to that lesson (lesson number is indicated in parentheses) and review the skill.

Language

For Questions 1–3, decide which punctuation mark, if any, is needed in the sentence.

1 She said, "I'll pay the bridge toll"; I was shocked!

   A ,

   B ?

   C "

   D None

2 Before I start working at my desk, I turn on the computer turn on the printer, and turn off the phone.

   A ,

   B .

   C ;

   D None

3 "Which of these projects," Luis asked, should we consider our number one priority?"

   A !

   B .

   C "

   D None

For Questions 4 and 5, choose the phrase that best completes the sentence.

4 Yesterday, my children and I _____ too early to see the main show.

   A was arriving

   B am arriving

   C will be arriving

   D had arrived

5 Some of the machines in the garage _____, but others had been overlooked.

   A were fixed

   B was fixed

   C has been fixed

   D is fixed

For Questions 6–11, choose the sentence that is written correctly and shows the correct capitalization and punctuation. Be sure the sentence you choose is complete.

6

   A I can't be anymore clearer than that.

   B I ain't got anything else to say.

   C What haven't you told me about yourself?

   D I haven't got nothing to say.

7

   A I rung the bell and left.

   B He had not swore to tell the truth.

   C Do you always throw your clothes around like that?

   D Barney gone East on route 195.

8

A The children have sitted in their chairs too long.

B Iowa City has always been my hometown.

C Walking through the building mumbling.

D Michael breaked his promise.

9

A Did he ask, "What do you got for your schedule this week?"

B I called the doctor and she ain't returned my call by noon.

C I seen his book called, *30 Days to a better vocabulary?*

D I saw a new set of knives in the drawer.

10

A Trimming the hedges, mowing the grass, and then I remove the weeds which is not my favorite things to do.

B Trimming the hedges, mowing the grass, removing the weeds.

C Removing the weeds, mowing the grass, trimming the hedges.

D Trimming the hedges, mowing the grass, and removing the weeds are not my favorite things to do.

11

A Nervous test-takers seen no chance for a good result.

B I done a great deal to do, nevertheless I will make time for our meeting.

C Bring these with you: your introduction, your statement of need, and your proposal for change.

D I done it right the first time.

The three paragraphs below contain numerous errors. Read each paragraph and answer Questions 12–21. In Paragraph III, you will also need to fill in the blank.

I. A cover letter always effects your résumé. Why? While your résumé states facts, the cover letter speaks direct to the person doing the hiring. Obviously, you want to grab that person's attention; otherwise, they may go right on to the next résumé.

12 Which word in the first sentence is an incorrect choice as a verb?

A résumé

B cover

C effects

D your

E No error

13 Which descriptive word is in the wrong form?

A grab

B next

C obviously

D direct

E No error

14 Which pronoun in the paragraph does not agree in number with the noun that comes before it?

A they

B you

C us

D your

E No error

15 Which mark of punctuation is incorrect?

A Obviously,

B Why?

C attention;

D résumé.

E No error

II. While writing your cover letter, you are including your personal strengths. The strengths need to relate directly to the job for which you are applying. Then of course your qualifications is backed up by the facts in your résumé. Each one, the cover letter and the résumé, need to be strong.

16 Which one of the sentences in the paragraph is incomplete?

A 1

B 2

C 3

D 4

E No error

17 In the third sentence, where should a comma or commas be placed?

A Then,

B backed up, by

C facts,

D Then, of course,

E No error

18 In the third sentence, there is a subject-verb agreement error. How would you correct it?

    A Change *facts* to *fact*.

    B Change *résumé* to *résumés*.

    C Delete *up*.

    D Change *is* to *are*.

    E No error

19 Look at the fourth sentence. Choose the answer that shows the correct subject and the verb.

    A cover letter need

    B résumé needs

    C each needs

    D each need

    E No error

III. Some people who are searching for jobs has come up with a very clever way to reach more people. They create and distributes 3 × 5 cards that hold a lot of important information. The card include name, phone number, job related skills, job objective, training/education/or certification, special skills. _____

It goes out attached to every résumé or application.

It is used as a business card.

It is given to people to whom the job-seeker is referred.

It is given to relatives and friends as well as the person's entire network.

It is left at the interview and attached to the thank you note that follows the interview.

20 In the first three sentences of this paragraph, there are three verb agreement errors (in number). Choose the answer that includes the three.

    A has, distributes, include

    B searching, has, hold

    C come up, include, training

    D reach, important, include

    E No error

21 Which of the following sentences would fill in the blank and best complete the paragraph

    A Always wear a suit to the interview.

    B Write a thank you note after each interview.

    C In addition, the card is used in a number of ways:

    D You will need a portfolio.

    E No error

For Questions 22 and 23, choose the answer that best develops the topic sentence.

22 Our grandfathers worked for companies that tended to stay the same for many years, but in our own work experience, that's not often the case.

   A Companies today strive for stability. They can afford to remain unchanged for the foreseeable future.

   B When change comes to your workplace, resist it with all your might. If you are strong enough, you'll win the battle.

   C When things change at work, tell someone that you know better. Suggest a way to keep all the old ways in tact.

   D Today, companies look for people who are comfortable with change. Employees who are cooperative and productive in the midst of change are highly valued.

23 To commemorate Black History Month, the class developed themes on the subject of historic contributions made by African American women in science.

   A Professor Dale Emeagwali (a-MAG-wali) contributed to the fields of microbiology, molecular biology, and biochemistry. Her greatest achievement, was the discovery of an enzyme found in the blood of cancer patients.

   B Professor Dale Emeagwali (a-MAG-wali) contributed to the fields of microbiology, molecular biology, and biochemistry. Her husband, Dr. Phillip Emeagwali, is often referred to as the father of the internet.

   C Professor Dale Emeagwali (a-MAG-wali) was unsuccessful in her attempt to prove that science can be understood by only a few of our school children. She returned to teaching.

   D Professor Dale Emeagwali (a-MAG-wali) is working hard with her husband to make some small contribution to science. She expects a breakthrough shortly.

Read the two sentences given in Questions 24 and 25. Then choose the answer that best combines those sentences into one.

24 The board members considered safety the most important issue. They thoroughly discussed fire evacuation routes.

  A The board members considered safety the most important issue and then they thoroughly discussed fire evacuation routes.

  B They thoroughly discussed fire evacuation routes while the board members considered safety the most important issue.

  C The board members considered safety the most important issue; therefore, they thoroughly discussed fire evacuation routes.

  D The board members chose fire evacuation routes. They discussed them.

25 I will get up earlier to open the office. You could open it since you live so much closer to town.

  A I will get up earlier to open the office and you could do it too since you live so much closer to town.

  B Either I will get up earlier to open the office or you could since you live so much closer to town.

  C Either I will get up earlier to open the office. Or you could.

  D I could get up earlier to open the office, you could open the office, you live closer to town.

Read the paragraphs in Questions 26–28. Then choose the sentence that best fills the blank in each paragraph.

26 _____. We suggest that you check our online manual of training courses. You will find many courses that will help you update your skills. Please contact the Human Resources Manager for more information.

    A Training is always much more fun in a classroom.

    B Our company offers many opportunities for gaining the skills you need.

    C There are very few courses to choose from.

    D Every employee we hire is fully prepared for all departments the day he or she starts the job.

27 On the other hand, you may have a specific training need. _____ In our manual, there are online courses of all lengths. Your need may be very specific and require only a few hours from start to finish. However, no matter what the length of the course, you will receive credit for it.

    A Sometimes, that need can be filled by a short term, online tutorial, or teaching session.

    B You must always go to another teaching location for the training course.

    C Our company does not believe in computer-based training.

    D Every course we offer is four to six weeks long.

28 Our online courses have a number of characteristics that make your training easier. First, courses are very easy to sign up for. After you are assigned a password, you can go online and start your training portfolio. Once you have found the training you want, you will be given very clear procedures to follow. _____

    A Immediately start the training.

    B The first item on the procedures list is to record in your portfolio the name of the training course you have chosen.

    C Always take a break at this point.

    D Don't do a thing until you call a friend.

To the Student: As you check your answers, record the results in this chart. Use the three columns next to the Item Answers to mark your answers as *Correct, Incorrect,* or *Skipped.* Use the other columns to record additional information you want to remember about the individual questions. Total the number of your answers in each column at the bottom of the chart. Then read the recommendations that follow.

Language Skills Assessment: Answers and Skills Analysis

Item Answers	Correct T	Incorrect X	Skipped O	I have a question about this item	I need instruction.	Refer to these lessons	Reading Skill Categories*
1 D						5	32
2 A						5	5
3 C						5	28
4 D						2	3
5 A						2	4
6 C						5	9
7 C						2	5
8 B						2	3
9 D						2	5
10 D						6	13
11 C						2	3
12 C						2	5
13 D						4	8
14 A						3	2
15 E						5	24
16 E						2	11
17 D						5	25
18 D						2	4
19 C						2	4
20 A						2	4
21 C						6	15
22 D						6	15
23 A						6	15
24 C						6	12
25 B						6	2
26 B						6	14
27 A						6	15
28 B						6	18
TOTALS	Correct	Incorrect	Skipped	Questions	Instruction	Lessons	Skills

* Key to Language Skill Categories

1 Usage
2 Antecedent Agreement
3 Tense
4 Subject/Verb Agreement
5 Easily Confused Verbs
6 Adjective
7 Adverb
8 Choose Between Adjective/Adverb
9 Use Negatives
10 Sentence Formation
11 Sentence Recognition
12 Sentence Combining
13 Sentence Clarity
14 Paragraph Development, Topic Sentence
15 Supporting Sentences
16 Sequence
17 Unrelated Sentence
18 Connective/Transition
19 Capitalization
20 Proper Noun
21 Name
22 Title of Work
23 Punctuation
24 End Mark
25 Comma
26 Semicolon
27 Writing Conventions
28 Quotation Marks
29 Apostrophe
30 City/State
31 Letter Part

Note: These broad categories of language skills are broken down into subcategories. Question numbers are aligned with the subcategory as well as the lesson to which you can return for a review.

Language Skills Analysis

Usage

Pronoun

Objective

Possessive

Antecedent Agreement	14	(See Lesson 2)
Tense		
Past	8	(See Lesson 2)
Future		
Perfect	4, 11	(See Lesson 2)
Progressive		
Subject/Verb Agreement	5, 18, 19, 20	(See Lesson 2)
Easily Confused Verbs	7, 9, 12	(See Lesson 2)
Adjective		
Comparative		
Superlative		
Adverb		
Superlative		
Choose Between Adjective/Adverb	13	(See Lesson 4)
Use Negatives	6	(See Lesson 3)
Sentence Formation		
Sentence Recognition		
Complete/Fragment/Run-on	16	(See Lesson 2)
Sentence Combining		
Adding Modifier		
Coordinating	24, 25	(See Lesson 6)
Subordinating		
Sentence Clarity		
Misplaced Modifier		
Nonparallel Structure	10	(See Lesson 6)
Verbosity/Repetition		
Paragraph Development	26 (Topic)	(See Lesson 6)
Supporting Sentences	21, 22, 23, 27	(See Lesson 6)

Sequence		
Unrelated Sentence		
Connective/Transition	28	(See Lesson 6)
Capitalization		
Proper Noun		
Name		
Geographic Name		
Title of Work		
Punctuation		
End Mark	15	(See Lesson 5)
Question Mark		
Comma		
Series	2	(See Lesson 5)
Appositive		
Introductory Element		
Parenthetical Expression	17	(See Lesson 5)
Semicolon		
Writing Conventions		
Quotation Marks	1, 3	(See Lesson 5)
Comma with Quotation		
End Marks with Quotation		
Apostrophe		
Possessive		
City/State		
Letter Part		
Date		
Address		

Salutation	
Closing	

To identify your areas of skills improvement in language, do three things:

1. Total your number of correct answers out of the 28 possible answers. You should have 90 to 95 percent correct (or 25 to 27 correct answers).

2. Total the number of correct answers in each subcategory of skills. For example, in the subcategory *Supporting Sentences,* there are 4 correct answers. You should have 4 correct answers.

3. Wherever your score is below 95 percent, go back to that lesson (indicated in parentheses) and review the skill.

Spelling

For Questions 1–20, choose the word that is spelled correctly and best completes the sentence.

1 We thought it was _____ to choose vacation weeks so early in the year.

   A unnecessary

   B unecessary

   C unnecesary

   D unecesary

2 The moviegoers stood in one _____ line.

   A continous

   B contenuos

   C continuous

   D continuius

3 Your work has made a _____ difference in the success of this department.

   A noticeible

   B noticeable

   C notiseable

   D notisable

4 The Human Resources Manager _____ me to the company's learning center for help in writing business letters.

   A refered

   B reffered

   C referes

   D referred

5 The directive stated, "Handle the changes _____."

   A expediently

   B expediuntly

   C expediantly

   D expedintly

6 Your _____ are not a problem; they have all been for serious illness.

   A abbsences

   B abcenses

   C absences

   D absunces

7 "_____ the day!" is a popular slogan.

   A sieze

   B siece

   C seize

   D seise

8 You need a _____ driver's license for this job.

   A valid

   B vallid

   C valud

   D vallud

9 Our country has faced many _____ in the past few years.

   A crices

   B crises

   C crisses

   D cryses

10 We expect _____ of materials to arrive at the receiving dock.

   A truckfuls

   B truckfulls

   C trucksful

   D trucksfulls

11 She is a _____ to our team's progress.

A   detriment

B   detrament

C   detrement

D   detrament

12 A _____ under the photo in the newspaper gave everyone's names.

A   capshon

B   capsion

C   capcion

D   caption

13 A room for 100 people will _____ all of us at the meeting.

A   acommadate

B   accommodate

C   accomadate

D   acommadate

14 Every time we hire a new employee in our small company, we make a _____ decision.

A   crucial

B   crusial

C   crutial

D   crusiel

15 Be careful; that ink is _____.

A   indelable

B   indellible

C   indellable

D   indelible

16 Your new plan has been an _____ for all of us.

A   insperation

B   innspuration

C   inspiration

D   inspuration

17 Those two computer programs are _____.

A   interchangable

B   intrachangeable

C   interchangeible

D   interchangeable

18 At Mike's company, 12 hours of entry-level training are _____.

A   compulsery

B   compulsory

C   compulsry

D   compulsury

19 He is well prepared for a job that requires _____ thinking.

A   analytical

B   anilitical

C   anilical

D   analytucle

20 With your help, I have been able to cope with many _____.

A   emergencys

B   amergencies

C   emergencies

D   emurgencies

Answer Key

1. A; unnecessary
2. C; continuous
3. B; noticeable
4. D; referred
5. A; expediently
6. C; absences
7. C; seize
8. A; valid
9. B; crises
10. A; truckfuls
11. A; detriment
12. D; caption
13. B; accommodate
14. A; crucial
15. D; indelible
16. C; inspiration
17. D; interchangeable
18. B; compulsory
19. A; analytical
20. C; emergencies

To the Student: As you check your answers, record the results in this chart. Use the three columns next to the Item Answers to mark your answers as *Correct, Incorrect,* or *Skipped.* Use the other columns to record additional information you want to remember about the individual questions. Total the number of your answers in each column at the bottom of the chart. Then read the recommendations that follow.

Spelling Skills Assessment: Answers and Skills Analysis

Item Answers	Correct T	Incorrect X	Skipped O	I have a question about this item	I need instruction.	Spelling Skill Categories*
1 A						2
2 C						2
3 B						3
4 D						2
5 A						3
6 C						2
7 C						1
8 A						1
9 B						2
10 A						3

	Correct	Incorrect	Skipped	Questions	Instruction	Skills
11 A						3
12 D						2
13 B						2
14 A						2
15 D						1
16 C						1
17 D						3
18 B						1
19 A						1
20 C						3
TOTALS	Correct	Incorrect	Skipped	Questions	Instruction	Skills

* Key to Spelling Skill Categories

1 Vowels   2 Consonants   3 Structural Units

Note: These categories of spelling skills are broken down into subcategories as well. On the next page, question numbers are aligned with the subcategories as well. Return to Section 5 to review the rules.

Spelling Skills Analysis

Vowel

Short	8
Long	7
Schwa	15, 16, 18, 19

Consonant

Variant Spelling	2, 6, 9, 12, 14
Silent Letter	
Double Letter	1, 4, 13

Structural Unit

Homonym	
Similar Word Part	5, 11
Root	10
Suffix	3, 17, 20

To identify your areas of skills improvement in the Spelling Section, do three things:

1. Total your number of correct answers out of the possible 20 answers. You should have 95 percent correct (or 19 correct answers).

2. Total the number of correct answers in each subset of skills. For example, in the subset *Schwa,* there are 4 correct answers. To score a passing grade, you should have 4 correct answers.

3. Keep a list of your spelling errors and follow the directions for improvement in the Study Tip on page 265.

Math

Part I: Computation

No calculators are permitted. Suggested time limit: 10 minutes. Start Time: _____

1 $60 - 24.8 =$

    A   352.0

    B   35.2

    C   84.8

    D   45.2

    E   None of these

2 $(5 + 3)(8 - 3) =$

    A   40

    B   13

    C   31

    D   61

    E   None of these

3 $0.75 \times 7.5 =$

    A   5.125

    B   5.625

    C   56.25

    D   5,125

    E   None of these

4 $\dfrac{7}{8} \div \dfrac{1}{2} =$

    A $\dfrac{7}{16}$

    B $1\dfrac{3}{4}$

    C $1\dfrac{3}{8}$

    D $3\dfrac{3}{4}$

    E   None of these

5 $6\,(7 - 5) + {-4} =$

    A   12

    B   16

    C   8

    D   33

    E   None of these

6 $5\dfrac{3}{4} + 12\dfrac{3}{8} =$

    A $17\dfrac{1}{8}$

    B $18\dfrac{1}{8}$

    C $16\dfrac{3}{8}$

    D $18\dfrac{3}{4}$

    E   None of these

7 $-12 \times -3 =$

    A   36

    B   −36

    C   −15

    D   15

    E   None of these

8 $5x\,(x + y) =$

    A $6x + 5xy$

    B $5x^2 + 5xy$

    C $5x^2y$

    D $5x^2 + y$

    E   None of these

9 $20 - (-10) =$

    A   10

    B   −10

    C   30

    D   −30

    E   None of these

10   10 percent of _____ = $90

    A $9.00

    B $9,000

    C $80.00

    D $100.00

    E   None of these

11   What percent of $30.00 is $6.00?

    A   60 percent

    B   150 percent

    C   5 percent

    D   20 percent

    E   None of these

12 $24 \div -3 =$

    A   −8

    B   −6

    C   8

    D   21

    E   None of these

13 $6^2 + 9 \div 3 - 5 =$

    A   36

    B   2

    C   34

    D   10

    E   None of these

14 $|{-5} \times 6| - |{-25}| =$

    A   −5

    B   55

    C   −55

    D   5

    E   None of these

15 $6\frac{1}{2}$ percent of $500.00 =

    A $35.20

    B $325.00

    C $32.50

    D $77.00

    E   None of these

16 $19c + c = 154 - 2c$

    A $c = 132$

    B $c = 7$

    C $c = 8$

    D $154 - 22c$

    E   None of these

17 $-6 - 24 \div 6 + 3 =$

    A   −8

    B   −7

    C   −2

    D $-3\frac{1}{3}$

    E   None of these

18.   What % of 24 is 18?

    A $33\frac{1}{3}\%$

    B   60%

    C   75%

    D   80%

    E   None of these

19. $4^2 - 3^2 =$

   A   1

   B   2

   C   −1

   D   7

   E   None of these

20. $3(a - 7) =$

   A $3a - 7$

   B   −21

   C $3a - 4$

   D $3a - 21$

   E   None of these

21. $-15 - (-10) =$

   A   −25

   B   −5

   C   5

   D   25

   E   None of these

22. $2\frac{1}{3} + 3\frac{1}{4} =$

   A $5\frac{1}{6}$

   B $5\frac{2}{7}$

   C $5\frac{7}{12}$

   D $5\frac{4}{7}$

   E   None of these

23. $\dfrac{24}{2.4} =$

   A $\dfrac{1}{100}$

   B $\dfrac{1}{10}$

   C   10

   D   100

   E   None of these

24. $(-3)(-12) =$

   A   −15

   B   15

   C   −36

   D   36

   E   None of these

25. $(5x)^2 =$

   A $25x^2$

   B $5x^2$

   C $10x$

   D $10x^2$

   E   None of these

Stop Time: _____

Math

Part II: Application

You may use a calculator. Suggested time limit: 30 to 35 minutes.
Start Time: _____

1 It takes approximately 1,480 watts of electrical energy to operate a desktop computer and its monitor for 4 hours. How many kilowatts is that?

    A   Less than 1 kilowatt

    B   Between 1 and 2 kilowatts

    C   Between 10 and 20 kilowatts

    D   More than 14 kilowatts

2 Find the width of a field that has an area of 4,800 square meters and a length of 120 meters.

    A   30 meters

    B   40 meters

    C   45 meters

    D   None of the above

3 In 2002, the estimated population of the United States was 287,367,280. Round this population statistic to the ten thousands place.

    A   287,368,000

    B   290,000,000

    C   287,000,000

    D   287,370,000

4 A machine shaft revolves at 245 rpm (revolutions per minute). It is necessary to slow it down by 20 percent. What will the rpm of the shaft be after the reduction? Choose the expression that will enable you to answer to this question.

    A $245 - (0.20 \times 245)$

    B $245 - (20 \times 245)$

    C $245 + (0.20 \times 245)$

    D $245 + (20 \times 245)$

5 What is the circumference of a swimming pool that has a radius of 6 feet? ($C = \pi d$. Use $\frac{22}{7}$ for π.)

    A $37\frac{5}{7}$ ft

    B   38 ft

    C   56 ft

    D   None of the above

Refer to this advertisement to answer Question 6.

> **Dinette Set: Take It Home Today for Only $159.00!***
>
> Dining Set: Take It Home Today for Only $54.20!*
>
> Table and Four Chairs Sale Price: $541.99 + 7% tax
>
> *Installment Plan: 10% down $49.99 per week for 12 weeks (including tax)

6 How much more will it cost to buy the dining set on the installment plan than it will to buy it on a cash basis?

   A $594.20

   B $579.92

   C $74.15

   D $104.30

7 Shawn wants to buy a CD player that costs $48.00. If he has already saved $30.00, what percent of the price of the CD player has he saved?

   A $62\frac{1}{2}$ percent

   B 50 percent

   C 75 percent

   D 57 percent

8 Driving on the North West Expressway, Debbie averaged 62 miles per hour for $3\frac{1}{4}$ hours. How far did she drive?

   A 195.2 miles

   B 201.5 miles

   C 120.25 miles

   D 200.25 miles

Questions 9 and 10 are based on the passage and diagram that follow.

LOOKING FOR A SHORTCUT

> A group of hikers stopped along the trail to make a decision. They studied their map to figure out the shortest route from where they stood to their Base Camp. They noticed that the two established trails leading to the Base Camp intersected perpendicularly. Further map reading, and use of a protractor and a compass, convinced the hikers they could take an off-trail shortcut through the woods that would lead, directly to their Base Camp.

$\overline{DA} \approx 15$ miles

$\overline{AB} \approx 8$ miles

$\overline{DB} =$ the shortcut

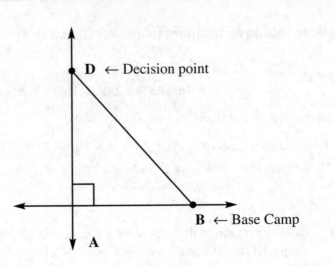

9 About how many miles do the hikers hope to *eliminate* from their trek by taking the off-trail shortcut?

    A   17 miles

    B   12 miles

    C   8 miles

    D   6 miles

10 In order to start heading southeast at the correct angle, the hikers needed to find the approximate value of ∠BDA. They placed a protractor on the map to measure the number of degrees in that angle. Which statement about the measurement of ∠BDA makes the most sense?

    A   ∠BDA = 45° or less

    B   ∠BDA = 46° or more

    C   ∠BDA ≈ 180°

    D   ∠BDA = Between 75° and 89°

11 Ed bought his dog a 10-lb bag of food. The first time she was fed, the dog ate $1\frac{3}{8}$ lb of food. How much dog food was left?

    A   8 lb

    B $7\frac{5}{8}$ lb

    C $8\frac{5}{8}$ lb

    D   None of the above

12 In an election, the winning candidate had 1,200 more votes than the loser. The total number of votes cast was 36,568. Select the pair of equations below that can be used to answer this question: How many votes did the winner receive?

    A   W = 2L + 1,200
           L = 36,568 − 12,000

    B   W = L + 1,200
           W + L = 36,568

    C   W = L − 1,200
           36,568 = L + 1,200

    D   W = L + 12,000
           L + W + 1,200 = 36,568

Refer to this bar graph to answer Questions 13 and 14.

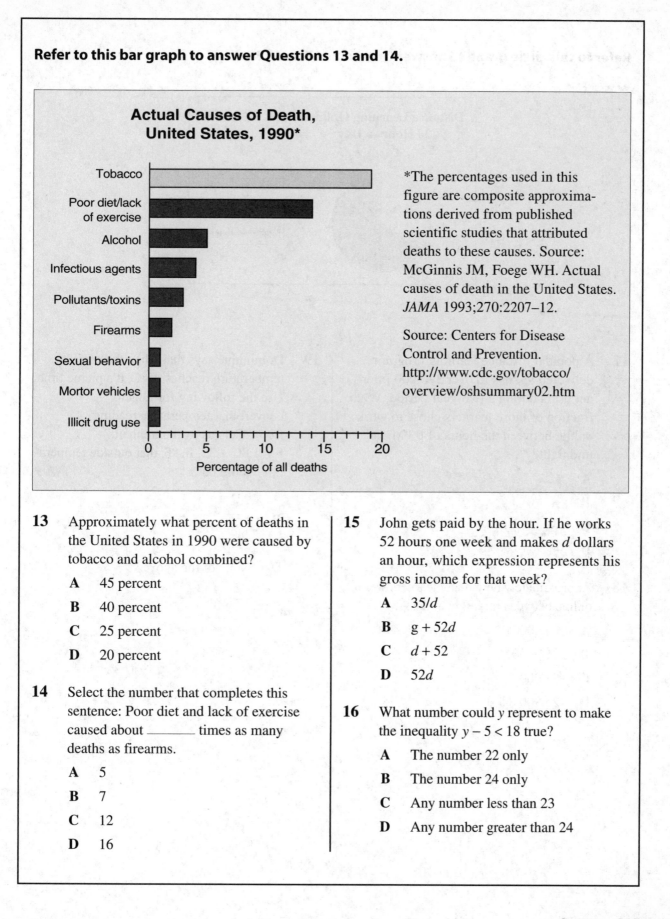

Actual Causes of Death, United States, 1990*

Tobacco
Poor diet/lack of exercise
Alcohol
Infectious agents
Pollutants/toxins
Firearms
Sexual behavior
Mortor vehicles
Illicit drug use

0   5   10   15   20
Percentage of all deaths

*The percentages used in this figure are composite approximations derived from published scientific studies that attributed deaths to these causes. Source: McGinnis JM, Foege WH. Actual causes of death in the United States. *JAMA* 1993;270:2207–12.

Source: Centers for Disease Control and Prevention. http://www.cdc.gov/tobacco/overview/oshsummary02.htm

13 Approximately what percent of deaths in the United States in 1990 were caused by tobacco and alcohol combined?

   A   45 percent

   B   40 percent

   C   25 percent

   D   20 percent

14 Select the number that completes this sentence: Poor diet and lack of exercise caused about _____ times as many deaths as firearms.

   A   5

   B   7

   C   12

   D   16

15 John gets paid by the hour. If he works 52 hours one week and makes d dollars an hour, which expression represents his gross income for that week?

   A $35/d$

   B $g + 52d$

   C $d + 52$

   D $52d$

16 What number could y represent to make the inequality $y - 5 < 18$ true?

   A   The number 22 only

   B   The number 24 only

   C   Any number less than 23

   D   Any number greater than 24

Refer to this circle graph to answer Questions 17 and 18.

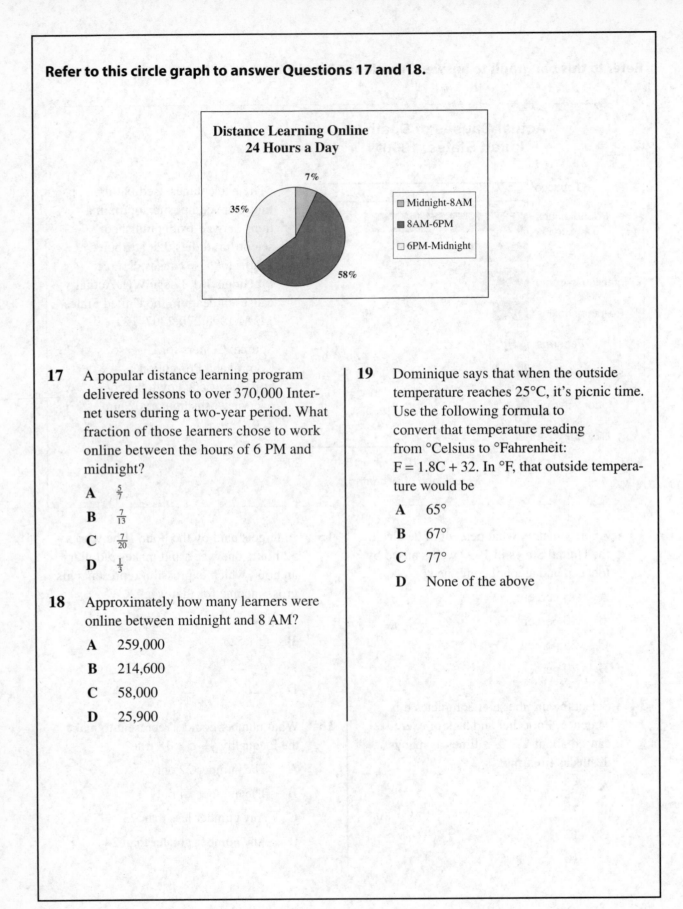

**Distance Learning Online
24 Hours a Day**

7%

35%

- Midnight-8AM
- 8AM-6PM
- 6PM-Midnight

58%

17 A popular distance learning program delivered lessons to over 370,000 Internet users during a two-year period. What fraction of those learners chose to work online between the hours of 6 PM and midnight?

   A $\frac{5}{7}$

   B $\frac{7}{13}$

   C $\frac{7}{20}$

   D $\frac{1}{3}$

18 Approximately how many learners were online between midnight and 8 AM?

   A   259,000

   B   214,600

   C   58,000

   D   25,900

19 Dominique says that when the outside temperature reaches 25°C, it's picnic time. Use the following formula to convert that temperature reading from °Celsius to °Fahrenheit: $F = 1.8C + 32$. In °F, that outside temperature would be

   A   65°

   B   67°

   C   77°

   D   None of the above

Use the data in this table and the information below to answer Questions 20–22:

Water Pump Rental Rates
Hoses and Connections Included

Pumps # Item	Flow Rate	Rate per Day	Pumps # Item	Flow Rate	Rate per Day
# 1	1.5 gal/min	$45	# 3	500 gal/min	$150
# 2	2.0 gal/min	$95	# 4	800 gal/min	$200

Torrential rains swept up the coast, leaving several low-lying properties under water. Terry and Rob woke to the sound of water gushing into their basement. Part of their house's foundation had caved in. When the water stopped rising, it covered the basement to a depth of 4 feet. They found a business that rented water pumps.

"How much water are we talking about?" asked the man at Liberty Rental. "Figure that out, and I can advise you which of these four pumps will do the job." He handed them a conversion table with this information circled: 1 cubic foot = 7.4805 gallons.

"Our basement measures 24 feet by 28 feet," said Rob. He took took out a notepad, a pen, and a calculator. Using the formula for the volume of a rectangular solid, $V = lwh$, Rob and Terry began to calculate. They hoped to rent a water pump with a flow rate that would remove the standing water as soon as possible—without emptying their wallets.

The manager offered them a deal: "If you can return the pump before noon, I'll only charge you for half a day, no matter which pump you choose. I'm sure I'll be able to rent it out again this afternoon."

20 Terry and Rob used the conversion chart and rounded the numbers to figure the approximate number of gallons of water in their basement. Which of the following expressions did they key into their calculator?

A 7.49×2800

B 7.48×27000

C 7.5×2700

D 7.4805×2670

21 They figured they had about 20,000 gallons of water to remove. Next, they looked at the flow rates of the four water pumps. How many gallons of water per hour can pump #3 remove?

A 30,000 gallons per hour

B 500 gallons per hour

C 5,000 gallons per hour

D 800 gallons per hour

22 Rob and Terry hurried home with pump #3. The pump did the job in

A about $3\frac{1}{2}$ hours.

B less than 1 hour.

C less than half an hour.

D about 2 hours.

23 Which three numbers will complete the spaces in the following number pattern?
100, 98, 94, _____, _____, 70, _____, 44

A 90, 86, 66

B 88, 82, 56

C 88, 80, 58

D 92, 88, 68

Refer to the following passage and line graph to answer Questions 24 and 25.

CARS, SPEED, AND STOPPING DISTANCE

"It takes the average driver about 0.75 second to react before he or she steps on the brakes. Once the brake pedal is depressed, it takes additional time for the car to come to a complete stop."*

Here is the formula for finding the total stopping distance of a car traveling on dry, level concrete when an alert driver is behind the wheel: Total Stopping Distance = $(1.1 \times s) + (0.06 \times s^2)$. s represents *speed* in miles per hour. $(1.1 \times s)$ represents the *reaction time distance,* in feet. $(0.06 \times s^2)$ represents the *braking time distance,* in feet.

Source: National Science Teachers Association.
http://www.nsta.org/Energy/fn_braking.html.

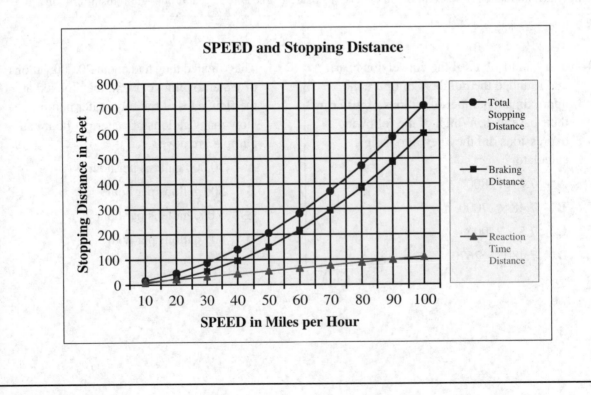

24 Use the Total Stopping Distance formula to calculate the total braking and reaction distance it takes a car to come to a complete stop when that car is being driven at 65 miles per hour under the controlled conditions described above.

A   310.5 ft

B   318.5 ft

C   321 ft

D   325 ft

25 Examine the relationship between the Stopping Distance and Speed as pictured in the graph. Look at the trend lines to help you complete this statement: As *speed* in miles per hour *doubles,* the *braking distance.*

A   increases by 29 feet.

B   doubles.

C   triples.

D   quadruples.

Answer Key

To the Student: Check your answers and record your results in this chart. Use the three columns next to the Item Answers to mark your responses as *Correct, Incorrect,* or *Skipped.* Use the other columns to record information you want to remember about the individual math problems. Total the number of your responses in each column at the bottom.

Answer Key and Skills Analysis: Part I, Computation

Item Answers	Correct	Incorrect	Skipped	Refer to these lessons.
1 B				1
2 A				5
3 B				1
4 B				2
5 C				5
6 B				2
7 A				3
8 B				6
9 C				3
10 E				4
11 D				4
12 A				4
13 C				5
14 D				6
15 C				4
16 B				6
17 B				5
18 C				4
19 D				6
20 D				6
21 B				3
22 C				2
23 C				1
24 D				3
25 A				6

Answer Key and Skills Analysis: Part II, Application

Item Answers	Correct	Incorrect	Skipped	Refer to these lessons.
1 B				10
2 B				11
3 D				1
4 A				12, 4
5 A				11
6 C				8
7 A				8
8 B				10
9 D				11
10 A				11
11 C				12
12 B				14
13 C				12
14 A				12
15 D				8
16 C				14
17 C				12
18 D				12, 4
19 C				10
20 C				9
21 A				10
22 B				8
23 C				14
24 D				14
25 D				12, 14

Analyze Your Results

1 Write the total number of your *correct* answers for Parts I and II in the spaces below.

2 Divide the number of correct answers by the total number of answers to figure your percentage of success.

Part I _____ Correct answers ÷ 25 total answers = _____ = _____%

Part II _____ Correct answers ÷ 25 total answers = _____ = _____%

Plan Your Review

This posttest gives you a good idea of the types of items you will find on the TABE, Level A, Forms 7 and 8. To be confident of doing well on this section of the TABE, your goal is to answer between at least 88 percent of the items correctly.

Recommendation

Review the lessons indicated for any item you answered incorrectly, skipped, or answered correctly but about which you still have questions. Then return to this posttest and reread any test item(s) you missed. Do you understand the correct answer(s) now?

If your answer is *Yes,* practice your new understanding:

- Check out math books at your public library or learning center.
- Browse math websites.
- Ask fellow students or a teacher about practice possibilities.

If your answer is *No*:

- Help yourself. Review the learning/study strategy tips in this book.
- Ask for help. A fellow student or your teacher will be happy to help.

 FYI

The TABE math test may include items for which you have not prepared. This will be true as well for other tests that cover content similar to the TABE. Take a deep breath if you see a problem that looks unfamiliar. Relax. Look at it again. Approach the problem logically. Try to use your common sense to solve it.

A | Testing Strategies and Tips

If you read and responded to questions regarding your test-taking "know-how" in Section 1, you have already learned about these test-taking strategies and tips. Each strategy/tip is followed by a brief explanation and/or an example of how to use it. If you did not respond to the questions in Section 1, you may want to go there after you familiarize yourself with these strategies/tips and see how you feel about your abilities. Using these strategies and tips will help improve your test-taking experience.

1. *Visualize success for self-confidence and best results.*

   Have you ever heard the term "self-fulfilling prophecy"? In essence, it means that if you think you *can* do something, you have a better chance of being able to, and if you think you *can't* do something, you have less of a chance of being able to. So, using the principle of self-fulfilling prophecy, tell yourself that you *can* do well. Talk to yourself in positive, not negative, terms.

2. *Prepare physically for the test day.*

   Even if you are prepared for the content of the test, you may not do well if you are not well rested. Go to bed early the night before, or spend a quiet evening at home (it's probably not a good idea to go out to a party).

3. *Identify key words in questions and directions.*

   During the test, look out for important words that will help you understand directions and the questions being asked. Don't rush through either the directions or the test questions, because you risk reading them incorrectly and choosing incorrect responses.

4. *Recognize pitfalls of multiple-choice tests.*

   Often the answers that you have to choose from in a multiple-choice test are similar. You must read each one carefully before you choose your answer.

5. *Use the process of elimination to check multiple-choice questions.*

   If you are having trouble deciding on an answer to a multiple-choice question, first look at all the possible answers and see if any can be eliminated. Sometimes an answer just doesn't fit and you can eliminate it from consideration. This will narrow down the number of items you have to choose from.

6. *Relax by using breathing techniques.*

When you are sitting down to take a test and feel tense or nervous, take a moment to take a few deep breaths. Inhale slowly through your nose and exhale slowly through your mouth. This will help calm your nerves.

7. *Take one-minute vacations to relieve stress during the test.*

Another way to reduce stress or nervousness during a test is to stop for a minute, close your eyes, and visualize a place that brings you peace or happiness. Try to envision being there or think about the sensation you feel when you are there. For example, if you love to be at the beach, try to see yourself sitting on the warm sand with the sun beating down on your face. Think of the sound of the gentle waves lapping at the shore. Feel better already, don't you?

8. *Pace yourself during the test to finish within the time limit.*

As much as you might love to spend more than a minute on your mini-vacation, you do need to be mindful of the time limits of a test. Before you start the test, make sure you know how much time you can spend on each section, and stick to it. Don't linger too long on any item; you can always go back to it if you have time.

9. *Know when to leave a question that is giving you trouble.*

As mentioned above, if you linger too long on an item you may end up having to rush through other questions. If you just can't answer the question, move on and return to it if you have the time at the end.

10. *Use any time that is left at the end to check your work.*

If you finish a test before the time allotted, go back to items you did not answer. Then proceed to check your work if you still have time left.

General TABE Information

The TABE is a multiple-choice test. The test is offered as either a Complete Battery or a Survey version in two forms (9 and 10) for Level A. The Survey version consists of 50 questions, half the number of questions of the Complete Battery version. The Complete Battery version consists of the following sections and number of questions:

- Reading—50 questions
- Mathematics Computation—25 questions
- Applied Mathematics—50 questions
- Language—55 questions
- Language Mechanics—20 questions
- Spelling—20 questions
- Vocabulary—20 questions

The TABE will demonstrate your readiness for job training, employment, or taking the high school equivalency exam.

APPENDIX

B Resources

English Language Reference Books

Bernstein, T. M. *The Careful Writer: A Modern Guide to English Usage*. New York: Atheneum, 1965.

Booher, D. D. *Communicate with Confidence: How to Say It Right the First Time Every Time*. New York: McGraw-Hill, 1994.

Brusaw, C. T., G. J. Alred, and W. E. Oliu. *The Business Writer's Handbook*. 5th ed. New York: St. Martin's Press, 1997.

Cazort, D. *Under the Grammar Hammer: The 25 Most Important Mistakes and How to Avoid Them*. Los Angeles: Lowell House, 1997.

Dutwin, P., and H. Diamond. *English the Easy Way*. 4th ed. Hauppauge, N.Y.: Barron's Educational Series, Inc., 2003.

Dutwin, P., and H. Diamond. *Grammar in Plain English*. 3d ed. Hauppauge, N.Y.: Barron's, 1997.

Dutwin, P., and H. Diamond. *Writing the Easy Way*. 3d ed. Hauppauge, N.Y.: Barron's, 2000.

Follett, W. *Modern American Usage: A Guide*. Edited and completed by Jacques Barzun and others. New York: Hill & Wang, 1998.

Godden, Nell and Erik Palma. Eds. (*McGraw-Hill, 11th edition, 2011*). *Grammar Smart: A Guide to Perfect Usage*. New York: Villard Books, 1993.

Kipfer, B. A. (editor). *Roget's International Thesaurus*. 7th ed. New York: Harper Collins, 2010.

Merriam-Webster Collegiate Dictionary. 11th ed. New York: Merriam-Webster, 2014.

Mersand, J., and F. Griffith. *Spelling the Easy Way*. 4th ed. Hauppauge, N.Y.: Barron's Educational Series, Inc., 2006.

Oliu, W. E., C. T. Brusaw, and G. J. Alred. *Writing That Works*. New York: St. Martin's Press, 1980.

Sabin, W. A. *Gregg Reference Manual*. 9th ed. New York: Glencoe McGraw-Hill, 2001.

Strunk, W. Jr., and E. B. White. The Elements of Style. 3d ed. Boston: Allyn & Bacon, 1975.

Turabian, K. L. *A Manual for Writers of Term Papers, Theses, and Dissertations.* 6th ed Chicago: University of Chicago Press, 1996.

Weiss, E. H. *The Writing System for Engineers and Scientists.* Englewood Cliffs, N.J.: Prentice Hall, 1982.

Information Technology

Refer to Section 2, Lesson 4 for information on accessing the Internet. Refer to Section 2, Lesson 4 for information on using your library for researching on the Internet.

Look into Distance Education/Learning

Distance education is the process of providing instruction when students and teachers are separated by physical distance but united by computers. Distance education is often offered together with occasional face-to-face communication. Learning has traditionally taken place in the classroom (face to face) or as home schooling. Distance education has created virtual classrooms, and it plays an important part in the learning experience.

In a traditional classroom setting, instruction is through lecturing and student-to-student and students-to-teacher interaction. More recently, computers have become the means of course delivery. Instructors and students send and receive assignments via e-mail. Communication is said to be *asynchronous* when people do not interact simultaneously (such as an online course). Communication is *synchronous* when interaction between participants (such as a class "discussion") is simultaneous.

Community colleges, universities, and online universities offer distance learning or "online" courses as a convenient way for students of all ages and at all levels to further their education.

Inquire at Your Workplace About E-Learning as a Training Solution

Many companies offer training as needed through the use of computer courses. Computer assisted instruction and online courses are important options to help learners master a specific skill.

Community Services

There are a number of resources you can find in the town where you live, such as:

- Your local library
- Your community center (for education and recreation)

- Your family services organization
- Your congressional representatives
- Your local school department
- Your local recreation department

Educational Opportunities

Find out about educational opportunities and options by calling the appropriate department of your local and state school system. Also, access your state's website for information. You may find some or all of the following:

- State Adult Education Department (may sponsor distance education)
- Adult high schools
- ABE/GED programs
- Career and technical high schools
- Special education programs
- State Educational Opportunity Center

In addition, local libraries frequently offer literacy and ABE/GED classes, as well as many other courses and programs.

Index

P

Pacing, 324
Paragraphs
    constructing, 253–260
    placement of sentences, 255–256
    topic sentence, 253–254
    transition words, 256–257
Parentheses, 244
Parts of sentence, 194
Parts of speech, 194. *See also specific parts*
Patterns (number sequence), 163–164
Percentiles, 160
Percents, 103–105
    as decimals, 103–104
    dividing, 103
    equivalent values, 104
Performers. *See* Subjects
Physical preparation for tests, 323
Place value, 88–90
    rounding to a place value, 92–93
Points, 134–137, 165
Political party preference, 152–153
Polygons, 148–151. *See also* Quadrilaterals; Triangles
    congruence, 148
    hexagon, 148
    octagon, 148
    pentagon, 148
    perimeter, 148
    similarity, 148
Posttests
    language, 292–303
    mathematics, 309–322
    reading, 281–291
    spelling, 304–308
Prefixes, 267–268
Prepositional phrase, 194
    descriptive phrases, 227–229
    pronouns, 228–229
Prepositions, 194, 228
Prisoner pie chart, 153–154
Probability, 159–163
    definition, 160
    experimental, 161
    theoretical, 161
Problem solving, 171–174
    backsolving, 172

Pronouns, 207, 209–213
    antecedents, 212
    groups, 209
    indefinite, 211–212
    possessive pronouns, 221, 244
    prepositional phrase, 228–229
Properties of numbers, 111–112
    associative property of addition, 112
    associative property of multiplication, 112
    cumulative property of addition, 112
    cumulative property of multiplication, 112
    distributive property for addition, 112
    distributive property for subtraction, 112
    property of 1, 112
    property of -1, 112
    property of zero, 112
    zero product property, 112
Property of 1, 112
Property of -1, 112
Proportions, 100–103
Punctuation, 232–247
    apostrophe, 243–244
    colon, 243
    commas, 234–238
    dash, 244
    end marks, 233
    hyphen, 243
    parentheses, 244
    placement with quotation marks, 241
    quotation marks, 239–242
    semicolons, 238–239
Pythagorean theorem, 139

Q

Quadrilaterals, 143–147
    kites, 143
    parallelogram, 143–144
    rectangles, 143–144
    rhombus, 143–144
    squares, 143, 145
    trapezoid, 143, 145
Qualification statements, 5
Quartiles of database, 160
Questions, 194
    multiple-choice, 323

Study tips
  apostrophes, 244
  capitalization, 233–234
  commas, 235–236
  fragments, 235–236
  language, 221, 228, 233–234, 235–236,
    241, 244, 251, 256
  paragraphs, 256
  possessive pronouns, 221, 244
  pronouns, 228
  quotation marks, 241
  reading, 29, 31, 47–49
  spelling, 266, 275
  subjects, 228
  words in context, 47–49
Subjects, 194–199
Subject-verb agreement, 196–199
  descriptive phrases, 227–229
Subtraction
  algebraic operations, 115–117
  distributive property for subtraction,
    112
  fractions, 98–100
  integers, 107
Suffixes, 268–269
Supports, learning, 8–9. *See also*
    Resources
  balancing barriers and supports, 10–11
  community, 9
  family, 8
  friends, 9
  neighbors, 9
Syllables, 267
Synonyms, 47

T
TABE, 181
  general information, 324
  goals, 1
  research, 2
  score, 2
  skill assessment, 2–3
  skill comfort, 3
  test taking, 3–4
  timeline, 2
Tables, 35–37, 156–158
  number, 152

Telephone message form, 24
Test taking, 3–4
  multiple-choice tests, 323
  strategies and tips, 17, 323–324
  time limits, 324
  time management, 324
Time management, 324
Titles, 30
Tone, 65
Topic sentence, 253–254
Transition words, 32, 256–257
Triangles, 138–143
  altitude, 138
  base, 138
  base angles, 138
  equiangular, 138
  equilateral, 138
  hypotenuse, 139
  isosceles, 138
  legs, 139
  median, 138
  Pythagorean theorem, 139
  scalene, 138
  sides, 139

V
Variables, 171
Verbs, 194–205
  action verbs, 206, 209–210
  being verbs, 206–210
  irregular, 201–202
  linking verb contractions,
    213–214
  linking verbs, 206–210, 220–221
  non-action verbs, 206–210
  tense, 199–203, 215–217
Visualizing, 323
Volume, 149–151
Vowels, 266

W
Whole numbers, 118–119

Z
Zero, 112, 118, 119
Zero product property, 112